Praise for Patrick Henry Hansen's
From Great Moments in History Series

"Patrick's link between history and sales is very entertaining, but more importantly, very relevant to modern sales and marketing professionals. If you are interested in dramatically improving sales results, read these books."

—Dr. Stephen R. Covey, author of *The 7 Habits of Highly Effective People*

"These exciting books of superb selling methods and techniques, told against a vast panorama of historical events, are not only entertaining, they also show salespeople specific ways to double their sales and double their income."

—Brian Tracy, author of *The Psychology of Selling*

"Patrick's use of history to teach modern methods of sales and marketing is remarkable—inspiring, captivating."

—Larry King, former host, CNN

"Patrick's understanding of sales, together with his wit, makes his book series extremely enjoyable and informative. I've been lucky enough to see some of his ideas applied to a sales organization. As a result, pipelines grew, morale improved and our sales team performed better than ever."

—Kyle Powell, Co-founder, *Novell*

"Bravo... a maverick approach to sales and marketing. Patrick's use of history is engaging, interesting, and informative—a blueprint for sales and marketing success."

—Gerhard Gschwandtner, Founder of *Selling Power Magazine*

"These are fantastic books. Not only are the sales concepts and marketing principles profound but the manner in which they are communicated is totally unique. I strongly recommend these books."

—Hyrum W. Smith, Vice Chairman of the Board, *FranklinCovey*

"Patrick reminds us that those who ignore history are condemned to repeat it. His use of classic scenarios informs present day practitioners. He communicates solid marketing principles, helping readers understand the past in an unforgettable manner."

—Dr. William D. Danko, co-author of *The Millionaire Next Door*

"Patrick is everything he promises, and then some—entertaining, engaging and extremely effective."

—Jack Solomon, VP Strategic Procurement, *Watson Pharmaceuticals*

"Fantastic! If you're interested in dramatically improving communication skills and sales results, learn from the masters of the past by reading these books."

—Ron McMillan, co-author of *Crucial Conversations*

"In a word… WOW! An irreplaceable tool in the sales process, these books will make you a more impactful, learned, and skilled professional."

—Clark Jones, Corporate Trainer, *Sinclair Oil Corporation*

"Our company engages in complicated negotiations with large corporations including BMW and Mercedes. We needed the best negotiation strategies possible and Patrick delivered. His expertise and passion for the topic was palpable. I strongly endorse his books, approach and content."

—Denis Kerrigan, Director of Global Learning, *Harman International*

"I have attended numerous sales trainings over my career and consider myself well read on the topic. I can say, unequivocally, this is the most effective sales approach available. The entertaining style and "real world" examples made it engaging, memorable and, most importantly, implementable."

—Ryan Rothe, Sales Director, *Research Now*

"I highly recommend Patrick's books and trainings to any organization looking to increase their overall sales results and negotiation effectiveness. Simply put, it's the most engaging and thought-provoking content I've seen."

—Chris Prekopa, Sales Director, *Time Warner Cable*

"My team has sang nothing but "Patrick Praises" from your books and training. It is really rare for my sales team to be this positive about training and about the trainer. You exceeded my expectations."

—Alison Hesse, Director of Sales, *Clear Channel Radio*

"The mixture of history coupled with PHI's ability to customize the B2B content to our industry gave our reps tools that they could immediately apply. One of our veteran sales reps said that in 40 years in the industry, this was the best training he has ever seen."

—Weston Winegar, Sales Manager, *Sutron Corporation*

"One of the first actions I made as a sales director at Mediacom was to have my team go through PHI's training. Although they were initially skeptical, they became disciples of the books, concepts and methodology."

—Dominick M. DePaola Jr., Sr. Director Enterprise Solutions, *Mediacom*

"I can honestly say, choosing your company to train our sales force was the correct choice and you made me look like a hero. Your books and training really hit home with our sales team."

—Scott Youmell, Sales Operations Manager, *Ranpak*

"Engaging, timely, well structured, and the ideas presented were solidly fleshed out. Well done, Patrick!"

—Marshall Chapman, Sales Manager, *Cates Control*

"Rarely does someone capture so many priceless truths in such an interesting way. Patrick's use of history as a teaching tool is fabulous."

—Rob Bishop, United States Congressman

"Patrick understands how people learn and what it takes to create new, more productive behaviors. His content, teaching style and follow up tools stand apart from the crowd. He has become one of our trusted advisors."

—Ken Clayton, Vice President, Worldwide Sales, *SolidWorks Corp.*

"Simply the most unique books I've read on sales and marketing. Patrick's use of history to teach sales and marketing is informative and inspiring."

—Robert Dilenschneider, author of *Moses: CEO*

"The books and trainings definitely lived up to their reputation."

—Lane Shelton, Executive Vice President, *Softmart*

"Nothing compares to the training that Patrick provided. As a sales manager I couldn't have asked for a better response."

—Terry Ray, Sales Manager, *Modern Tech*

"I was skeptical about Patrick's books and trainings (honestly, they sounded too good to be true). Not anymore. They far exceeded our expectations."

—Christian Smith, VP Sales, *eProject*

"In a word, brilliant. The most effective approach I've seen in 30 years of corporate experience."

—Bill Schjelderup, President, *Companion Corporation*

"Patrick's insight, paired with his teaching approach and implementation tools, has given our sales force more confidence in securing fair and equitable contracts that provide sustainable relationships with our clients."

—Eric K. Pritchard, Senior Vice President Pricing, *Valassis*

ALSO BY PATRICK HENRY HANSEN

Power Prospecting: Cold Calling Strategies for Modern-Day Sales People

The DNA Selling Method: Selling Strategies for Modern-Day Sales People

Winning Sales Presentations: Presentation Strategies for Modern-Day Sales People

From Great Moments in History

Sales-Side Negotiation

NEGOTIATION STRATEGIES FOR MODERN-DAY SALES PEOPLE

Patrick Henry Hansen

BRAVE PUBLISHING, INC.

Dedicated To

My mother, Sharon Reva Corner,
for inspiring me to never settle for mediocrity.

ACKNOWLEDGEMENTS

Winston Churchill once said that writing a book is an adventure. "To begin with it is a toy and an amusement. Then it becomes a mistress, then it becomes a master, then it becomes a tyrant. The last phase is that just as you are about to be reconciled to your servitude, you kill the monster and fling him to the public."

Writing this book has indeed been an adventure, but it has not been a road traveled alone. As with each of the books in the *From Great Moments in History* series, there have been numerous people who have helped in the endeavor. Special thanks to Matthew and Heather Moore for their meticulous editing skills, principle development, and insightful content review. Thanks to Brian Tracy and Dr. William Danko for their professional critique. And to my friends Larry Brooks, Darren Dibb, Kevin Dibb, Zac Fenton, Tyler Hansen, Glen Lassen, Clint Sanderson, Stephen Kunzler, and David Stephens—for their insight and "in the trenches" feedback. And to a quintessential American entrepreneur, Bill Schjelderup, for his undeviating optimism and support.

CONTENTS

FIGURES

HISTORICAL REFERENCES

- Roman senator, Gauius Popillius Laenas negotiates the retreat of Syrian monarch Antiochus Epiphanes and his army of 30,000 soldiers. (v)
- Julius Caesar defeats Celtic Chieftain, Vercingetorix. (1)
- Prussian general Carl von Clausewitz revolutionizes military theory with the publication of his book, *On War*. (8)
- Feared gunfighter Harry Alonzo Longabaugh (The Sundance Kid) and Robert Leroy Parker (Butch Cassidy) raid the West. (17)
- Foreign policy adviser Henry Kissinger exercises power over Winston Lord. (19)
- Queen Elizabeth builds, balances, and maintains power with the British aristocracy, Parliament, and foreign diplomats. (23)
- Napoleon Bonaparte uses the sale of Louisiana to empower France and weaken England. (26)
- A northern corporal finds three cigars wrapped in paper that contain the battle plans of Confederate general, Robert E. Lee. (30)
- World War II German general Erwin Rommel prowls the deserts of North Africa. (35)
- Ho Chi Min and the Northern Vietnamese spend nine months haggling about the size and shape of the negotiation table with President Nixon's peace delegation in the 1974 Paris peace talks. (37)
- General George S. Patton's Eighth Army defeats Rommel's German Panzer Division. (40)
- Northern Vietnamese officials stockpile information about American soldiers during the Vietnam War to use on POW's during interrogations. (44)
- Meriwether Lewis and William Clark negotiate a contract with French trapper Toussaint Charbonneau and his fifteen year old Shoshone wife, Sacagawea. (45)
- Michelangelo defies the power of God on Earth, Pope Julius II. (48)
- John D. Rockefeller Jr. negotiates the sale of a Minnesota ore track with J.P. Morgan. (49)
- The Carter Administration's obsequious attitude toward the Soviet Union leads to diplomatic disaster. (50)
- Private John Shields negotiates the price of battle-axes in exchange for corn to feed the starving members of the Lewis and Clark expedition. (57)
- Roman general Publius Scipio battles Carthaginian general Hannibal Barca. (61)

- Famed art dealer Joseph Duveen fails to manipulate Henry Ford. (71)
- Henry Kissinger uses his knowledge of Israeli history to influence diplomats at a Middle East peace summit. (80)
- Lord Baden-Powell, founder of the Boy Scout movement and former British spy, uses clandestine espionage tactics to secure information about foreign military installations and weaponry. (85)
- British tides lead to the destruction of Julius Caesar's naval fleet in his first invasion of Britain. (87)
- English monarch Alfred the Great uses unconventional tactics to defeat the invading Scandinavian Vikings. (91)
- Ardent abolitionist Charles Sumner is brutally beaten in the Senate chamber by proslavery representative Preston Brooks. (95)
- Financial icon J.P. Morgan negotiates the price of a pearl scarf pin. (109)
- "Babe" Ruth negotiates with Red Sox owner, Harry Frazee. (112)
- Legendary art dealer Joseph Duveen is outwitted by J.P. Morgan. (114)
- Carthaginian general Hannibal Barca outwits the Romans and secures the escape of his army. (131)
- Abraham Lincoln pacifies a belligerent critic with reason and rationale. (140)
- Russian revolutionary Kondraty Ryleyev is executed by Russian Czar Nicholas I. (146)
- Sir Francis Drake and his English "sea dogs" defeat the Spanish Armada. (149)
- Aaron Burr shoots and kills founding father Alexander Hamilton in the most infamous duel in U.S. history. (152)
- British Intelligence trains falcons to destroy carrier pigeons bringing messages over the English Channel to Nazi spies. (154)
- Prussian premier Otto von Bismarck orchestrates the downfall of the Austrian empire and the rise of Prussia. (181)
- Financial titan J.P. Morgan negotiates the purchase of Andrew Carnegie's steel enterprise for $300 million dollars. (188)
- Queen Elizabeth issues a political treatise providing rationale for intervening on behalf of Dutch Protestants in their war against Spain. (191)
- Theodore Roosevelt's campaign manager negotiates the use of a copyrighted presidential photograph in the election of 1912. (196)
- British prime mister Neville Chamberlain succumbs to the negotiation tactics of Adolf Hitler. (199)
- British negotiators trade a nutmeg forest in the Spice Islands for the

Dutch controlled island of Manhattan. (201)
- Jericho prostitute Rahab negotiates the safe passage of her family from the onslaught of the Israelite army. (202)
- Henry Ford negotiates the purchase of door handles for his Model T. (209)
- George Lucas negotiates the merchandizing and licensing rights to his characters in *Star Wars*. (210)
- Nineteenth century art dealer Ambroise Vollard uses eccentric strategies to sell his art. (218)
- Ely Callaway introduces Big Bertha golf club. (225)
- James Monroe negotiates the purchase of the Louisiana Territory from France. (227)
- Moses receives the Ten Commandments from Jehovah. (235)
- Roman consul Marcus Crassus is crushed in the battle of Carrhae—the worst military defeat in Roman history. (236)
- Willing to sell his new ticker system to Gold & Stock for $3,000, Thomas Edison negotiates a price of $40,000. (238)
- United States President James Polk negotiates the procurement of Oregon Territory in 1846. (244)
- British monarch Queen Elizabeth I, develops an elaborate system of quid pro quo with the most influential people in England. (247)
- Outnumbered, surrounded, and cut off from reinforcements, Caesar's general Marcus Octavius defeats an army of Pompey in the Roman civil war. (252)
- Benjamin Franklin develops a self-improvement system. (254)
- Abraham Lincoln experiences nine political defeats before being elected President of the United States. (257)

For more information regarding historical references, see the Selected Bibliography.

Introduction

In 168 B.C., disputes over dynastic successions among Egypt's royal family reached a climax. Because the quarrels had so weakened the country, Syrian monarch Antiochus Epiphanes decided to seize the moment. With an army of 30,000 soldiers, he invaded Egypt, quickly overrunning its defenses. Antiochus then marched on Alexandria where the royal family had fled for protection. In desperation, Egypt appealed to Rome and asked for an army to repel the invading Syrians.

The Romans received the Egyptian appeal with great dismay. The Punic Wars to the south had exhausted Rome's treasury and constant skirmishes with Celtic tribes to the north had depleted the Roman armies. But, the Roman senate reasoned that nobody knew that—least of all the Syrians. The Romans dispatched one of their most prestigious members, ex-consul Gaius Popillius Laenas, who carried with him the *fasces*, or bundle of sticks, that for centuries had symbolized Roman power.

Senator Laenas arrived in Alexandria in the fastest boat possible. When he arrived, he didn't make a ceremonial appearance before the Egyptian royal family. Instead, he immediately left the city and headed east in the direction of the invading Syrian army. Because Senator Laenas was an old man, he traveled slowly, relying on a tall staff to help him walk. After several hours, he encountered the vanguard of the Syrian army.

Shocked at the appearance of a lone Roman senator standing in the road in front of them, the advance guard stopped, and soon the entire Syrian army behind them came to a complete halt. Within a few minutes, Antiochus and his entourage rode up from the rear to investigate the delay. Seeing the Roman senator standing in the middle of the road, they angrily dismounted and approached him.

"What are you doing in Egypt?" demanded the Syrian monarch.

The aged senator replied, "Your majesty, I believe the question is, what are you doing in Egypt?"

The king laughed defiantly and with a dismissive tone replied,

"Go back to Rome, old man."

The senator didn't move. The king stopped laughing.

"Who do you think you are? Behind me stands an army of over 30,000 men."

The senator stood unimpressed. "Behind you stands only a visible and rather small army. Behind me stand the invisible legions of Rome. In the name of the Senate and the People of Rome, I command you to go home."

Trembling with rage, Antiochus furiously glared at the senator and reached for his sword. In the moment of hesitation, Senator Laenas stepped forward and with the end of his staff began to draw a circle in the dirt around the Syrian king. After he completed the circle, he returned to his position and looked Antiochus in the face.

"Step out of the circle in any direction but east, and you will answer with your kingdom and your life."

Staring at the old man in his dusty toga, Antiochus stood transfixed. Even through the dust and dirt, the Syrian monarch recognized the senator's purple-bordered toga and did not need to be reminded of what those bundles of sticks represented. The king studied Senator Laenas. The senator waited, his eyes never moving from their solemn gaze in the direction of Antiochus. Time passed, and the sun grew hotter. The king's captains began to shift their weight in growing anticipation.

Suddenly, the king did an about-face, stepped out of the circle, and headed east. Without a word, he remounted his horse and wheeled around to the rear of his army. His captains began shouting orders to reverse course.

Senator Laenas stood alone in the middle of the road and watched the Syrian army withdraw to the east. When he could no longer see the dust from the retreating army, he turned around and began the long walk back to Alexandria.

Negotiation—an Ancient Art with Contemporary Application

One bold man defying an army of 30,000 soldiers? How could he have possibly reversed the Syrian king's course of action? Did Senator Laenas really have the power and the means to defeat the Syrian army? If he didn't, why did the Syrian king concede and retreat?

The reason is simple: Senator Laenas was a master negotiator. All major, historic events involve key figures engaged in epic negotiations; from the ancient struggles between the Hebrews and Egyptians, to the fourteenth century clashes between England and Scotland. Even modern history is dominated by negotiation. World War II may have been avoided had British Prime Minister Neville Chamberlain been as skilled and adroit a negotiator as Senator Laenas. Adolf Hitler was aware of Chamberlain's weaknesses and obtained through negotiation what he could not win with war.

Fundamental components of both ancient and modern negotiation are embodied in the historic encounter between King Antiochus and Senator Laenas. All of the contemporary elements of negotiation promoted today are present in this brief but historic account:

- Power
- Calculated risk
- Strategy
- Countertactics
- Concessions
- Consequences
- Perceived power
- Premeditated boldness
- Tactics
- Title & position
- Symbols, dress, & appearance
- Self control & demeanor

Despite the scientific accomplishments and social advancements of humanity over the centuries, principles of negotiation have remained virtually unchanged. They may be couched in different terms, but if we were to observe an ancient negotiation between a Babylonian king and a Persian prince, we would witness negotiation tactics similar to those used by today's businessmen and women.

Note on Historical Content

Too many countries, too many businesses have been destroyed by not studying history.

—Donald Trump

George Santayana said, "Those who cannot remember the past are condemned to repeat it." Oliver Wendell Holmes, Jr., remarked, "A page of history is worth a volume of logic." Cicero observed, "To be ignorant of what happened before you were born is to remain forever a child." Most of us hear these quotes from time to time; nevertheless, how many of us actually recall specific lessons from the past and apply them to our personal and business lives? We know of Rome's decadence, the French aristocracy's arrogance, and Stalin's brutality, but what can we learn from this knowledge that can help us in business and negotiation?

Actually, quite a lot. Behind these events are great lessons of history. History's little and big stories provide instruction of immense importance. Historic negotiations embody, for example, components of strategy, tactics, and power. They act as textbooks for modern students of negotiation. If you want to be a successful negotiator, learn from the masters of the past.

Nothing beats personal experience, of course, but learning from others' experiences comes in a competent second. The risk in learning only from personal experience is that too often, we draw conclusions from too little data—we learn too much from too little.

Because history emphasizes important principles, I reference numerous historical events throughout this book. Each chapter in each of the *From Great Moments in History* books begins with an historic event or experience that illustrates a particular point or principle. These lessons and events are worth learning precisely because they have something to teach.

The Purpose of This Book

Negotiation is a primary component of successful selling. *Without* effective negotiating skills and strategies, sellers unnecessarily offer price concessions, which in turn drives down profitability. *With* effective negotiating skills and strategies, sellers not only hold (and sometimes even increase) profitability margins, they also simultaneously create satisfied customers.

The purpose of *Sales-Side Negotiation* is to instruct sellers in the science of negotiation; specifically, negotiation from the sales side of the table. Although the principles are applicable for all types of negotiation, the context of the book is sales. Its content provides sellers with a structured process and clear methodology to conduct successful negotiations, avoid unnecessary discounts, and prevent unwarranted price concessions.

Integrity: The Foundation of Sales-Side Negotiation

A young Englishman searching for the secret of success sought the advice of a wealthy businessman in London.

"Go over to the window, look out, and tell me what you see," said the businessman.

"I see the marketplace," the youth replied.

"Now go look into the mirror and tell me what you see."

"Well, naturally, I see myself."

"In each case you were looking through a pane of glass. Tell me, what is the difference?" the businessman asked.

"The window is a clear pane of glass that allows me to see out and see the people in the marketplace. The mirror has a backing of silver that reflects my image."

"Therein lies the secret of success: When you let silver come between you and the people in the marketplace, you are only going to see yourself."

Sales-Side Negotiation is not a program of clever gimmicks or manipulative techniques. It is a program based on values, trust, and integrity. It is *customer-centered* and designed to help salespeople stop thinking in terms of products and features, and start thinking in terms of buyer needs, goals, and objectives. Using the principles in *Sales-Side Negotiation* sales people develop meaningful relationships and advance buyers through the sales cycle using honest, effective negotiation strategies.

Negotiating with integrity is not only the right thing to do, it is the smart thing to do. Because buyers make assessments about the character and integrity of sellers, it is imperative to demonstrate honesty and integrity throughout the sales process. Buyers need to know that sellers are trustworthy. "Am I dealing with Vinny the back slapping, plaid-jacketed, used-car salesman trying to sell me a pink Yugo, or is this someone I can trust?" As the great sales educator Zig Ziglar says, "The most important persuasion tool you have in your entire arsenal is integrity." Without integrity, salespeople severely limit their ability to establish honest rapport and build long-term relationships with clients.

Note on References

A traditional *Sales Cycle* consists of four steps. Each step requires a different skill set. To help sellers master each skill set, *Patrick Henry International* provides training programs and books that specifically address each stage of the selling process.

Sales Cycle	Book Title
1. Prospecting	*Power Prospecting*
2. Investigating	*The DNA Selling Method*
3. Presenting	*Winning Sales Presentations*
4. Closing	*Sales-Side Negotiation*

Each book provides a comprehensive assessment of the chosen topic. Combined, the books offer sellers and managers a reference library that addresses each step in the selling process.

Because each stage of the sales cycle is part of an overall process rather than an isolated event, each of the books in the *From Great*

Moments in History series reference each other in footnotes.

Note on Format

Where there is a need for special emphasis, one of three alert windows is used:

> **Note**: A "Note" is an idea, concept or principle that is highlighted for clarity and impact.

> **Caution!** The "Caution" window makes sellers aware of potential negotiation mistakes to avoid.

> **The Point?** "The Point" focuses the reader on the prominent principle or main idea of the section or chapter.

Thank you for your interest in promoting and exercising sales-side negotiation concepts. I hope you will draw upon your own experiences to personalize and adapt the material to fit your own business or situation.

Best Regards.

Patrick Henry Hansen

---

part one I

Seller-Negotiators

CHAPTER 1

Selling—Your Most Important Negotiation Skill

—————❧●❧—————

While wintering in northern Italy in 52 B.C., Julius Caesar received news that Vercingetorix, the most capable Celtic leader of his day, had united the Gaulic tribes in rebellion against Roman rule. Caesar's predicament was that his army was cut in two—half wintering in northern Italy, the other half in northern Gaul (modern France) while Vercingetorix occupied the middle.

Caesar immediately marched his northern troops toward Vercingetorix. Divided, outnumbered, in hostile territory, and with a limited supply line behind him, Caesar defeated his famed Celtic opponent in the battle of Alesia. Caesar went on to defeat the various Celtic tribes of Gaul and Britain, and over an eight-year period, he subjugated all of modern France, Switzerland, Austria, western Germany, Belgium, Holland, and southern England. He defeated his former political ally and son-in-law, Pompey, in the Roman civil war, engaged in over forty battles against armies larger than his own, and on more than a dozen occasions, he barely escaped with his life. His military prowess led him to utter his famous, "Veni, vidi, vici" (I came, I saw, I conquered).

—————❧●❧—————

Because Caesar's military conquests are unrivaled in world history, military and non-military historians alike study and question the reasons for his overwhelming achievements. Many scholars attribute his success to his engineering feats of constructing bridges, siege towers, and highly accurate missile throwing equipment. Others ascribe his success to Roman weaponry—the seven-foot javelin, the gladius (a short, two-edged sword), and the scutum (an oblong, four-by-two foot shield). Some say it was little more than his extraordinary boldness. Caesar personified the Roman maxim, "Fortuna favet fortibus" (fortune favors the brave).

Although reasons vary, one conclusion consistently stands out among the students and scholars of Julius Caesar—without question, he was the most skilled military commander of his time.

The difference between Caesar and his counterparts was not bravery, cowardice, or effort. The difference was skill and tactics. Caesar's military tactics were superior to his opponents' tactics because the Romans were cerebral. Instead of rushing into battle, they used a systematic approach to warfare. They were innovative and introduced legionary battle methods that were more advanced than German and Celtic phalanx methods. They were meticulously organized and used fighting techniques that could be repeated from one battle to the next.

Skill separated Julius Caesar from his counterparts and distinguished him from his enemies. Skill made him triumphant. His battlefield skills and methodologies brought him repeated victories over his less skilled opponents.

Just as in Caesar's ancient battle methods, skill is the determining factor that separates a winning negotiation from a losing negotiation and is what differentiates an elite negotiator from a mediocre negotiator.

The Importance of Developing Negotiating Skills

How often are commissionable dollars and company profits lost by a lack of negotiation skills?

Because a growing number of buyers are receiving negotiation training, there is a corresponding need for sellers to learn how to counter buyer negotiation tactics aimed at securing discounts and price allowances. It is no longer an option for sellers to neglect acquiring effective negotiation skills.

While many companies hire professional purchasing agents to "do their bidding," other businesses that consistently make high value or high volume purchases send employees to negotiation seminars to learn how to negotiate discounts and drive prices down. Because of these skilled negotiators, many sellers unwittingly play into the hands of trained buyers by not recognizing buyer-negotiator tactics.

> **Caution!** Unprepared, untrained sellers who run into prepared, trained buyers are at a severe disadvantage in negotiation.

Sellers should not resent this process. They should embrace it. It is a buyer's job to ask for discounts and price concessions. Buyers know that if they don't ask, they won't receive a better price. Buyers who have attended negotiation seminars have been taught that they have nothing to lose and everything to gain by asking for price concessions. Experienced sellers expect and prepare in advance for buyers to request discounts.

Fortunately, with appropriate training and practice, recognizing and combating buyer negotiation tactics is not difficult. Even novice sellers can learn to minimize discounts and negotiated price concessions.

Skilled sellers develop professional buyer-seller relationships without giving away profitability or offering unnecessary price concessions. In order to accomplish this, they recognize commonly used buyer negotiation tactics and strategically neutralize those tactics with effective countertactics. By implementing advanced sales and negotiation skills, such as trading concessions instead of donating concessions, they avoid giving away profitability and commissionable dollars. In short, successful sales professionals sell through negotiation.

The Role of Skill in Negotiation

In *Patrick Henry International's* corporate trainings and executive retreats, we ask participants "What is the purpose of business?" We get a plethora of answers from "To make customers happy," "To meet the needs of the market," "To serve our clients," or "To make money." While all of these responses are partially correct, none of them reveals the true purpose of business. The answer is not complicated. In fact, it's found in a single word: *profitability. The purpose of business is to be profitable—to increase profitability.* Businesses cannot achieve any of the lofty goals and ideals as previously noted without good, old-fashioned Adam Smith profit.

There are only three ways known to man to increase profitability:

1. Increase Sales
2. Increase Sales Margins
3. Decrease Costs

That's it. In order to increase profitability, you can increase sales. You can increase sales margins. You can decrease costs, or you can do a combination of the three. Is it possible to do all three simultaneously? Absolutely. Ways to increase sales are addressed in *Power Prospecting, Winning Sales Presentations,* and *The DNA Selling Method.* This book focuses on increasing the difference between the cost of goods sold and the price of the good or service. In other words, the profit margin.

> **Note**: The most effective way to increase sales is to improve selling skills. The most effective way to increase sales margins is to improve negotiation skills.

The Negotiation Skill Scale

Can we agree that some sales and negotiations are going to be *won*, regardless of the skills of the seller? Can we agree that some sales and negotiations are going to be *lost*, regardless of the skills of the seller? Can we also agree that some sales and negotiations are going to be *won or lost* by the skills of the seller?

Of course, the answer to each question is yes. The logical conclusion is this: the controlling factor of a successful negotiation is the skill of the seller. It is the primary factor in maintaining and increasing sales margins.

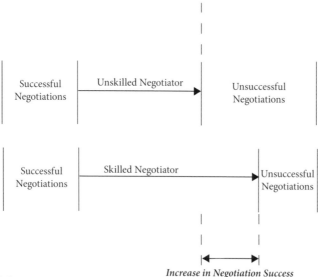

The Negotiation Skill Scale

Figure 1.1

Skills determine the level of success a seller-negotiator experiences. The "width" of the middle tier of the skill scale (see Figure 1.1) is what Stephen R. Covey, author of *The 7 Habits of Highly Effective People*, calls the "circle of influence." Because sellers control, influence, and determine their skill level, they also control, influence, and determine their negotiating success. Skilled negotiators expand the middle tier and shrink the unsuccessful tier.

> **The Point?** Skill is power. The more negotiation skill a seller acquires, the more power a seller has to influence the outcome of a negotiation. Skills constitute the base of negotiation success.

Increasing Sales Margins

Many sellers have asked me how being an effective negotiator helps increase sales margins rather than just maintain sales margins. Good question.

When companies with a team of direct sellers average a 10 to 20 percent discount ratio, they are discounting far more than necessary to make sales. For example, let's say ABC Corporation generated $5,000,000 in sales last year, and let's assume the price of their product was $100,000. If they made 50 sales at full price, that would add up to $5,000,000 in gross sales. Unfortunately, that's not how it typically works. Most companies will make around 60 sales at an average price of $85,000 to reach their $5,000,000 in sales. In other words, their average discount rate will be about 15 percent.

If we were to cut the discount rate of ABC Corporation by just 5 percent, its sales would increase by $250,000. Assuming the cost of goods sold remained the same, that is $250,000 of *pure profit*. This is what I mean by increased sales margins.

> **Note:** Because the cost of a sale remains identical with or without a discount, price concessions go to the bottom line of profitability every time.

I consulted with a software company that averaged a 25 percent discount rate prior to implementing our sales processes and our "death to discounts" program. We trained the sellers in advanced sales and negotiation skills, and we created a strict discounting policy. We carefully tracked sales, and after just one year, we cut the discount rate by 20 percent. What was the company's result? Sales increased, sales margins increased, and as a result, so did corporate profitability.

The most effective and consistent way to increase sales margins is to increase selling and negotiating skills.

Selling is Negotiating

From the beginning of the sales cycle to the signed contract, everything you do as a seller has an impact on negotiation. Every question you ask, every answer you offer, every decision you make, every skill you utilize, and every presentation you deliver, adds or diminishes your ability to effectively negotiate.

Many sellers fail to recognize their role as negotiators and view negotiation as an activity engaged in by union leaders, corporate executives, and lawyers. Regrettably, some sellers over simplify negotiating by flippantly equating it with the kind of haggling activity found at a flea market. The truth is, negotiating is an integral part of every day selling. Selling is negotiating.

In Summary

Although selling and negotiating are considered separate disciplines, in reality they are extensions of the same branch, appendages to the same body.

Because of the impact negotiation has on sales, it is no longer optional for professional salespeople to acquire negotiation skills. Skills—real, substantive, negotiation skills—are what separate high-caliber sales professionals from mediocre sales representatives.

> **The Point?** How you sell is as important as how you negotiate.

CHAPTER 2

The Sales Cycle

Because principles of combat are equally applicable in sales and negotiation, books such as *The Art of War* by Sun-Tzu and biographies of General George S. Patton and Sir Winston Churchill are found on most CEO's bookshelves. Carl von Clausewitz's writings are no exception. His principles of military theory are directly applicable to sales and negotiation.

———————

Carl von Clausewitz revolutionized military theory in 1832 by publishing his book *On War,* which outlined absolute theories of warfare that are still studied and used by military leaders today.

As a young man, Clausewitz joined the Prussian army's fight against Napoleon. He was so disgusted with the Prussian monarch's accommodation of the French that he continued his fight against the French Emperor with the Russians. In 1815, however, he reunited with the Prussian army and served in the Waterloo campaign, assisting in Napoleon's final defeat.

Analyzing the campaigns of Napoleon, Clausewitz wrote, "Direct annihilation of the ene-my's forces must always be the dominant consideration... Once a major victory is achieved, there must be no talk of rest... but only the pursuit of going for the enemy again, seizing his capital, attacking his reserves and anything else that might give his country aid and support." Clausewitz reasoned that after war comes negotiation and the division of territory. However, when only a partial victory has been won, a country will inevitably lose in negotiation what it won by war. Therefore, Clausewitz argued, military leaders should focus exclusively on the annihilation of their enemy in order to empower post-war negotiations and diplomacy.

Like Carl von Clausewitz' observation that what takes place

on the battlefield will dominate what takes place at the negotiation table, intelligent negotiators know that what takes place in the selling process will determine what takes place in the negotiation process. In other words, *what happens prior to the negotiation is as important as what happens during the negotiation.* For that reason, strategic negotiators focus first on selling and then on negotiating.

The Natural Evolution of a Sale

Selling is a process which has a natural flow with a beginning, middle, and end. Sellers who ignore the natural evolution of a sale and engage in the wrong sales behavior at the wrong time won't reach their full potential. For example, if sellers immediately jump from prospecting to closing, they will miss vital selling steps such as discovering critical needs, identifying problems, and building value prior to a presentation or negotiation.

There are four steps in the sales cycle:

1. Prospecting
2. Investigating
3. Presenting
4. Closing

Each stage of the sales cycle has its own sub-stages and accompanying selling steps and behaviors. For example, the prospecting stage focuses on lead generation activities, referrals, cold calling, qualifying, client introductions, and initial appointments. Even though each selling stage requires specific skills to address the issues at hand, the objective of each stage of the sales cycle is the same: *advancing the sale to the next stage of the sales cycle.* Keep in mind that measured performance at each stage is the only way to determine success.

The Sales Cycle

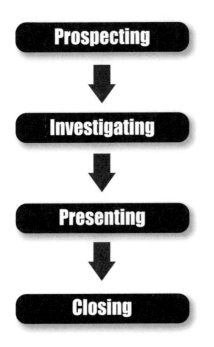

Lead generation, cold calling, obtaining referrals, initial meetings, discovery-qualification questions.

Information gathering, questioning, understanding buyer needs and problems, identifying primary buying motives, need-problem questions, ascertain-pain questions.

Presenting capabilities, demonstrating value, proposing solutions, submitting proposals, providing references.

Preventing and overcoming objections, following up, gaining commitment, obtaining agreement, negotiating.

Figure 2.1

The Prospecting Stage

Prospecting is the first step of the sales cycle and has an enormous impact on a seller's success. The quantity and quality of prospecting results determine the volume and caliber of sales a professional will make.

Unfortunately, many sellers downplay the importance of prospecting—especially the influence prospecting has on negotiation. Sellers set the tone of the sale during the prospecting stage and build the foundation for the remainder of the buyer-seller relationship. This means that sellers who know how to effectively prospect build power (the most important factor in negotiation) from the outset of the buyer-seller relationship.

In every step of the sales process, power is either built or diminished. Prospecting is no exception to this rule. The power a seller establishes in the initial interactions with a buyer will have a direct effect on the success or failure of a negotiation.

The Investigating Stage

No selling skill has more impact on negotiation than the ability of a seller to identify a prospective buyer's needs, problems, and pains. That bears repeating. **Nothing you do in the selling process is more important to negotiation than discovering needs, identifying problems, and isolating pain.** If we continue the application of Carl von Clausewitz' military theories to negotiation, the investigation stage of the sales cycle is the equivalent of initial battle stages in warfare. (How you conduct the investigation stage of the sales cycle is discussed in great detail in *The DNA Selling Method*).[1]

Needs fuel the sales process. Without first identifying the needs and problems of buyers, sales professionals cannot sell to needs. In other words, they cannot address the issues that give value to the product or service being sold. Without first establishing value, sellers set themselves up for a long and difficult negotiation process.

Like the aggressive post battle pursuit addressed by Clausewitz, sellers should not stop the investigation stage of the sales cycle after simply identifying buyer needs and problems. Instead, sellers should analyze and develop those problems into pains that warrant action.[2]

---

1. See Part 2 in *The DNA Selling Method* for a detailed discussion of *The DNA Selling Method*—a sales questioning methodology used to qualify prospects, identify buyer needs and problems, and illustrate the benefits of problem resolution.

2. See *The DNA Selling Method* to learn how to develop needs and problems into pains that warrant purchasing action.

Pain justifies purchasing decisions, so the more pain a seller identifies, the more he or she can resolve. The more pain a seller resolves, the more power a seller has in negotiation.

> **Note**: Ascertaining the level of pain a prospect is experiencing helps determine and develop the urgency of a sale. The more pain prospects experience, the more money they are willing to pay for products and services to resolve those pains.

The Presenting Stage

The presentation is the apex of the sales process and usually determines who wins and who loses.[3]

Like the investigating stage of the sales cycle, the presentation stage is extremely important to the negotiation process because it gives the seller an opportunity to show how he or she can solve pains and problems. This gives sellers a chance to "separate from the pack," distinguish themselves from other vendors, and develop competitive differential advantages. Establishing competitive preference is vital because some basis of favorable differentiation is imperative to justify existing or higher prices.

Sellers who deliver compelling presentations create a value perception in the minds of buyers. Good presentations increase the perceived value of proposed solutions. Poor presentations diminish the perceived value of proposed solutions. The more value buyers perceive, the more disposed they are to purchase at higher prices. An effective presentation encourages buyers to believe the product or service is worth the published price and reduces demands for discounts.

During a recent business trip to Texas, I had an experience that illustrates my point about presentations. I needed a pair of sunglasses, so I went into a shopping mall, found a sunglass kiosk, and asked to

---

3. To learn how to deliver successful presentations, see *Winning Sales Presentations*.

try on a few pair. The salesman immediately began up-selling me on the benefits of better glasses. He pulled out a pair of Oakley sunglasses and delivered a presentation on the benefits of using high quality sunglasses. He told me that not only would I see better and experience little glare, but the Oakleys were also more durable, flexible, and had a better warranty than most sunglasses. I was sold. I walked into that mall expecting to pay $20 to $50 for a pair of sunglasses, but because of the impact of the salesperson's presentation, I was convinced that the quality and benefits justified purchasing a more expensive pair of sunglasses. I ended up paying $220 for a pair of high-end Oakleys.

When it comes time to negotiate, the power of a presentation will have a direct impact on a salesperson's ability to negotiate from a position of strength. An effective presentation justifies price, differentiates the product, and gives sellers negotiating muscle.

The Closing Stage

The closing phase of the sales cycle is the natural conclusion to a well-executed communication process. Closing is a logical progression of the sales process and should happen if a seller has done an adequate job in the preceding stages of the sales cycle. The purpose of closing is to overcome objections and gain a firm commitment from the buyer to purchase the proposed good or service.

> **Caution!** Sellers should not begin closing or negotiating before identifying needs and establishing clear benefits associated with proposed solutions.

Because closing is the most negotiated portion of the sales cycle, *how* a seller closes is extremely important.

In high-value sales, pressure closing techniques can actually harm the success of a negotiation. Buyers who have to potentially face negative consequences for the wrong decision, such as losing a job or suffering public embarrassment or a reprimand, are not receptive to pressure in regard to a purchasing decision. Pressure techniques intensify the fear and stress of making a poor decision, generating buyer resistance and decreasing the likelihood of closing a sale.

Buyers involved in high-value purchases do not make decisions based on sudden emotions or impulses. For instance, if a salesperson at a clothing store tells you that you look fabulous in a particular suit and that it is the last one of its kind in stock, you might be easily persuaded to purchase the suit. On the other hand, if you are purchasing a $250,000 back up system for an accounting department in a large corporation, you are not going to be persuaded by traditional closing techniques.

High pressure, manipulative closing tactics have no place in high-value sales as they reduce respect, diminish relationships, and decrease the likelihood of closing the sale. Although high pressure closing techniques can be successful in small, low-value sales, they are irritating to professional buyers and should be avoided in high-dollar sales.

> **Note**: Manipulative pressure tactics are inversely effective as the size of a sale increases. As the size of a sale grows, so does the risk. When a sale involves a high-dollar item, the risks and consequences of a bad decision become more significant.

Traditional Closing Techniques and When to Use Them

As I mentioned earlier, traditional closing "tricks of the trade" can be effective in sales that do not involve long sales cycles or high-value purchases. For example, I managed a team of sales professionals who sold technical solutions that ranged between $25,000 and $1,000,000 dollars with a sales cycle six to eighteen months long. When I first managed this group of salespeople, I worked with representatives who used traditional closing techniques on potential and existing clients. Not only did these tactics not work, they strained existing customer relationships and lost winnable sales. Buyers were feeling pressured rather than persuaded. I received phone calls from both prospects and customers saying things such as, "I never want to talk to that sales rep again," or "I don't know who hired that guy, but if he calls here again we are dropping your product."

When I started my sales consultation business, I worked with numerous clients whose various products and services ranged from a few dollars to hundreds of thousands of dollars. Because of my background in the technical industry, I was jaded against using traditional closing techniques. I hated them. My experience had taught me that they rarely worked and typically cost more than they gained. I was, however, wrong. As I began consulting clients who sold low-dollar items, such as herb and vitamin supplements, specialized mattresses, and radio advertisements, I learned very quickly that traditional closing techniques can be extremely potent.

Traditional closing techniques that can be effective in low-dollar sales include:

The Assumptive Close: Sellers simply assume the sale has already been made. "I'll go ahead and write this order up and leave the mattress with you tonight. Your wife is going to love it!"

The Add-On Close: Sellers assume the primary purchase and add on less expensive, additional accessories. "John, in addition to the snow blower, you will also need a few bags of rock salt to keep the sidewalks safe." When the buyer agrees to the rock salt, they've also agreed to buy the snow blower.

The Alternative Close: Sellers infer the buyer's intent to purchase and offer alternative options such as, "Will you be paying with cash or credit card?"

The Prescription Close: The seller summarizes the problem, and then prescribes the solution. "Based on what you've told me, I would recommend the following…," or "Here's what you're going to need."

The Last Chance Close: Sellers insinuate that if the buyer does not act immediately, the opportunity will pass him or her by. "Wow! I just realized that there are only two booths left, so I'll get you registered for the trade show today."

The Thermometer Close: "We've covered a lot so far, and there is still more to show you, but on a zero-to-ten scale, zero meaning you have no interest in my service and ten meaning you have already decided to buy my service, where do you stand?"

The Authorization Close: After addressing questions, the salesperson takes out the agreement, places a check mark where the customer needs to sign, and slides it over to her saying, "Mary, if you will authorize this with a signature, we'll get the order process started."

The Trial Close: Sellers use questions to feel where the seller is in regard to making the purchase and determine the prospect's buying temperature. The trial close is designed to get reactions rather than commitments. "How does this sound so far?" "What are your thoughts?" "Is this what you were looking for?" "Does this make sense to you?"

The Return Serve Close: When the buyer asks a question, sellers reply with a question. "Does this include training?" "Would you like us to include training?" "Is this available in black?" "Would you like it in black?" "Can I pay in monthly installments?" "Would you like to pay in monthly installments?"

The Impending Close: Sellers imply that buyers need to act immediately to seal the deal at the current price. "You had better get your order in now because the price is going up on the first of the month." This tactic sells the benefits of taking immediate action.

The Throw In Close: The seller offers to throw in something for free to encourage the buyer to make the purchase. "Tim, if you purchase today, I will include training at no extra cost." The additional items or services make buyers feel that they are getting a better value for their dollar.

Although traditional closing tactics can be effective in low-dollar sales, most prospects are experienced enough to recognize closing techniques. For that reason, sellers need to be cautious about how they use traditional closing tactics.

> Note: Keep in mind that people love to buy, but they hate to be sold.

People don't want to feel pushed or cajoled into making a purchase. They want to be encouraged and convinced, not pressured. They want to make their own decisions, and they resent being pushed too hard.

Cerebral sellers use closing tactics in a forthright and honest manner. They recognize that if they make the buyer feel manipulated, buyers will not only resent the tactic, they will also resent the seller.[4]

The Better You Sell, the Less You Will Negotiate

To subdue the enemy without fighting is the acme of skill.

—Sun Tzu

Butch Cassidy (Robert Leroy Parker) and The Sundance Kid (Harry Alonzo Longabaugh) were two of the most famous outlaws the American West produced. Together they led the Hole-in-the-Wall Gang through Utah, Nevada, Wyoming, and Montana in some of the most infamous railroad and bank robberies in American history. While it was Butch who provided the

---

4. For a detailed analysis of effective and ineffective closing techniques, see *The DNA Selling Method*.

brains behind the robberies, it was Sundance who provided the necessary firepower. His reputation as an expert marksman and skilled gunfighter instilled fear in the lawmen who pursued him. Sheriffs and posses alike knew he was a bad man to tangle with in a fight—especially a gunfight.

Ironically, while Sundance was considered one of the most feared gunfighters in the Old West, there is no record that he ever killed anyone. Apparently, he was such a skilled gunfighter that no one dared challenge him. Both outlaws and lawmen alike had an overwhelming fear of his fast draw, so they dared not cross him. In one of history's most bizarre twists, the most famed gunfighter in the American West's history never had to engage in a serious gunfight!

In like manner, the more skilled a salesperson is, the less he or she will ever have to negotiate. *Winning a sale without a formal negotiation is the ultimate sign of a skilled negotiator.* That might seem like an oxymoron at first glance, but it's not if you view selling in the appropriate light. In reality, the entire selling process is one giant negotiation. Winning a sale is simply a natural conclusion to a well-executed selling process. It's what should happen if you've done your work in the preceding stages of the sales cycle.

In Summary

It would be impossible to exaggerate the impact the selling process has on negotiation. Sellers with effective prospecting skills build power. Sellers who unearth needs, problems, and pain develop a precedent for buying. Sellers who make powerful presentations establish value in the minds of buyers. Salespeople who are serious about being better negotiators focus first and foremost on improving their sales skills.

> **The Point?** Sellers who develop advanced selling skills minimize the need for discounts and price concessions and put themselves in a position to successfully negotiate.

CHAPTER 3

Seller Power

———◦►●◄◦———

During the Nixon Administration, President Nixon's foreign policy adviser, Henry Kissinger, requested a detailed government report concerning the Vietnam War from Winston Lord. Winston Lord worked on the report for days, but after he submitted the report to Kissinger, it was returned with the notation, "Is this the best you can do?" Lord reworked the report and resubmitted it. Again, it was returned with the same notation. After redrafting and resubmitting the report a third time, it was again returned with the same notation. Furious, Lord returned the report to Kissinger with a notation of his own, "Damn it, yes, it's the best I can do." To which Kissinger replied, "Fine, then I guess I'll read it this time."

Henry Kissinger was able to exercise this kind of power because Mr. Lord didn't know it existed.

———◦►●◄◦———

Understanding and Recognizing Power

Power from the standpoint of experience, is merely the relation that exists between the expression of someone's will and the execution of that will by others.

—Leo Tolstoy

Power is difficult to define. It's like defining love. It has different meanings to different people. It is defined by personal experience, not a dictionary.

Power comes in many shapes and sizes. It can be based on a person's position, such as a CEO or elected official, or it can be technical, based on specialized skills and training like those of an architect or attorney. Personality affects power. We've all dealt with people who are powerful based solely on their personality, charm, wit, or charisma. Power can be exemplified by mental, physical, or emotional means. It can be established with symbols, dress, and demeanor. It can be gained or lost with a single word, sentence, or act. It is in constant flux and is never static.

> **Note:** Power is the most influential factor in negotiation. Understanding, recognizing, and exercising power is an important dynamic in any negotiation.

As we saw in the historic clash between Senator Laenas and King Antiochus, power is both real and perceived. It is both actual and abstract. It is both valid and invalid, depending on how it is used. Antiochus recognized and acknowledged that Senator Laenas was powerful because of what he represented, not because of his actual strength. In reality, even what he represented (Rome) did not have the ability to back his bold assertions.

What Senator Laenas did was by no means limited to his experience. Similar scenarios happen every hour of every day when people project power they don't actually have. Even from a seemingly powerless position, *pretense* can wield power behind the shield of *perception*. What's amazing is that people in positions of real power (like King Antiochus) often fail to use it! Sellers often have enormous power over buyers but are too timid to use it. By not tapping into the power they possess, they leave dollars on the table.

Motive and cognition aside, power is always present throughout the selling process. Sometimes power is exercised intentionally, sometimes unintentionally. While some buyers utilize power consciously, others use it unconsciously. Power can influence a sale or negotiation by intent or by accident. The point is that one way or another, power is always exercised.

Ultimately, our individual experiences define power for us. To some, power equals authority, and to others it means control or strength. Regardless of our exact definition, power exists and is a very real part of sales and negotiation.

> **The Point?** Power (the ability to influence people's opinions, perceptions, and decisions) is exercised to one degree or another in every relationship and is an integral part of the negotiation process.

The Power Scale

Almost everyone knows that piranhas are dangerous, man-eating fish, the Boston Tea Party resulted from high taxes, chameleons can change colors to match their surroundings, the Hippocratic Oath is required of doctors, and that hemophiliacs bleed to death. A common mistake we make, though, is to accept these and similar assertions at face value. They are based more on folklore than on fact.

Similarly, many sellers carry a heavy bag of assumptions on their shoulders about how much power and influence they have compared to buyers. Often times, sellers assume that buyers are all-powerful and that they have complete control over the outcome of a sale. That is simply not true. In fact, most of the assumptions sellers make about buyer power are incorrect. Sellers frequently overestimate the power of their counterparts and underestimate their own power.

Excluding the power of the actual product or service being sold, there are ultimately only two sources of power in purchase related negotiations:

1. The power of the buyer
2. The power of the seller

Typically, but not always, buyers have the most power in the initial stages of the sales cycle, while sellers have the most power in the later stages of the sales cycle. In other words, each has more influence than they realize. Why? Because early in the sales cycle, buyers may not be aware of the magnitude of the problems they are experiencing, and sellers have not yet had an opportunity to present their solutions, demonstrate value, or differentiate themselves from competitors.

A colleague of mine who sells accounting solutions shared a story with me that clarifies my point. He delivered a presentation to a buyer who initially treated him poorly. *Prior* to the presentation, the buyer had invested little or no time evaluating my colleague's program and did not recognize the impact it would have on his business. *After* my colleague delivered a presentation that demonstrated how his program would improve the accounting process for his business, the buyer recognized the value of the offer and purchased the program.

In the initial stages of the sales cycle, the buyer had more power. After the presentation, the seller had more power.

Power and Skill

In 1931 Gandhi visited Italian dictator Benito Mussolini, complete with the goat that accompanied him on his travels. Mussolini's children mocked the incongruous figure, but Mussolini reproved them: "That man and his goat are shaking the British Empire."

Not only did Gandhi have power, but he knew how to exercise it.

There is an inverse importance (not a relationship) between power and skill in negotiation. Negotiating skills become less important as more power is acquired. Regardless of the skills of a negotiator, if his or her counterpart has an overwhelming amount of power, skills will have a limited impact on the outcome of a negotiation.

> **Note**: Power is the single most important component of negotiation, even more important than skill. The more power a negotiator has, the less relevant skills become.

This in no way diminishes the importance of having and exercising negotiation skills. Quite the contrary. Rarely, if ever, does one party have a monopoly on power. Typically, power is up for grabs, and it is the skill of the buyer or seller that grabs it. Skill is what harnesses power. Skill is also what implements power. The skills of the negotiator determine how power will be exercised. Perceived power in particular is ineffectual without the skills to use it. Think about Senator Laenas.

His perceived power was effective because he had the negotiation skills to exert power that wasn't even real.

In the case of sales-side negotiations, sellers have to build power. It is rarely just handed to them. How do they build power? With skill. It is the skill of the seller that builds, maintains, and balances power. Skill also retrieves power when it is lost.

While power is the most important element in negotiation, it's not enough. Successful negotiators need both power and skill. Sellers possessing both are much more successful negotiators and command greater respect from their counterparts.

> **The Point?** Combined, power and skill are the hallmarks of a successful negotiator.

Building, Balancing, and Maintaining Power

Elizabeth Tudor was the daughter of King Henry VIII and Anne Boleyn. She was a slender, pale, red-haired girl who had been declared a bastard by her ruthless father, held prisoner through much of her childhood, and was accused of high treason as a teenager. Upon the death of her half-sister, Mary I, in 1558, Elizabeth ascended the British throne.

Queen Elizabeth learned at an early age that outward, superficial things—including all the trappings of power—are fragile, transitory and subject to change even by trivial accident. Although she was only twenty-five when she became Queen of England, Elizabeth fully appreciated the dynamic, fluid nature of power. Her royal inheritance made it seem that fortune and authority were foregone conclusions, but Elizabeth realized that circumstances could readily change overnight. She knew that her own mother, queen one day and adjudged conspirator the next, was beheaded as an accused, adulterous traitor. She saw her own fortunes change with the deaths of Edward VI and Mary I.

When Elizabeth was crowned in 1558, England was a religious, diplomatic, and economic mess. She inherited the short-sited economic policies of her father, diplomatic disasters with France and Spain, and the intolerant religious bigotry of her Catholic half-sister, Mary I. (Mary burned over three hundred Protestant leaders as heretics, earning her the sobriquet, Bloody Mary).

In 1558, England was the ugly step-child of Renaissance power. Yet, by the time Elizabeth died in 1603, England was the richest and most powerful nation in Europe and well on its way to becoming the most dominant empire in the history of the world. What was her calculus for success?

What guided her through forty-five years of rule? The answer is *power*. Elizabeth built, balanced, and maintained power throughout her reign. She understood that a leader cannot stand aloof from the game of command but must actively engage in it, mastering the changing chessboard of power. She devoted time and effort to creating and maintaining a persona and reputation that enhanced her royal office. She was constantly vigilant in building power with British aristocrats, balancing power with Parliament, and maintaining power with foreign diplomats. She impressed on her subjects, nobles, and foreign dignitaries an image of strength and control that demanded respect. Elizabeth's deliberate use of power made her the greatest monarch in British history.

——————————

Like Queen Elizabeth, sellers should have three objectives with regard to power:

1. Build Power
2. Balance Power
3. Maintain Power

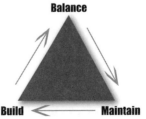

Figure 3.1

Building Power

To achieve power, sellers have to build power. Power is not something a seller acquires by osmosis. Because buyers and sellers perpetually maneuver throughout the sales process, it is important to view negotiation as part of an overall selling process, not a one time meeting.

Remember, how a person sells is as important as how a person negotiates. Everything a salesperson does prior to the negotiation either builds or diminishes power. Certain actions almost always increase one's power, while others decrease it. With that in mind, sellers should be cognizant of building power throughout the selling process by continually attempting to develop personal and corporate credibility, providing compelling presentations, and clearly establishing the value of the proposed product or service. All of these activities build power.

> **Note**: Negotiation is a process, not an event. Every step of the sales cycle, from the cold call to the close, either builds or diminishes power. To be an effective negotiator, first focus on building power by being an effective seller.

The more power sellers establish during the selling process, the more power they have during the negotiation process. Very often, when sellers do an adequate job of building personal, product, and corporate power, buyers completely bypass the negotiation process and adhere to the seller's purchasing terms. If enough power is established, buyers expect to pay the proposed price.

I sold corporate sales training to a committee of executives for a major U.S. call center. Prior to the scheduled presentation, they reviewed my marketing literature and prepared a detailed list of questions to ask me. After providing me with enough time to make a PowerPoint presentation, they grilled me on the specifics of the proposed trainings. I impressed them with the potential increase in sales they would experience by implementing *The Patrick Henry International Selling System*. When the question and answer period was completed, one of the committee members blurted out, "This can't be cheap!" (Terrible thing to say if you're a buyer, by the way). I passed out my published price list, outlined the pertinent trainings and kept quiet. Because of the events that transpired prior to the price discussion (in other words, the selling process), I never had to negotiate price. The impact of the presentation left them expecting to pay full price.

> **The Point?** The best negotiation is the one you never have. One sign of an excellent seller is that he or she rarely has to formally negotiate.

Balancing Power

It is necessary from the very nature of things that power should be a check to power.

—Baron De Montesquieu

On July 4, 1803, the *National Intelligencer* of Washington reported that Napoleon had sold Louisiana to the United States. Napoleon's decision to sell not just New Orleans but all of Louisiana to the United States at a measly three cents per acre seemed insane to European diplomats and many French officials, but Napoleon was delighted with the sale, and rightly so. He held the title to Louisiana, but no power to enforce it. "Sixty million francs for an occupation that will not perhaps last a day!" he exulted. He was fully aware of what he was giving up and what the United States was getting. In the midst of a massive European power struggle with England, Napoleon empowered the Americans at England's expense by selling Louisiana. "The sale assures forever the power of the United States, and I have given England a rival who, sooner or later, will humble her pride." Napoleon used the sale of Louisiana to balance the scale of power in favor of France against his primary military rival, England.

Like Napoleon's masterful gambit with the sale of the Louisiana Territory to the United States, skilled sellers purposefully balance power with buyers.

At our negotiation trainings, I use the power scale to illustrate the concept of balancing power.

Buyer Power

Seller Power

Figure 3.2

Buyers consistently exercise power that tilts the scale out of balance. The key is to ensure that power is balanced. (In Chapter 4 we will address exact methods sellers can use to build, balance, and maintain power).

With the addition of our fourth child, my wife and I decided to purchase a new Chevrolet Suburban. We made an offer to the salesman, and he took it back to his manager for approval. Upon reviewing our offer, the manager hollered out, "What! Not a chance!" and yelled it loudly enough for us to hear it (a buyer tactic called *Pretended Anger* discussed in Chapter 9). When the salesman came back with a counter offer, I, of course, balanced power by hollering back, "What! Not a chance!" loudly enough for the manager to hear it. (Incidentally, we negotiated a terrific price).

Unfortunately, there are many sales and negotiation courses that instruct sellers to "dominate" the selling and negotiating process. Although "dominating sales" sounds empowering to sellers, it's actually dangerous. For instance, if a buyer dominates the sales process by making heavy time investment demands on the seller, power is out of balance. If a seller uses strong-arm tactics to manipulate and control the buyer, power is out of balance. It is essential not to dominate buyers, but to build and balance power.

You might ask yourself, "What's wrong with dominating a sale? Who cares if I have more power than the buyer?" Good question— easy answer. Buyers who are dominated by sellers feel manipulated, and experience what is commonly referred to as "buyer remorse" or "post purchase syndrome." Buyers who feel pressured or controlled into making purchases typically end up resenting the seller, returning the product, or spreading negative word-of-mouth. For long-term, healthy buyer-seller relationships, power should be balanced, not monopolized.

Like sellers, buyers constantly exercise power. There is nothing wrong or inappropriate about that. It's perfectly healthy. Buyers should exercise power. It's part of the symbiotic relationship between buyers and sellers. Do not attempt to eliminate or corner power, but to balance it—to make sure it's not being exercised for or against you in a way that is dominating or overly controlling.

Buyer Power

Seller Power

Figure 3.3

It is important to note that power is not always leveraged strategically or deliberately. Power can be exercised intentionally or unintentionally, consciously or unconsciously. In the end, it doesn't matter why power is exercised. It only matters how.

> **Note**: You build power with effective selling skills. You balance power with effective negotiation skills.

A subtle, yet common strategy buyers use to tilt the power scale in their favor is negotiating on their "home turf." As sports fans know, home teams have a decided advantage over competitors. Because most negotiations take place at the buyer's facility or location, sellers are at a disadvantage from the outset. The buyer is the host, controlling the atmosphere and physical setting of the negotiation. To balance power, a seller should attempt to schedule the negotiation at a neutral facility such as a hotel lobby or restaurant.

I met with a business owner who had a large office. He had purposefully built his desk area on an eight to twelve inch platform. I was seated in a small, cloth chair while he sat in a large, leather chair. As I sat across from him, he literally looked down on me. In order to balance power, I stood up and paced the room as I spoke to him.

My point is that you should always attempt to balance power.

During our negotiation trainings, a consistent question we field sounds something like this, "How do you know if power is balanced? I mean, I like your scale and all Mr. Hansen, but I don't know if it will actually help me build or balance power."

The power scale is not meant to build power. It's meant to conceptualize power, to help sellers comprehend the role of power between buyers and sellers. We use the power scale to help make sellers aware of power and to emphasize the importance of balancing it.

As far as knowing whether or not power is balanced, that is an excellent, but loaded question. To know if power is balanced (or unbalanced), a seller must first recognize power. Once he or she recognizes power, then the seller must understand the various sources of power. Once a seller understands the sources of power, he or she can recognize whether or not power is being built or diminished, and if power is balanced.

Once sellers distinguish sources of power (see Chapter 4), they can look to those sources to determine whether the power scale is in or out of balance. Experienced sellers get to the point where they instinctively feel when power is out of balance.

Maintaining Power: Don't Give Power Away!

In September of 1862, Confederate general Robert E. Lee seized the initiative and invaded the North. He understood that with a decisive victory on northern soil, European nations would recognize the Confederacy and provide badly needed military and civilian supplies. European nations, threatened by the growing power of the United States, were eager to see its demise. With European backing, the war would, for all intents and purposes, be over, and the South would triumph as an independent nation.

Northern general and notorious procrastinator George McClellan battled Lee, but was no match for the bold and daring Confederate general. Fate intervened on McClellan's behalf, however, when an Indiana regiment camped in a field that had been occupied by Confederates a few days earlier. As one of the soldiers sprawled his bedding on the field, he noticed an envelope lying in the grass. Inside the envelope were three cigars wrapped in a piece of paper. Elated, the soldier unwrapped the cigars to show his comrades. As he prepared to light one of the cigars, he looked closely at the paper. What he found changed history.

Lee had written a copy of the marching orders for his army on the papers. The orders contained information about Confederate battle plans and locations. Galvanized by this discovery, General McClellan promptly went on the attack. The results devastated Lee. Using the captured information, McClellan repelled the invading Confederates at the Battle of Antietam, the bloodiest single day in American history. Over five thousand Americans were killed and nearly twenty thousand more were wounded, including Corporal Barton W. Mitchell, the soldier who found the three cigars wrapped in a Confederate battle plan.

—————➤◊◊◄—————

Taking a cue from Lee's painful example, not only is it important to build and balance power, it is also important to retain it. Information is a powerful tool and should not be casually revealed or inadvertently communicated to potential counterparts.

Sellers give power away to buyers every hour of every day by making unwise statements or providing buyers with unnecessary information. Ill-advised statements communicate to buyers, "I'm negotiable" and severely diminish power. Some sellers actually lead off their sales pitch with statements such as, "Of course, our prices are negotiable." "Since you are one of our better customers...," "There is a discount schedule," or, "Just for you, Jim..." Each of these statements empowers buyers and weakens sellers.

> **Caution!** Do not advertise your willingness to make concessions. Avoid statements that indicate a lack of commitment to your price. Don't disclose discount opportunities with phrases that scream, "Lets haggle!"

Many sellers unintentionally equip buyers with the power of information by providing buyers with unnecessary information. Imparting too much information should be completely avoided. Examples of giving away too much information might include volunteering information about your price structure, discussing personal information in which you reveal that you are having a bad sales month, that you are under pressure from your manager to meet a specific quota, mentioning upcoming specials or previous discounts, or that you are having a production or delivery problem. All of these disclosures give power away. These and similar statements can potentially arm counterparts with information that can be used to tip the power scale in their favor. When it comes time to negotiate, buyers can use the revealed information to beat up the seller.

Early in my career, I had a buyer ask me if the software program I was demonstrating had any "bugs" or limitations. Being young and naïve, and thinking that openness would eventually work to my benefit, I said, "Yes, a couple." I briefly discussed with him a few of the limitations, confident he would see, on the total scale of things, the value of our product. Unfortunately, although he saw enough value in the product to make the purchase, he demanded a discount "because of potential limitations and problems we might experience with the 'bugs.'" I learned a valuable lesson that day: Don't voluntarily empower buyers at your own expense.

Fortunately, giving away power is a two way street. Buyers also give power away. Remember the man who blurted out after my presentation, "This can't be cheap"? Inadvertently, he let me know that he thought my offering had tremendous value, tipping the power scale in my favor. I used that insight to stick to my price. I knew, in their minds, the value of the program justified the price. Sometimes buyers will come right out and say, "We've researched the market and we think your product is the one that best meets our needs." That buyer just handed you power on a platter. Having that information equips you with immense power. (Whether you use it or not depends on your skill level). You now know that they think you are the best. Can you use that information when negotiating? Of course you can.

The opposite, lack of information on the buyer's part, is also empowering to the seller. That's why it's critical to control the flow of information and not accidentally give away information that can be used against you. The point is to know when to remain silent and safeguard your power.

> **Caution!** When buyers ask about issues that can potentially empower them at your expense, remember the adage, "Sometimes being dumb can be smart." Don't volunteer information that can be used against you.

How you feel about your price is also important because it will be communicated either verbally or non-verbally to the buyer. The correct words can be used, but if they are expressed in a timid or faint-hearted way, it can invite negotiation. Be confident in your price.

In Summary

Wherever I found the living, there I found the will to power.

—Frederick Nietzsche

I remember the first time I listened to someone explain the importance of power with regard to selling. I was sitting in a training conference with a team of technical sales professionals. Our sales manager was conducting sales training and kept referring to the impact power had on the selling process. My first thought was to disregard his statements as hyperbole, completely non-apropos to selling. Instead, I focused on his more "concrete" training and traditional selling skills. As I engaged in my everyday selling activities, however, I kept running into situations in which I felt powerless. I didn't feel that I had enough influence to control my own destiny. I felt like a skilled beggar. It was extremely frustrating.

We had a corporate summer camp a short time after this first meeting, and the issue of power came up again. I immediately perked up. After feeling powerless with buyers for a few months, the topic of power suddenly held meaning for me. I listened intensely, and I asked questions. By the end of the meeting, I felt like a new seller. Just understanding the role of power "empowered" me. It changed my life, specifically my selling life. Since then, I have felt in total control of my destiny. Success became a conscious choice, not a result of someone else's decision.

Power is real. It is not some abstract concept to motivate sellers. It is not a hypothetical construct conjured up by some scholastic academic who has never spent a day "on the streets." It is a tangible element in the selling and negotiating process.

The Point? Successful negotiators don't treat the subject of power lightly. They purposefully build, balance, and maintain power throughout the selling and negotiating process.

CHAPTER 4

Sources of Seller Power

In 1942, German field marshal Erwin Rommel prowled the deserts of North Africa like a "desert fox." His skills and tactics as a military commander were unmatched by his British counterparts. Rommel had a reputation for lightning speed attacks (called *blitzkrieg*) and deceptive maneuvering that struck terror into the hearts of his enemies. Even when his supply lines were cut off, his forces depleted, and British tanks outnumbered his own by five to one, entire cities would evacuate at the news of his approach. His reputation preceded him, inspired the resolve of his men, and demoralized the will of his enemy.

General Rommel had power and knew how to use it.

Power increased General Rommel's presence and exaggerated his strength. His power was both real and perceived. The very fact that he had a reputation of power gave him more power. It influenced battle, and it influenced the war. It was tangible in the hearts and minds of his troops as well as his enemies—the Allies.

Identifying Seller Power

> For God hath not given us the spirit of fear; but of power, and of ... a sound mind.
>
> —Timothy 1: 7

Many sellers labor under the mistaken dogma that they are at the mercy of buyers who have ultimate control over the sales process. Sellers often feel powerless since buyers can ultimately say "Yes" or "No" to the purchase of goods or services. This powerlessness is often exacerbated when buyers make price or product related demands on sellers. Fortunately, those sellers' assumptions are incorrect. Multiple sources of power exist that sellers should utilize to exercise, balance, and maintain power.

The six primary sources of seller power are:

1. The Power of TIME (Time, Investment, Money & Effort)
2. The Power of Information
3. The Power of Options
4. The Power of Differentiation
5. The Power of People and Pressure
6. The Power of Experience and Expertise

Sources of Seller Power

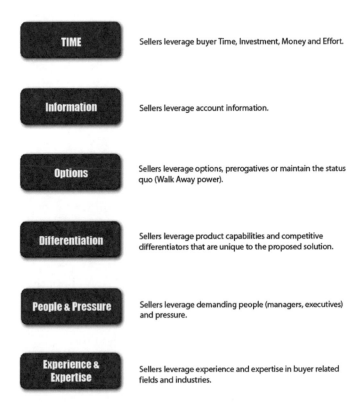

Figure 4.1

The Power of TIME (Time, Investment, Money & Effort)

⟫●⟪

During the Paris peace negotiation between the United States and the Northern Vietnamese, Ho Chi Min instructed his team of delegates to delay the negotiation as long as possible. Aware of the growing political turmoil surrounding the Vietnam War, and in an attempt to diminish the will and power of the United States delegation, Ho Chi Min duped President Nixon's diplomats into devoting excessive amounts of TIME (Time, Investment, Money & Effort) into the negotiation. By investing TIME, Ho Chi Min knew that the United States delegation would not be willing to walk away from the negotiation and would be more prone to acquiesce to his demands. Using ploy after ploy to prolong the process (his team spent nine months arguing about the size and shape of the negotiation table) Ho Chi Min dominated the negotiation.

⟫●⟪

When sellers leverage buyer resources by having the buyer invest time, money, and effort into the sale, sellers exercise the power of TIME. This process is often referred to as "skin in the game" and is sometimes called the power of commitment. Sellers encourage buyers to commit so much TIME into the sales process that it becomes difficult for buyers to walk away from the sale. Like the Nixon delegation in the peace negotiation with Ho Chi Min, the buyer has enough vested in the project that when it comes time to negotiate, walking away without making a decision is not a rational or viable option.

Time is money. When buyers invest time in a project, they are investing money in a project. When buyers spend TIME investigating a product, they often become married to that product and actually turn into "account sponsors" or "product champions" on the seller's behalf. *The more TIME buyers invest in a seller's product, the more partial they become to a seller's solution.*

When buyers make TIME demands, sales professionals should make counter demands to balance power. Professional sellers require purchasers to invest equivalent time, money, and effort into the sales process. They don't let TIME become a lopsided investment. Like Newton's third law of motion, they require an "equal and opposite" effort from the buyer. Throughout the sales cycle, they ask, "Who has more skin in the game?", or "Who has invested more time, energy, money, and effort?"

> **Note**: No investment = no commitment. If buyers don't invest time, money, and effort into investigating, researching, and reviewing goods or services, they have little mental or emotional commitment to the sale.

Sales professionals exercise and balance the power of TIME by having buyers engage in the following or similar activities:

- Taking phone calls
- Viewing websites, marketing literature, brochures, YouTube videos, online demos, or webinars, downloading PDF's, listening to podcasts, etc.
- Accommodating sales trips and site visits
- Attending demonstrations and presentations
- Attending breakfast, lunch, or dinner meetings
- Reviewing and responding to proposals
- Returning voice mail calls
- Replying to emails
- Filling out questionnaires
- Calling references
- Answering questions
- Analyzing, creating, and evaluating RFP's

Once buyers invest significant amounts of TIME, they will have difficulty walking away from the sale—and professional sellers know it.

The harder you work, the tougher it is to surrender.

—Vince Lombardi

When buyers make either innocent or calculated TIME requests that tilt the effort scale out of balance, sellers should counter with corresponding TIME demands.

For example, a potential client requested that I fly to their corporate site in New York. Because of the TIME involved, I requested that he purchase half of the plane ticket. I also requested that all of the decision makers be present and that an outline of the proposed agenda with a list of names and scheduled attendees be emailed to me prior to my departure. These activities required the buyer to put TIME into the sale and balanced power.

> **Caution!** If sellers neglect to balance power by exercising the power of TIME, when it comes time to negotiate, the seller will have all of the investment—the buyer will have all of the power.

One of my business mentors is a master negotiator. He understands power better than any executive I've associated with. He was a business and sales consultant for major U.S. and international companies including multiple Fortune 500's. One of his potential clients showed great interest in his consultation services and requested that he fly to his corporate headquarters to make a presentation to the executive team, at his own expense. Excited about the opportunity, but concerned about the hard costs involved in the sale, my mentor realized that when it came time to negotiate terms, he would have all the "skin in the game," and they would have none. Consequently, he stated to the contact person, "I would be happy to make the presentation. However, so that I don't waste your time or mine, I need the entire executive team, including those from your headquarters in ABC City, to attend the presentation." They agreed and spent (invested) the funds to bring in their entire executive team from all across the nation. By the time of the presentation, the prospective buyer had invested significant amounts of time, money, and effort in the project. Because he exercised the power of

TIME, and reciprocated demands, he balanced power. The result? He won the contract and negotiated an extremely lucrative agreement.

Strategic negotiators use the power of TIME to balance power. They recognize buyer demands that necessitate time, money, and effort—and, in turn, require buyers to match those efforts.

It should be reiterated that it doesn't matter if buyers intentionally or unintentionally get sellers to invest TIME. Once sellers invest time and effort in the process, buyers have the power to leverage that TIME against the seller. The key is to balance power by convincing the buyer to commit equivalent amounts of TIME throughout the sales process.

> **The Point?** Mutual commitment requires mutual investment.

The Power of Information

Rommel, you magnificent bastard, I read your book!

—General George S. Patton

The power of information is illustrated by the WW II experience of General George S. Patton in North Africa. In early 1941, Hitler sent an expeditionary force commanded by General Erwin Rommel to North Africa to bolster the struggling Italian army. With the U.S. army's landing on the island of Sicily, a great military showdown was inevitable between two equally genius commanders, German general Erwin Rommel and United States general George S. Patton. A student of warfare, Patton studied his opposition and its leadership. He read Rommel's book on tank warfare, and he mastered Rommel's battle tactics and strategies. When the two armies finally met for battle, Patton anticipated Rommel's tactics and outmaneuvered him. Patton's knowledge of his opponent was a vital element in defeating the Nazi's most prized and decorated general.

———————

> **Note:** Always try to know more about your counterparts than they know about you.

The power of information rests in knowledge. Sellers exercise this power when they obtain account information that can be leveraged to advance the sale, enhance product or service capabilities, and prevent discounts and negotiated price concessions.

Sales professionals exercise the power of information with:

Account information	Critical needs, buyer interests, existing pains, product problems, production problems, performance problems, dilemmas, unresolved issues, dissatisfactions, etc.
Company information	Struggling or booming? Market share, product successes or failures, financial situations, turnover, existing customer base, etc.
Buyer information	Inexperience, low performance, managerial pressure to solve problems, promotions, deadlines, failures, successes, etc.
Competitor information	Existing products in use, product or service disadvantages, pricing structures, market reputation, inferior features or capabilities, size, etc.

Purchasing information	Funding methods, budget amounts, decision-makers, decision deadlines, potential lost funds if not spent, timeframes, etc.

I was involved in a large sale in Jackson, Mississippi, that illustrates the power of information. Because of the size of the sale, multiple vendors were invited to deliver a presentation to a committee of over forty people. It was one of the largest presentations I had ever participated in. Prior to the presentation, we conducted site visits to each of the locations involved in the sale. We toured their facilities, and we asked need-problem questions. We volunteered to help out on the "front lines" to experience first hand some of the problems being experienced. In short, we equipped ourselves with first hand information which we used to customize our presentation to the exact needs of the committee members.[1] We exercised the power of information. It was a beautiful strategy, with one problem. Minutes before the presentation was delivered, our projector broke! We had no way of providing the participants with a live demonstration of how our software could solve their problems.

Because of the size of the committee, each of the selected vendors was provided a one-hour presentation time slot to show his or her product, so there was no second chance. We were forced to deliver the presentation without showing the software. We were devastated, but we knew we had only one shot and needed to make the most of the opportunity. For that reason, in lieu of showing the software, we centered our presentation, in great detail, on the client's needs and problems that we had identified on our site visits. Using the power of information, we referenced the names of the people we visited. We addressed specific problems and examples we had experienced while volunteering at their facilities. We talked about how our product would solve their problems, and we discussed the unique capabilities of our software solutions.

It was a landslide victory.

---

1. To learn how to conduct a successful site visit, see Chapter 4 in *Winning Sales Presentations*.

Because of the information we gained in pre-presentation site visits, we were able to verbally demonstrate what our competitors could not. When our competitors heard what had happened, they were shocked. They could not believe we were overwhelmingly selected without "showing" our product. They were so bitter about the experience (and because of the size of the sale), that they even threatened the buyer with a lawsuit.

We won that sale because we developed power in the investigation stage of the sales cycle. We won that sale because we gained first-hand information during our pre-presentation site visits.

When it came time to purchase our program, the buyer hired a professional purchasing agent to negotiate the terms of the agreement. Because of the overwhelming response of the committee to purchase our product, we had enough muscle to stand by our published price list. In other words, we had negotiation power. We were also aware that, because the buyers had committed so much TIME in the evaluation stage of the buying cycle, starting the process over would cost them thousands and thousands of dollars.

As a result of building and exercising the power of information, they purchased at full price.

> **The Point?** The more information sellers have about buyer needs, buyer problems, and competing vendors, the more power sellers have to successfully negotiate.

Knowledge and information are powerful negotiation tools. Knowledge of products, markets, and competitors builds credibility, but remember that the opposite is also true. Ignorance diminishes credibility and empowers competitors.

When sellers are aware of buyer needs, problems, and pains, they are equipped with negotiation power. When sellers know of dilemmas, dissatisfactions, or unresolved issues, they can use that information in the selling, presenting, and negotiating process. When buyers threaten to purchase inferior products or services, informed sellers can counter with explanations of how competing products cannot solve their pains and problems. When buyers "cry poverty" with *Sympathy* (a buyer tactic addressed in Chapter 9), sellers who have inside information concerning stock prices, financials, profits, or other related financial data can counter with informed responses.[2] Information about competitive weaknesses or pricing is useful when buyers try to lower prices by using competing prices. Knowledge about funding methods, decision deadlines, budget amounts, and other buying information enables a seller to make better decisions and negotiate from a position of strength.

> **Note**: Exercise the power of information by ordering one share of your potential client's stock. As a shareholder, you will receive press releases, financial reports, and other useful "insider" information about the company and its performance.

During the Vietnam War, the North Vietnamese gathered news releases from local American newspapers about young men serving in the war. Vietnamese officials stockpiled the information in case some of the men became their prisoners of war. Some of them did. Unfortunately, many American prisoners were broken by Vietnamese interrogators with the help of this information about family members and home—a horrible example of the power of applied research.

Knowledge is power; the more you know, the more advantage you can have. This is why generals trade troops for information and why spies are such an intricate part of warfare. In the Persian Gulf War, our ini-

---

2. Standard financial reports about most public companies are available free of charge on the Internet at www.freeedgar.com.

tial strikes were to knock out the information and command centers and blind the opposition.

Gain as much information as possible about buyers to enhance win capability and ensure that false or inadequate information cannot be leveraged against you. The more you know about your prospect, the more negotiating power you have.

> **Note:** The hit show *Pawn Stars* on the History Channel is a great illustration of the impact information can have on a negotiation.

The Power of Options

On November 4, 1804, Toussaint Charbonneau, a French Canadian trapper, walked into the winter camp of the Lewis and Clark expedition at Fort Mandan. He had with him two Shoshone women who had been captured by a Hidatsa raiding party. Charbonneau had won the women (who he took as wives) in a bet with the warriors who had captured them. Lewis and Clark were eager to acquire the services of Charbonneau because his wives could speak the language of the mountain tribes. The wives could translate to Charbonneau; he could then speak French to George Drouillard (a member of the expedition who was fluent in French and English) who would then pass it to the captains in English.

Charbonneau was aware of the communication difficulties Lewis and Clark experienced dealing with the Sioux. Inadequate, incomplete, and incompetent translation had nearly led to full-fledged war. Charbonneau was also aware that Sacagawea was critical to the expedition's dealing with the Shoshones, a tribe rich in horses—horses the expedition needed to continue its objective to find a route to the Pacific Ocean in the spring.

On March 11, 1805, Lewis and Clark sat down with Charbonneau to make a contract.

Aware of the enormous contribution his wives could offer as translators, Charbonneau took the high ground and tried to dictate the terms. The captains explained that he would have to pitch in and do the same work the enlisted men had to do in addition to standing a regular guard. Charbonneau scoffed at the offer and replied that he would not share in the physical duties of the enlisted men. Agitated at Charbonneau's arrogance, Lewis ordered him to leave Fort Mandan immediately, taking his family with him. Lewis and Clark then began discussions with Joseph Gravelines, a trapper familiar with many of the tribal languages.

After four days of living in the Mandan Indian village, Charbonneau sent a message to the captains "to excuse his simplicity and take him into the service." Whether or not he came to his senses on his own or a fellow trapper told him what a fool he was for risking exclusion on a chance-in-a-lifetime opportunity, no one knows. However it happened, Charbonneau was ready to crawl in order to participate in the great adventure. The captains sent word to him to come to the fort for a discussion. He showed up on March 17, and they offered the position to Charbonneau and one of his wives. Charbonneau chose Sacagawea, who was fifteen years old and six months pregnant.

———⟫●⟪———

Lewis and Clark were not only expert explorers, they were also shrewd negotiators. Unlike Charbonneau, they had extensive experience negotiating with suppliers, traders, and tribal leaders. They understood, implicitly, the danger of conceding to ultimatums, so when Charbonneau made his demands, Lewis and Clark exercised the power of options by kicking him out of the camp—a clear signal that they had other options and that they were going to proceed on the journey with or without him.

Similar to the demands of Charbonneau, many buyers attempt to intimidate sellers by making price related ultimatums. Like Lewis and Clark, highly effective negotiators balance those demands by exercising the power options.

Unfortunately, the power of options is most often interpreted as strictly a buyer power. After all, what options does a seller have with a buyer who has the ultimate ability to say "Yes" or "No"? I've heard it before. "Why don't we just skip the bull and move on to something more realistic and cut out the warm fuzzy, happy-clappy, 'make me feel empowered' motivational sales talk? We all know that only buyers have options. I mean, what options could a seller possibly have over a buyer?"

We all understand that the power of options is exercised by buyers when they choose a competitor, announce delays or holds on a project, threaten to *not* purchase a seller's goods or services, or do nothing and make no decision whatsoever. We also know that buyers use the power of options as leverage against sellers. For these reasons, it is the power most feared by sellers.

Is this fear justified? Do sellers have options? Do sellers have prerogatives? Do sellers have any power to say "Yes" or "No" or walk away from a sale? Of course they do. Look at my previous software example. Power was balanced in our favor because of the overwhelming response of the committee, and because of the TIME involved in the evaluation process. It wasn't realistic for the buyer to walk away from the sale because they had too much time, money, and effort invested in the project. If, during the negotiation process, they had been belligerent or overly demanding, we could have threatened to walk away, leaving the committee members without the product they desired and costing their organization exorbitant sums of time and money to start the process over.

> **Note**: Always be prepared to walk away from a sale.

Many sellers have a limited vision of their power in comparison to buyers. Sellers often imagine that buyers do not have to make a decision, that they can just say "No" or "Not right now" and merrily go on with life. This is not always the case. Many buyers are forced to make purchasing decisions because of personal, production, quality, financial, or other related pressures.

Sellers sometimes forget that there are times when buyers *must* make a purchase. The *cost of not* buying can be greater than the *price* of the product or service. Often times, buyers have budgets that must be spent or they will lose the funds. They have deadlines that have to be met. They have problems that need to be solved and emotional needs that have to be filled. Sellers often ascribe more options to buyers than they truly have.

Sellers can also reduce or negate buyer options (and thus power) by communicating features, capabilities, and benefits unique to their good or service. The more needs a seller fulfills, and the more benefits a seller offers, the less competitive options a buyer has. Not all solutions are equal. If one solution is superior to another, the other options become less viable. The fewer options a buyer has, the less power a buyer has and the more power a seller has.[3]

―――⟶⊰●⊱⟵―――

During the Renaissance, there was an abundance of talented artists. There was, however, a shortage of patrons willing to finance the artists. The primary obstacle to an artist's success was finding the right patron, and Michelangelo was no exception.

Fortunately, Michelangelo was not only a master painter, he was also a master businessman. His patron was Pope Julius II. The Pope hired Michelangelo to build a marble tomb. The two of them quarreled over the design of the tomb, and Michelangelo left Rome in a fit of disgust. This was a major act of defiance on the part of Michelangelo. At the time, the Pope represented God's power on Earth.

To the amazement of the papal court, however, the Pope did not fire Michelangelo. Instead, he begged the famed artist to return. He realized that Michelangelo could find another patron, but that he could not find another Michelangelo.

―――⟶⊰●⊱⟵―――

―――――――

3. See Chapter 9 in *Winning Sales Presentations* to learn how to effectively communicate competitive differential advantages.

Sales professionals exercise the power of options by projecting and exercising:

Options	If necessary, walking away from the sale or negotiation. Not "snapping" at every request of a buyer. Ensuring buyers know the seller's time is valuable, their goods and services are in high demand, and that other clients are requiring their time.
Prerogatives	Controlling and influencing dates, times, locations, and timeframes.
Status Quo	Letting buyers know their success is not dependent or reliant on one particular account. If it's not mutually beneficial, having the ability to walk away from the sale.

———

In the early 1900's, J.P. Morgan, founder of U.S. Steel Corporation, sought to purchase a large Minnesota ore track owned by John D. Rockefeller. Unwilling to negotiate directly with Morgan, Rockefeller sent his son, John D. Jr., to negotiate the terms of the purchase. As soon as John D. Jr. sat down, Morgan pressed him, "Well, what's your price?" John D. Jr. paused and then shrewdly responded, "Mr. Morgan, I think there must be some mistake. I did not come here to sell; I understood you wished to buy." John D. Jr.'s response communicated to Morgan that his price was non-negotiable and that he was willing to walk away from the sale if Morgan was unwilling to pay the full price.

———

The primary way sellers exercise the power of options is by projecting demand and avoiding any indication of being desperate. Desperate sellers project that they have no options, or that they are unwilling to walk away from the sale. The "I'm willing to do whatever it takes to earn your business or make the sale" attitude conveys an image of weakness rather than strength and destroys a seller's status as an equal. When sellers present themselves as equals, they demand a level of respect from buyers necessary to establishing balanced, long-term relationships. To build, balance, and maintain power, sellers must subtly communicate that they do not need that particular prospect's business. If a buyer makes unreasonable demands, a seller might respond with, "We would love to do business with you, but this deal is just not for us. Let's get together later with something we can agree on."

I delivered a presentation to a group of educators in the state of Washington. After the presentation, one of the attendees came up to me and said, "The guy who presented before you offered a fairly substantial discount." I responded, "How much?" She replied, "Twenty-five percent." She then made a statement that forever changed my opinion of discounts. She said, "He must be pretty desperate." The poor guy thought he was making a positive impact by offering a discount when in reality he was projecting weakness. He communicated a message of desperation rather than a message of strength. (See Chapter 12 for more information regarding the dangers associated with discounting).

During the Carter Administration human rights became the central objective of American diplomacy. Popular though it was, Carter's human rights advocacy soon led to diplomatic troubles. Soviet spokesmen denounced it as an "unsavory ploy." When the Kremlin angrily protested a State Department report criticizing the persecution of Soviet dissidents, Carter flinched. He told reporters that the statement had not been cleared with him and that he wished to avoid "aggravating" relations with Moscow. Subsequently, in his meetings with Soviet officials, Carter behaved obsequiously. His conciliatory attitude toward Moscow only seemed to wet the Kremlin's appetite. Convinced that they would experience nothing more than a verbal condemnation from the Carter Administration, the Soviet Union invaded Afghanistan. Seeing Carter's disastrous accommodation of the Soviets, Americans turned instead to Ronald Reagan, who promised to prosecute the Cold War more aggressively than ever.

—————

Neediness, Meekness, and Weakness

It is important that you do not appear weak, desperate, needy, or obsequious to buyers. Do not be Mr. Milquetoast or become a "yes man." Rid yourself of happy-face pins, particularly those that read: Have a nice day! Throw away those bumper stickers informing other drivers that you brake for small animals. Being overly friendly is the kiss of death in negotiation. Like the Reagan Administration's attitude toward the Soviet Union, you must appear to be forceful—an attribute that people associate with power, authority, and expertise.

> **Note**: In mandarin China, the *k'o-t'ou*, or kowtow, was a ritual shown to a superior by formally kneeling and touching the head to the ground. Far too many salespeople perform the equivalent of a modern kowtow by yielding to every whim of a buyer.

Neediness is especially dangerous in a negotiation. Buyers who perceive neediness have less respect for the seller, are less responsive to requests, and are more aggressive when making demands. Neediness will always have a dramatic, negative effect on buyer behavior. More bad deals are signed and more sales are lost because of neediness than because of any other factor. In order to avoid showing need, you must never feel it. You do *not* need this deal. You might want it, but you do not need it.

Sellers who exercise the power of options communicate confidence and strength. People have more confidence in purchases they make from confident people. People like to buy from strong sellers and strong businesses. It's just a natural part of the human psyche. We like to buy from people who project strength. We like to buy from people and businesses in high demand. Sheepish sellers and weak companies do not provide buyers with confidence or a sense of certainty regarding the purchase.

When buyers make time demands, sellers should always let them know that they are extremely busy and that their product is in high demand. Can the seller accommodate the buyer's request? Of course, but it might take a little extra time or a schedule shuffle.

> **Caution!** Sellers should never communicate that they need business, have time on their hands, or that they are struggling financially.

I made a software sale to a gentleman whose perception of sellers was, to put it mildly, less than favorable. He immediately began making TIME demands, acting as if I were just sitting at my desk waiting for him to call so that I could end my boredom. He "told" me when I was going to meet with him to discuss our product. Even though I could easily have rescheduled my calendar to meet his demands, I chose not to. I told him I was not available on the date he selected and suggested an alternative date. He immediately responded, "Nope. I need you here on X date." Accordingly, I informed him that due to *High Demand* (a seller countertactic discussed in Chapter 10), I could not meet on X date, that I had other clients making heavy demands on my time to get our product implemented. He again refused. I finally said to him in a firm but cordial manner, "Mr. Prospect, in all due respect, slavery ended a long time ago. If you want to discuss how our product can help your company achieve X, then we will have to meet on Y date." I think he fell off his chair. He was accustomed to pushing sellers around and having them jump when he said jump. He ended up being a very nice man, and we developed a productive relationship. He just needed to be pushed back a bit. He needed to have his power balanced. I chose to use the power of options to do it.

Remember the saying, "That which is easily obtained is lightly esteemed." Don't let buyers take you for granted, dominate you, or push you around. Project power and confidence by making counter TIME demands and controlling or influencing scheduling decisions.

Obviously, exercising the power of options is easier when a salesperson has a full pipeline of opportunities from which to choose. It's just a reality in sales. Without prospects, you have limited options. Salespeople with a small number of accounts have difficulty exercising the power of options. This is one reason prospecting is so critical. Salespeople who avoid prospecting limit the number of accounts they deal with and, therefore, limit their ability to build and exercise power.[4]

The person who cares the least about the outcome has the most power in negotiation. As noted authors Roger Fisher and William Ury state, "*The more easily and happily you can walk away from a negotiation, the greater your capacity to affect its outcome.*"[5]

Remember that the objective is to get what you want by threatening to walk away. The objective is not to walk away. Similar to General George S. Patton saying to his troops, "Keep the objective clear. The objective is not for you to die for your country. It's for you to get the other side to die for their country."

> **The Point?** Sales professionals who are able and willing to walk away from a sale gain enormous negotiation power. Sellers who have walk away power exercise greater control and influence over a negotiation than sellers who don't.

For sellers worried about the risk of walking away, using the protection of a *Third Party* as a backup can minimize the risk (see Chapter 10). Introducing a new negotiator such as a manager or executive, is a comfortable way to reopen a negotiation.

---

4. See *Power Prospecting* to learn how to build a pipeline of qualified opportunities.

5. Roger Fisher, William Ury, *Getting to Yes* (New York: Penguin Books, 1991) 110-111.

The Power of Differentiation

Emphasizing competitive advantages is the foundation for building and exercising the power of differentiation. Because most sales involve competitors, successful sellers focus on unique and exclusive product or service benefits.

Unfortunately, traditional salespeople lack the will and skill to effectively address competitor weaknesses. In many sales, the only difference between sellers is the company name on the business card. This is why cerebral sellers insert unique selling propositions (exclusive features and capabilities) and the strongest competitive strengths possible into their proposals and presentations. They make clear and definitive capability differentiations by using the words "unique," "only," and "exclusive." For example, "We are the *only* supplier that provides this service." "This is a benefit provided *exclusively* by X product." "Our twenty-four hour, seven day a week technical support is totally *unique* in the industry."

Categories of differentiation include:

Product Uniqueness: features, functionality, and benefits exclusive to the represented product or company.

Distribution: distributing goods and services in ways that offer advantages over competitors. (Dell Computer, Mary Kay, and Amazon.com are prime examples of using distribution as a differentiator).

Customer Service: providing prompt attention, timely responses, after hour services, expert assistance, and a friendly staff. (Southwest Airlines and Ritz Carlton Hotels are good examples of using customer service as a differentiator).

Specialization: providing goods and services that cater to a specific segment of a market. (Apple Computer uses specialization as a differentiator by catering to the printing, graphic design, and film industries).

Market Dominance: utilizing brand name recognition, accessibility, performance capacity, and market-place muscle as differentiators. (Microsoft, Intel, and Wal-Mart are examples of market dominance differentiators).

Competitive differentiation separates sales wins from sales losses. If buyers see products as essentially interchangeable, they will make purchasing decisions based solely on price. Effective sellers do more than affably communicate the features and functionality of their good or service. Instead, they focus on differentiations that emphasize unique selling points and competitive advantages.

> **The Point?** The more critical the problem, and the more unique the solution, the less a salesperson will ever need to negotiate.

The Power of People and Pressure

I observed a sale in which a couple wanted to purchase an expensive household product. It was obvious that they desperately wanted the item but would have to stretch to find the funds to make the purchase. They worked the salesperson over pretty hard, but he didn't budge. He used a common closing tactic that sealed the deal. He informed the couple that, not only could he not offer a discount, but the price of the product was going up. The thought of a price increase pressured the couple into making the purchase.

Pressure, which comes in all shapes and sizes, can create negotiating power. We all feel pressure to buy when we hear statements like, "This offer is only good for fifteen days." "The price goes up January first," or "This option expires on October 10th." Deadlines induce action. Used appropriately, they create seller power.

> **Note**: Raising the price is an excellent negotiation tactic to use on the chronically indecisive. Threatening to raise the price helps buyers understand that they will get a better deal today than if they wait until tomorrow.

Obviously, deadlines are not the only source of pressure. Buyers are often under pressure to enhance performance and resolve pending problems. Buyer urgency eliminates the luxury of drawn out negotiations with the attendant demand for concessions.

People can also create pressure. Demanding executives, managers, and bosses can drive people to solve problems or enhance performance. I worked with a buyer who informed me that his job was on the line if he didn't solve a particular problem in his organization. It was a serious problem. He looked to me for help. Price was completely irrelevant, and we never once discussed deviating from our price list or delivery terms. The pressure he felt from people within his organization equipped me with immense power.

Sales professionals exercise the power of people and pressure by identifying and leveraging sources of pressure. Examples include:

- Project deadlines
- Funding that will be lost if not spent
- Performance evaluations and bonuses
- Project evaluations
- Demanding business leaders and managers
- Pending sales
- Production problems
- Threatening contracts
- Demanding customers
- Difficult accounts
- Declining revenues

Although people and pressure are positive sources of seller power, they need to be dealt with tactfully. If you are aware of the existing people and/or situations that are creating the pressure, it is usually sufficient.

Caution! People and pressure power should not be leveraged in a threatening or manipulative fashion. It is a delicate power that should always be exercised in a professional manner.

The Power of Experience and Expertise

On February 4, 1805, Meriwether Lewis noted in his journal that his expedition was about to run out of meat. The immediate problem of scanty provisions threatened the lives of his men and progress of their journey. In addition to sending out a hunting party, Lewis turned to Private John Shields for help. Private Shields was a skilled blacksmith who had set up a forge and bellows inside the winter fort where he mended iron hoes, sharpened axes, and repaired firearms for the Indians in exchange for corn. By the end of January Shields' business was at a complete standstill. The market for mending hoes had been satisfied, and Indian firearms had been repaired. Shields needed some new product or service to attract business.

The obvious answer was arms—not firearms (the captains forbade the sale of rifles or pistols to the Indians), but battle axes. The battle axe was highly prized by the Indians, and Shields could easily make them. He went to work, getting his sheet iron from an abandoned stove and cutting timber to provide wood to make a charcoal kiln to expand production capacity. Still, he couldn't turn out battle axes fast enough.

The Indians were skilled traders who drove hard bargains, but because they were not skilled in metal working, they were at a severe negotiation disadvantage. After some haggling, a price was set: eight gallons of corn for each axe.

Because of his experience and expertise as a blacksmith, Private Shields was able to sell his battle axes at a premium, secure enough corn to feed the entire Corps of Discovery for a month, and stave off a potential disaster for Lewis and Clark.

Experience and expertise have an almost magical effect on negotiations. The more experience and expertise a person has, the better his or her chances for conducting a successful negotiation. Like Private Shields' blacksmithing skills—the greater the expertise of the seller, the more people are willing to pay for the good or service.

Have you ever purchased a product when you had no clue regarding how it worked? Why, then, did you buy? Chances are you purchased it because of the expertise of the seller. In other words, you had confidence in the seller's proposal and accuracy of his recommendation.

In the previous example, the seller looked to me for help alleviating the people pressure he was feeling. He approached me because he believed I could solve his problem. He sought my help because he perceived competence and expertise in me. He trusted my judgment, recommendations, and opinion. But, it was more than just trust in me. He placed his trust in the reputation of the company I represented. Our corporate name and product reputation preceded me. When he called me, he didn't ask for my personal credentials. He didn't ask for our corporate history or financial statements. He assumed we had the capabilities to solve his problems.

The trust this man placed in me is a common trait we all share. For instance, I have been using the same mechanic for eight years because I trust his judgment. I trust his character, and he has experience and expertise that I lack. I rely on him to explain to me what needs to be done to my vehicles. In essence, he has power over me. Because he has always taken the time to explain what parts needed to be replaced and why, and because he has never made an expensive decision without first obtaining my approval, I have confidence in his recommendations. His experience and expertise actually prevent me from bartering with him. I would be absolutely powerless to use reason and rationale to cut his prices. I could threaten him with competition, but he is so busy and always has so much business (power of options), he probably wouldn't even notice if I no longer used his services.

Sales professionals exercise the power of experience and expertise by:

- Understanding buyer needs and pains

- Communicating experience and expertise

- Using language that reflects an in-depth comprehension of product, industry, and market terminology

- Having knowledge of a buyer's situations and problems

- Making appropriate, credible solution recommendations

- Communicating past experience with other clients relevant to the buyer's current situation

In some cases, buyers are unaware of the seriousness of the problems they are experiencing, and occasionally they are unacquainted with available solutions. They might lack industry experience and require consultation, counsel, and guidance from an experienced seller.

Experience and expertise build power. A sales consultant's knowledge, proficiency, and experience add credibility to proposed solutions. When sellers exhibit experience and expertise, buyers are less likely to make cost related or price reduction demands.

In Summary

We confide in our strength, without boasting of it; we respect that of others, without fearing it.

—Thomas Jefferson

Sellers have multiple sources of power to influence the outcome of sales and negotiations. Like an archer with a quiver full of arrows, sellers have an abundance of power they can exercise to build, balance, and maintain power. The power of TIME, the power of Information, the power of Options, the power of Differentiation, the power of People and Pressure, and the power of Experience and Expertise can all be exercised during the selling and negotiating process.

part two

BUYER-NEGOTIATORS

CHAPTER 5

The Buyer Cycle

Roman general Publius Cornelius Scipio and Carthaginian general Hannibal Barca were two of the most brilliant military strategists in history. They were contemporaries destined to face each other in battle. Both were military leaders' sons raised from boyhood with the sole mission of destroying the other's country. Both were appointed the top command of their country's armed forces on the deathbeds of their fathers. Scipio's father, in fact, was nearly killed in battle by Hannibal but was saved at the last moment by his seventeen-year old son, Scipio. Both Scipio and Hannibal were also convinced they were reincarnations of Alexander the Great destined to lead their countries to world power. Obviously, they had much in common.

No commonality, perhaps, surpassed their meticulous habits of study and preparation. Both Hannibal and Scipio were military scholars and cared more about books and knowledge than they did about pleasure and entertainment. For all of their similarities, however, there was one great difference. Hannibal was arrogant and underestimated his counterpart's intellect. Scipio, on the other hand, never underestimated the genius of Hannibal. Scipio, in fact, spent close to sixteen years documenting and studying the military campaigns and tactics of Hannibal while Hannibal did nothing of the sort. This lack of study proved the weakness that led to Hannibal's ultimate defeat.

Hannibal struck Scipio's armies first in a surprise attack across the Alps. Along his way, he wreaked havoc on Roman defenders. Scipio recognized that Hannibal's crushing momentum in Italy could not be stopped, so he decided to mimic Hannibal's strategy and send an invasion force to strike at Carthage itself. When Scipio's army reached Sicily, Carthage panicked and sent an emergency fleet to Italy to retrieve Hannibal to prepare a defense.

In 202 B.C., the two great adversaries squared off at Zama, a fortification just southwest of Carthage, North Africa. Under a flag of truce, the two generals attempted to negotiate a peace settlement. According to Greek historian Polybius, Hannibal offered to relinquish all attempts to conquer territories outside of Africa if Rome would agree to the same outside of Italy. Carthage would withdraw to Africa, and Rome could keep everything else. Scipio, however, having studied the life and campaigns of Hannibal, knew Hannibal's burning hatred for Rome and intractable desire to conquer his foe. He also knew that Hannibal would not make such a concession if he were confident of victory. Scipio declined Hannibal's offer and the following morning the two armies met on the field of battle to resolve the matter.

The two armies were evenly matched, each side with about thirty-five thousand men. However, Scipio was by far the more prepared commander. His deep respect for Hannibal, and his years of study and preparation were about to pay off. During the battle, Scipio predicted Hannibal's every move. He anticipated every tactical thrust, maneuver, and strategy the experienced general threw at him. By day's end, the student overcame the master.

Hannibal was forced to capitulate, and Rome became the undisputed power of the Mediterranean world. Scipio would forever after be known as Scipio Africanus.

Twenty-one centuries later, two equally genius commanders faced off only miles from where Scipio and Hannibal did battle—General George S. Patton and German General Erwin Rommel. The result was the same. Patton's extensive study of Rommel's tank warfare methods allowed him to predict and overcome Rommel's surprise attack at the Battle of El Guettar, setting the stage for Rommel's defeat in North Africa.

―――⟫●⟪―――

Recognizing the Buyer Cycle

Those of us who are professional sellers know much more about selling than we do about buying. Yet, our livelihood depends on our ability to understand buyer behaviors and influence buyer decisions. Like generals confronting the tactics and methods of their counterparts, sellers need to study, recognize, and understand the natural process that buyers go through before making a purchase.

In order to effectively negotiate, sellers must first understand the decision-making process buyers experience when purchasing goods and services. Sellers with a firm grasp on buyer processes and decision psychology have a huge advantage over competing sellers who don't. The more a seller understands the buyer cycle, the easier it is to influence the purchasing decision. *With* a clear understanding of the buyer cycle, a seller is positioned to implement the appropriate selling and negotiating skills at the appropriate time. *Without* a clear understanding of the buyer process, a seller's ability to influence the outcome of both sales and negotiations is severely limited.

Understanding the Buyer Cycle

There are two systems at work in a sale—the seller cycle and the buyer cycle.[1] The buyer cycle mirrors the seller cycle in its order of progression, and it consists of four stages:

Buyer Cycle		Seller Cycle
1. Need/Problem Identification	→	1. Prospecting
2. Pain or Gain Verification	→	2. Investigating
3. Product Evaluation	→	3. Presenting
4. Product Acquisition	→	4. Closing

Seller behaviors should reflect buyer behaviors. For example, if a buyer progresses to the evaluation stage of the buyer cycle and a seller hammers on the fact that the buyer has a problem that needs fixing,

---

1. To learn how to shorten the sales cycle, see *The DNA Selling Method*.

the buyer will recognize the seller is clueless about the buyer's position. The buyer has already identified the problem, experienced the consequences of the problem, and is ready to evaluate solutions to resolve the problem.

> **Note**: You cannot know where you are in the selling process unless you know where your client is in the buying process.

In the mid 1990's, I worked for a technology company that was experiencing severe communication problems between the development team, technical support staff, and sales personnel. With the advent of commercial email, we immediately saw the implications email could have in cutting costs, improving communication, and increasing productivity. We contacted email vendors and invited them to present their products and technology. The first presenter wasted almost his entire, allotted presentation time explaining why our company needed email. He did not ask questions or show any unique capabilities. He delivered a traditional "show up, throw up" sales presentation.[2] In other words, he failed to realize where we were in the buying cycle. We did not need convincing that our company needed email. We had already realized that before we contacted vendors, so we were beyond the need-problem identification stage of the buying cycle. We were in the product evaluation stage.

In contrast, his competitor came in, asked a few preliminary questions and identified where we were in the buyer cycle. He accurately determined that we were beyond the need of hearing a sales pitch about the generic benefits of using a common, corporate email system. We needed concrete demonstrations of his product and technical capabilities—which he provided.

The opposite situation can also transpire. Sellers often prematurely demonstrate product features and capabilities (thinking the buyer is

---

2. To learn how to avoid "show up, throw up" presentations, see *Winning Sales Presentations*.

The Buyer Cycle

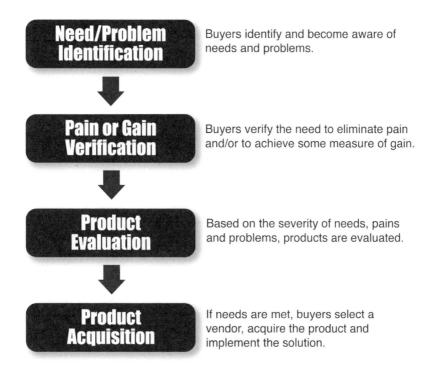

Need/Problem Identification — Buyers identify and become aware of needs and problems.

Pain or Gain Verification — Buyers verify the need to eliminate pain and/or to achieve some measure of gain.

Product Evaluation — Based on the severity of needs, pains and problems, products are evaluated.

Product Acquisition — If needs are met, buyers select a vendor, acquire the product and implement the solution.

Figure 5.1

in the product evaluation stage) when prospects are in the problem identification stage of the buying cycle. This can lead to premature presentations, confusion, and ultimately lost sales.

The Point? Awareness of the buyer cycle is the first step in influencing the buyer cycle. When sellers recognize the buyer cycle, they can adjust their selling behaviors and make intelligent time investment and skill implementation decisions.

Need/Problem Identification

The need/problem identification stage of the buyer cycle occurs when buyers first become aware of needs, problems, difficulties, and/or dissatisfactions. Needs and problems create two elements essential to successful sales-side negotiation:

1. Legitimacy
2. Urgency

Needs and problems create legitimacy. The more needs a buyer has and the more problems a buyer experiences, the more justification the buyer has making purchases to fill the need or eliminate the problem. The more serious the problem is, the more legitimate the purchase. The more legitimate the purchase, the more power sellers possess when introducing and proposing solutions.

Needs and problems also create urgency. Urgency equips sellers with power and is an extremely effective negotiation tool. The greater the need and the bigger the problem, the more urgently a solution is needed. The more urgent the need for a solution, the less room a buyer has to haggle over price or negotiate discounts.

Pain or Gain Verification

Although buyers identify needs, in many cases, the needs are not critical enough to warrant action. In other words, the buyer might recognize that he or she has a need, but might not see enough "gain" to act upon it. For buyers to take action, they must first see clear and compelling reasons to do so.

Obtaining some measure of gain is the motivating factor behind every purchase. When benefits exceed price, prospects have an incentive to buy. Examples include return on investment, increased revenue, decreased costs, pain elimination, or personal gain.

The same is true with problems. The implications of a problem might not appear serious enough to warrant immediate action because it doesn't cause enough pain. When problems are trivial or minimal, buyers stay at the problem identification stage of the buyer cycle. If the problem is a hiccup and not a heart attack, buyers typically just live with it.

> **Note**: The pain formula: P(N)=A. Pain leads to needs. Needs lead to action. Potential buyers will not change unless the pain of staying the same is greater than the pain of change.

If the need is critical, and the problem causes enough dissatisfaction to warrant action, the buyer has progressed to the pain verification stage of the buyer cycle. The buyer has verified both the existence of the need or problem and the general source of the pain. Based on the seriousness of the problem and the magnitude of the pain, the buyer decides whether or not to evaluate potential solutions to alleviate the pain. In other words, buyers verify the pain that justifies the action in the pain verification stage.

Problem ⇨ Pain

Many sellers have a hard time distinguishing between problems and pains. Problems are situations that present perplexity or difficulty. The problem is the source of the pain. Pain is the result or consequence of the problem. For example, my neighbor's sprinkler system broke while he was on vacation, leaking water into his back yard. Because of the duration of his vacation, his water bill was hundreds of dollars. The problem was the broken sprinkler system. The pain was forking out the money to pay his water bill.

Why is it important to recognize the difference, and what does it have to do with sales-side negotiation? It is important to recognize pain because the more serious the pain, the more urgent the solution. The more urgent the solution, the more power the seller has to negotiate from a position of strength. Clearly, the more pain buyers feel, the less bargaining power they have to negotiate discounts and price concessions.

> **The Point?** No pain = no change. If buyers don't feel pain, they have no incentive to change. The better job a seller does unearthing needs, problems, and dissatisfactions in the selling process, the higher the likelihood for negotiation success.

Product Evaluation

Once pain has been verified, buyers move to the product evaluation stage of the buyer cycle. In this stage, buyers assess potential solutions in order to eliminate the problems and pains they are experiencing. Evaluation criteria are established, and often, multiple vendors are invited to engage in the sales process.

Problem ⇨ Pain ⇨ Evaluation

In the product evaluation stage, buyers shop. In some cases, buyers ask for RFP's (requests for proposal), RFI's (requests for information), URS's (user requirement specification), and other formal evaluation forms. Vendors are asked to present to the decision-making person or committee. Products are evaluated, risks are assessed, and costs are determined. If a particular solution fits the needs, budget, and objectives of the buyer, a vendor or product is selected.

In the buyer cycle's product evaluation stage, sellers have a chance to emphasize competitive advantages, distinguishing their products from other vendors and build competitive preference. Why is this important in negotiation? *Because, the more critical the need, and the more unique the solution, the less a seller will ever need to negotiate in the first place.*

The more problems and pains a seller resolves, the more power he or she possesses to justify existing and higher prices. In other words, the stronger the solution, the more muscle the seller has to negotiate.

For example, if a buyer has three primary needs (identified as A, B, and C), and vendor one fills need A, vendor two A and B, and vendor three fills all three needs—A, B, and C, vendor three will have the most negotiation power. By the same token, if need C is the most critical need, vendor three has enormous negotiation power because he is the only vendor who provides it.

Previously, I mentioned a presentation we received that demonstrated the unique capabilities of a particular corporate email program. At the conclusion of the presentation, we cut the salesman a purchase order. We did not haggle over price, nor did we attempt to chip away at his proposal. We wanted his solution, and he demonstrated that his product would solve the problems we were experiencing. Because of the impact of his presentation, he did not need to engage in a lengthy price negotiation.

Product Acquisition

After products are evaluated, a decision is made (or a vendor is selected), and payment plans are established. The solution is implemented and performance is evaluated. Based on the performance of the solution, buyers determine the value of the purchase decision.

Problem ⇨ Pain ⇨ Evaluation ⇨ Acquisition

The product acquisition stage is the most negotiated stage of the buyer cycle. In the acquisition stage of the buyer cycle, formal negotiations are usually conducted.

Many buyers choose to negotiate terms after a vendor has been selected. Buyers often wait until after a decision has been made to negotiate the details of the deal (It's called *Nibbling*, a buyer tactic discussed in Chapter 9). After a sale is made, many buyers pile on additional "requests" such as free shipping, licensing adjustments, delivery timeframes, add-ons, throw-ins, etc.

In Summary

Effective sales-side negotiation strategies begin with a clear understanding of how people buy. If sellers attempt to negotiate too early in the buyer cycle, they don't negotiate from a position of strength. Sellers must not begin negotiating prior to identifying needs or problems to resolve because they won't have enough justification or leverage to negotiate from a position of power. It's akin to laying all of your cards on the table before your opponent places a bet or opts to fold.

In Chapter 12, I will address why sellers should negotiate as late in the buyer cycle as possible. Negotiating late in the buyer cycle provides sellers with an opportunity to identify needs and problems, establish legitimacy, develop unique solutions, and differentiate themselves from competing vendors—all of which build power and increase the likelihood of a favorable negotiation.

> **The Point?** By recognizing the different stages of the buyer cycle, sellers avoid negotiating too early in the buying process, giving away power, and ultimately losing winnable sales.

CHAPTER 6

The Buyer Method

———⟶⁑◈⁑⟵———

The post World War I years were hard on everyone, including art dealers. Big art buyers were simply not buying, and art dealers, such as Joseph Duveen, who catered to the richest tycoons in America were unable to sell. Incapable of making it any longer on his own, Duveen partnered with a number of other art dealers who pooled their resources to go after the richest men in America. Henry Ford became their first and primary target because he had not yet ventured or invested in the art market.

Duveen devised a plan to assemble a list of "The One Hundred Greatest Paintings in the World." They would present them in one sweeping offer to Henry Ford who was one of only a handful of individuals wealthy enough to make such a purchase. With one purchase, Ford could have made himself the possessor of the world's greatest art collection. Duveen and his colleagues worked for weeks on a three-volume set of books that contained reproduc-

tions of the beautiful paintings and scholarly text accompanying each painting.

As Duveen's group approached the residence of Henry Ford in Dearborn, Michigan, they were surprised at the modesty of his home and surroundings. Ford received them in his study and examined the reproduced paintings. As he turned the pages of the art books, he showed signs of wonder and delight. He was impressed. After making a lengthy evaluation of the paintings, he turned to the art dealers and said, "Gentleman, beautiful books like these, with beautiful colored pictures like these, must cost an awful lot." "But Mr. Ford!" explained Duveen, "we don't expect you to buy these books. These books are a present to you." Duveen then explained that they were hoping Ford would buy the actual paintings that the reproductions in the books depicted. Ford refused.

Duveen left Dearborn a defeated man. He had prided himself on being a master art salesman and was accustomed to manipulating the upper class by preying on their weaknesses—weaknesses such as pride, insecurity, jealousy, and greed. But Duveen's approach did not work with Henry Ford. Although Ford was the wealthiest man in America in 1920, he was an unassuming man who felt more at home with blue collar workers than he did with upper class, white collar bankers, businessmen, and sophisticates.

The mistake that Duveen made, and what he failed to recognize in his first meeting with Henry Ford, was that Ford was not really evaluating the art—he was evaluating Duveen. Ford wanted to determine what kind of man he was dealing with and whether or not Duveen was just another urbane peddler preying on the rich. Ford's primary evaluation did not surround the quality of the art. It surrounded Duveen's character. The blunder Duveen and his cronies made was attempting to sell their art without first selling themselves.

Five Criteria Buyers Evaluate

Not only do buyers go through a consistent *buying cycle* when purchasing goods and services, they also follow a predictable purchasing pattern. It's called the buyer method. The buyer method represents the criteria buyers use before making a decision.

Buyers consistently evaluate five things when deciding on a particular product or service, and typically in this precise, psychological order as indicated in *Figure 6.1*.

The Sales Representative

What you are thunders so loudly in my ears I cannot hear what you say.

—Emerson

The first evaluation buyers make is not about a product or service. It is about the salesperson. As Ford's example demonstrates, outside of pur-

The Buyer Method

Representative	Honesty, character, attitude, knowledge, experience, etc.
Company	Reputation, dependability, status, size, stability, etc.
Product	Quality, features, capabilities, functionality, etc.
Price	Rates, fees, charges, costs, affordability, etc.
Value	Benefits, gains, worth, utility, importance, consequences, risks, etc.

Figure 6.1

chasing shelf products from retail stores, the first thing buyers instinctively do is size up the person representing the good or service.

No matter the circumstances, buyers make immediate judgments about the salesperson dealing with them. Is the salesperson nice looking or unattractive? Is he dressed appropriately, or does he look like a gang member who needs to pull his pants up? Is she knowledgeable and smart, or illiterate and uneducated? Is he helpful and courteous, or rude and discourteous? Does she listen or talk too much? You get the idea.

Most importantly, buyers evaluate salespeople regarding trust and character. Early in the sales cycle, buyers make quick assessments about the honesty, character, and experience of sellers. Prospective buyers typically decide within the first few minutes of contact whether or not they trust the seller enough to proceed to the next level of the selling process. This is especially true when selling over the phone.[1]

Without trust, sellers severely limit their ability to establish rapport and build long-term relationships. B*ecause of the prominent role of trust needed for a sale, a salesperson's character contributes more to success than any high-powered sales skill or fancy negotiation technique.* In fact, without integrity, sales skills and negotiation techniques are often interpreted as manipulative and duplicitous.

It is character and honesty that give life to professional sales and negotiation skills.

> **Note**: Sellers are subject to Napoleonic Law—guilty until proven innocent. Most buyers are automatically suspect of salespeople. Sellers must overcome this stigma by projecting and exercising character early in the sales relationship.

When sales progress to the point of negotiation, character, integrity, and experience are negotiation components that can work for you or against you. If sellers establish relationships based on trust and character, buyers are inclined to trust motives and recommendations. They are unmistakably more receptive to capability claims, product presentations, decision suggestions, and price proposals. Once trust is established, buyers are less suspicious of sellers and less resistant to price.

The Company

After a buyer develops a positive impression about the seller, he or she evaluates the company. Is the company as honest as the seller? Will it back its commitments? Will it deliver as promised? Is it dependable? Does it have a good reputation? Is it financially stable? Will it honor its warranty? Buyers ask these questions when they evaluate a company.

---

1. See Chapter 18 in *Power Prospecting* for a detailed analysis of how to effectively build credibility and character in the initial stages of a cold call.

Sellers who provide positive information about their company help buyers make favorable decisions. The company's dependability, history, market position, financial stability, brand status, and service reputation all either build or diminish power and credibility.[2]

> **Note**: The stronger you position your company in the selling process, the more power you will have in the negotiation process.

In the 1960's and 70's, IBM established a reputation as the epitome of corporate stability. To this day, IBM is commonly referred to as "Big Blue." Because of IBM's corporate reputation, buyers felt safe purchasing their goods and services. IBM played heavily on their corporate reputation and used it to intimidate competitors and sell their products at higher prices. They perpetuated the pithy marketing slogan, "No one ever gets fired for going with IBM." Their corporate reputation gave them selling and negotiating power.

When it comes time to negotiate, your company's reputation will either be an ally or an enemy. If your company has a reputation for outstanding service and high quality, buyers won't expect you to sell at prices on the same level as competitors with a reputation for poor service or low quality.

If you establish a professional, reputable corporate image, buyers will be at a psychological disadvantage when negotiating purchasing terms. Mentally, they will expect to pay more and negotiate less.

The Product or Service

After buyers are comfortable with the character of the seller and the reputation of the company, they evaluate product features, capabilities, and benefits. They determine whether or not the proposed solutions resolve problems, eliminate pain, or fill emotional needs.

---

2. See Chapter 8 in *Winning Sales Presentations* to learn how to effectively communicate corporate credibility.

Obviously, this is an important juncture in the selling process. Buyers have no incentive to change from the status quo if the product doesn't address needs, resolve problems, or eliminate pain. The more problems resolved and the more pain eliminated, the more motivated buyers are to purchase goods or services.[3] The more problems a seller identifies as needing resolution, the easier it is to justify price proposals. The more pain a product or service eliminates, the more rationale a seller has to negotiate favorable purchasing terms.

> **Note**: Product features and capabilities are only useful if they address buyer needs and pains. Regardless of how "cool" or nifty a feature or capability is, it is of no value to a buyer who can't use it.

Successful sellers make use of features and capabilities to create value, justify prices, and build power—not to "show up and throw up" on buyers.[4]

The Price

The fourth evaluation buyers make prior to making a purchase is price. Once buyers are confident that they are dealing with a reputable seller and stable company, and once they've decided the product or service meets their needs, they evaluate price. How much is it? What fees are involved? What charges can I expect? What rates are available? How much is the warranty? Is this a sale price? Is there a finance package that comes with it? Is it affordable? These are all price related evaluation questions.

Notice that price is the fourth evaluation criteria and not the first. Price is not the number one factor people use to evaluate goods and

---

3. See *The DNA Selling Method* for more details concerning how to identify and develop buyer needs and problems.

4. See Chapter 12 in *Winning Sales Presentations* to learn how to use *The Sales Messaging Matrix* to differentiate features, advantages, and benefits.

services (I address this issue in Chapter 14). Price is simply one of multiple factors evaluated.

Tired of running out of space on my desk top, I decided to shop for a desk that would accommodate multiple books, papers, accessories, and a computer without getting cluttered, muddled, or unorganized. I visited both furniture stores and office supply stores. I finally found a desk that was the size and quality I was looking for. After opening the drawers and evaluating the features of the desk, I asked the salesperson, "How much?" He quoted me a price that seemed a bit high, but reasonable. I agreed to pay the price, but negotiated free shipping. The truth is, I really wasn't overly concerned about price. I had found what I wanted in a desk, and I bought it. Having a large, accommodating desk was so important to me that I initially didn't even look at price. I first found what I was looking for, made sure it was a quality product, and then asked about price. In other words, price was the last criteria I used in my purchasing evaluation.

Keep in mind that price is meaningless without context, such as a need you fill, a problem you solve, or pain you eliminate. If you offer a price before identifying needs or problems to solve, it is useless. This is why the product or service evaluation stage of the buyer cycle is critically important. It is your product presentation or demonstration that gives meaning to your price. Your price will only have meaning when compared to how it affects a buyer's existing circumstance. You build the context during the selling process and prior to discussing price.

Value

Once the price of a product or service is established, buyers determine value. Value is calculated by comparing the utility of a good or service to the price. Buyers determine value by asking themselves questions such as, "What benefits are derived from the purchase and do they outweigh the cost?"

Note: Contrary to popular belief, people don't buy because of price. They buy because of value. Buyers want more than a good price. Until they are convinced of the value of the proposed good or service, no price will be right.

Price can be a double-edged sword. It is nothing more than the projected worth of a product or service, i.e., the value. Sellers project value with price. For this reason, sellers should be cautious when introducing the price of their good or service. If the price is too low, buyer suspicions are sometimes aroused. Low prices can potentially lead buyers to become skeptical of the quality of the good or service. Having a low price can actually hurt your chances of winning a sale if it diminishes the perceived value of the offer.

I worked closely with a major construction company that was bidding on a large, industrial project. They worked on the proposal for weeks, working out the material and labor costs, insurance, equipment, etc. They really wanted the deal, so they slashed costs in every corner of the proposal they could find. They lost the bid. When they asked the buyer why they lost, the answer they received shocked them. They were indeed the lowest bidder. So why did they lose the sale? The buyer assumed the lowest bidder offered the lowest quality. To be safe, they chose the "middle" bidder.

Be careful what your price communicates.

The more value buyers associate with goods and services, the less price resistant they become. The more value buyers perceive, the more power sellers have. The more power sellers have, the more favorable the negotiated outcome will be.

The Point? Don't sell price. Sell value.

In Summary

Negotiating is an integral part of the buying process. Virtually all buyers follow a consistent buyer method when purchasing a good or service. Recognizing the buyer method helps sellers become better negotiators. Why? Because, like selling, buying is a process. It has a natural flow and logical order of progression. Sales professionals who have a firm grasp on the buyer method are better negotiators because they understand the appropriate sequence of events that should take place *prior* to negotiating. Understanding the buyer method allows sales professionals to sell the right feature (themselves, their company, their product, or their value) at the right time and in the right order.

CHAPTER 7

Buyer Power

On June 5th, 1967, Israel preemptively attacked Egypt by air and by land. In less than three hours, the Israeli Air Force destroyed over 85 percent of the Egyptian Air Force. With total air command, the Israeli army advanced to the Suez Canal with minimal losses. In what was later called The Six Day War, Israeli forces occupied Sinai, the Golan Heights, and the region between the 1948 border and the west bank of the River Jordan.

In 1975, Henry Kissinger was sent to Israel to help negotiate the return of the Sinai desert the Israelis had seized in 1967. The negotiations were intense, and it was impossible to reach agreement on some points. During the meeting, and in the middle of a tense negotiation, Kissinger broke off discussions. To the surprise of those around him, he decided to go sightseeing. Accompanied by Israeli diplomats, Kissinger paid a visit to the ruins of the ancient fortress of Masada, known to all Israelis as the place where seven hundred Jewish warriors committed mass suicide in 73 A.D. rather than surrender to Roman troops. The Israelis immediately recognized the significance of the visit and understood the message Kissinger was attempting to communicate: They were courting mass suicide if they did not compromise some of their entrenched territorial positions.

Kissinger was able to indirectly accuse the Israeli diplomats of courting disaster because of his knowledge of Israeli history. He forced them to consider the seriousness of their territorial stances because of the power of CIA (Counter Intelligence & Account-information).

Sources of Buyer Power

Like Henry Kissinger, intelligent negotiators recognize and utilize *multiple sources of power*. The primary sources of power that buyers exercise are:

1. The Power of TIME (Time, Investment, Money & Effort)
2. The Power of Information
3. The Power of Options

Notice that the sources of buyer power are also the primary sources of seller power (as addressed in Chapter 4). It should come as no surprise that both buyers and sellers share sources of power. In fact, in order to balance power, both parties often have to tap from the same sources.

Sources of Buyer Power

TIME — Buyers leverage Time, Investment, Money & Effort against the seller.

Information — Buyers leverage Information against the seller.

Options — Buyers leverage Options, Prerogatives or the Status Quo against the seller.

Figure 7.1

The Power of TIME (Time, Investment, Money & Effort)

When buyers leverage seller resources by having them invest time, money, and effort into the sale, the buyer exercises the power of TIME. Buyers persuade sellers to commit so much TIME into the sale that it becomes difficult for sellers to walk away. When sellers invest significant amounts of TIME, they lose walk away power. The seller has so much vested in the project that when it comes time to negotiate, he is at a severe negotiating disadvantage and is vulnerable to price demands and negotiated discounts. In other words, the power scale is out of balance in favor of the buyer.

Buyers exercise the power of TIME by having sellers engage in the following or similar activities:

- Making numerous phone calls
- Sending literature, brochures, and marketing collateral
- Leaving numerous voice mails
- Sending emails
- Traveling to buyer locations
- Providing multiple presentations
- Attending breakfast, lunch, or dinner meetings
- Preparing and revising proposals
- Creating competitive comparisons
- Answering questions
- Filling out RFP's

Of course, these activities are completely legitimate and in many cases necessary to win sales. I'm not suggesting sellers shouldn't engage in these activities. I'm suggesting that sellers should maintain an awareness of the TIME investment required to fulfill these activities. Sellers need to be aware that sinking large amounts of time and effort into a sale can equip buyers with tremendous negotiating power. They need to be aware of TIME and make sure the buyer is equally invested.

I worked with a salesperson who gave numerous presentations to a particular company. After each presentation, the prospect would string him along and say he needed to give the presentation to yet another committee member who couldn't make it to the last presentation, or to an executive, or to another department now involved in the decision. It was ridiculous. The seller traveled hundreds of miles and spent hundreds of dollars each time he traveled to make the presentation. Each time he made a presentation he had more invested in the sale. With each presentation, he became more "married" to this particular account. Fortunately, he won the deal, but when it came time to work out the price and establish licensing terms, he didn't have a prayer. He was so wrapped up in the sale and had put so much time and effort into the process that he immediately acquiesced when they threatened to issue another RFP and start the process over if he didn't concede to their terms. (A buyer tactic called *Lost Ground*—see Chapter 9). He left thousands of dollars on the table because he never balanced power by equalizing the TIME the buyer put into the sale.

It doesn't matter whether a buyer purposefully or unintentionally gets a seller to invest TIME. Once sellers invest significant amounts of time and effort into the process, buyers have the power to leverage that TIME against the seller. The key, of course, is to balance power by getting the buyer to commit equivalent amounts of TIME into the process.

I learned this lesson the hard way as a young man entering the radio industry. During my junior year in college, I became upset at the university I was attending for financially supporting a politically active group that was using school funding to ridicule university standards and students in the most embarrassing and inappropriate ways possible. I approached the administration to see if they were aware of the "projects" they were financially supporting. They were not only aware of it, but they also had staff members from the law school sponsoring many of the activities. They actually expressed anger at me for bringing it to their attention. I was so frustrated by their dismissive response and lack of willingness to address the issue openly that I decided it was time to "Cross my Rubicon." I went to the local radio station and purchased an hour of airtime and started *The Patrick Henry Hansen Show*.

I had never been behind a microphone in my life. To pay for the airtime, I went out and hustled up business by soliciting a dozen or so local companies to sponsor the program. After just a few weeks, I generated enough funds to pay for the airtime, and I started making excellent money, especially for a college student.

The show became popular enough that I extended it to two hours and persuaded even more businesses to advertise. It was great! Right up to the point where I started butting heads with the station manager. When he began making demands concerning my program, guests, and content, I initially resisted but felt powerless. After all, he could pull my show at any time, right? Looking back, I understand that power was way out of balance. I had invested so much time in obtaining sponsors, creating ads, reading and studying current events, lining up guests, publicizing the show, even advertising my program in the university paper, that I had all the "skin in the game," and the station had none. I made no demands on the station. I never asked them once to invest time to train me, line up guests, or even promote the show.

What was worse, the station manager actually became envious of my growing radio popularity and financial success. As soon as he had a chance, he began renegotiating my contract. He upped the price of the airtime. Being young and inexperienced, I didn't understand how to negotiate or combat his ruthless negotiation tactics. I had invested so much time, money, and effort in the show (not to mention the emotional investment), that the thought of walking away was out of the question. So I caved. I didn't realize there was anything else I could have done.

Eventually, the problem became serious enough that I dropped my program at that station and moved to a bigger and better station. My point is that *I* had invested *all the TIME*. I had everything in the basket. I actually made myself powerless by putting so much TIME into my show and never asking for anything in return from the station. They had nothing invested in my program. When it came time to negotiate terms, I was not in a position to win.

The same thing happens in sales. Sellers get sucked into investing significant amounts of TIME into particular sales. Buyers make both innocent and calculated TIME requests that tilt the effort scale out of balance. When sellers negotiate, they have all the "skin in the game" while buyers have all the power in the game.

The Power of Information

————⤛●⤜————

In 1908, Lord Baden-Powell founded the Boy Scout movement by publishing *Scouting for Boys*. He founded the Wolf Cubs in 1916 and was acclaimed world chief scout in 1920. Interestingly, the revered scout leader had a clandestine past. He was a spy in the British military, the James Bond of his day. Born in London, he joined the army in 1876 and conducted undercover espionage missions in India, Afghanistan, and South Africa. He won fame for his bravery and courage during the battle of Mafeking in the South African Boer War. He was a master of disguise and developed innovative methods of spying. His most novel spy tactic was using coded art. Equipped with a butterfly net, sketchbook, and false beard, he would disguise himself as a naturalist wandering the targeted country in search of animals, insects and botanical discoveries. He would conceal diagrams that disclosed military installations, armaments, and large scale weaponry with what appeared to be innocent drawings of butterflies, grasshoppers, and other insects. His stealthy surveillance and mastery of spy techniques inspired him to publish an account of his experiences in a book entitled *My Adventures as a Spy*.

Lord Baden-Powell's undercover reconnaissance equipped the British military with knowledge and information that gave them a strategic edge in battle. His research and covert missions also provided intelligence that was used in diplomatic negotiations.

————⤛●⤜————

The second most common source of buyer power is the power of information. Like the espionage efforts of Lord Baden-Powell, the power of information is exercised when buyers obtain intelligence that can be leveraged against sellers. The concept of the power of information is captured nicely in the popular saying, "Knowledge is power."

In any industry or endeavor, knowledge is of supreme importance. This is why professional athletic teams study film of their opponents and countries spend immeasurable amounts of money and take huge risks to finance spies—to gain information.

Prospects use counter intelligence to obtain freebies, throw-ins, and various price concessions and exercise the power of information with data about:

Products	Weaknesses, shortcomings, vulnerabilities, prices, delayed releases, production problems, delivery problems, etc.
Company	Low sales, struggling market share, recent wins (a previous precedent for discounts) or losses (potential reason to discount), unhappy customers, recent turnover, small clientele, financial struggles, size, etc.
Sales Reps	Inexperience, low performance, managerial pressure to make quota, recent losses or failures, recent wins, etc.
Competitors	Competitive advantages, additional features, capabilities or benefits, market reputation, corporate size and stability, etc.
Pricing	Competitive pricing, previous prices, understanding margin and price structures, previous discounts, etc.

Knowledge and information are powerful negotiation tools. When buyers are aware of product shortcomings, they can use that information to obtain discounts. When buyers (or existing customers) are aware of corporate information such as struggling market share or unhappy customers, they can use that information to beat up sellers on issues like price, delivery terms, or licensing agreements. When experienced buyers recognize they are dealing with a rookie salesperson who is unfamiliar with products or market demands, they can use that insight to demand discounts or price allowances.

Competitive information is a notorious buyer negotiation tool. Many buyers make a conscious habit of mentioning the price, unique features, or specific product advantages of competing vendors in front of sellers to create FUD (fear, uncertainty and doubt) that is used to obtain discounts.

Information about previous sales also equips buyers with power. If a buyer obtains information about previous discounts to other clients, he or she has a legitimate reason to expect the same discount. "You gave so-and-so a discount. I assume you'll be giving us the same price?"

Oddly enough, the concept of the power of information was ingrained in my mind years ago when I read Julius Caesar's commentaries while waiting for a business flight from New York to Salt Lake City. I was perusing the history section of a bookstore in the JFK airport and came across one of the most fascinating books I've ever read.

Julius Caesar recorded his campaigns against the various Gallic and Celtic tribes in Europe in a book called *The Conquest of Gaul.* In it, he describes his first attempt to conquer the island of Britain in 55 B.C.

It happened to be a full moon that night, at which time the Atlantic tides are particularly high—*a fact unknown to the Romans.* The result was that the warships used in the crossing, which had been beached, were waterlogged, and the transports, which were riding at anchor, were knocked about by the storm, without the soldiers having any chance of interfering to save them. A number of ships were shattered, and the rest, having lost their cables, anchors, and the remainder of their tackle, were unusable, which naturally threw the whole army into great consternation…

On learning of this incident, the British chiefs who had assembled after the battle to execute Caesar's commands put their heads together. Knowing that Caesar had no cavalry, ships, or corn, and inferring the weakness of his forces… they decided that their best course was to renew hostilities, to hinder the legions from obtaining corn and other supplies, and to prolong the war into the winter.[1]

Caesar's lack of information concerning the treacherous tides of Britain, and his limited knowledge of the channel currents led to the destruction of his naval fleet. It caused additional loss of needed soldiers, prolonged the war, and Caesar himself was almost killed. Information concerning Caesar's wrecked ships rallied his enemies and emboldened the British chiefs to continue fighting for their freedom from Roman rule.

As Caesar later admitted, he would have been far more successful on his initial invasion of Britain had he conducted navigational reconnaissance of the tides and currents of what is now called the English Channel. Caesar did not make the same mistake twice and conquered southern Britain with a second invasion in 54 B.C.

Counter intelligence and information was as important a weapon to Caesar as was his most sophisticated battle weaponry.

> **Note**: Information is power. The more information buyers have about you, your company, your competitors, and your price structure, the more power they have to negotiate discounts and concessions.

---

1. Julius Caesar, *The Conquest of Gaul* (New York: Penguin Books, 1982) 101.

Armed with counter intelligence and information that includes product or corporate weaknesses and vulnerabilities, buyers are equipped to
make your negotiation experience a difficult one. The opposite is also
true. A lack of information on the side of your counterpart empowers
you, the seller, and will make your negotiating experience an easier
one. This is why it is critical to control the flow of information and not
inadvertently give away information that can be used against you.

The Power of Options

Sellers most fear the power of options. The power of options is exercised when buyers threaten to *not* purchase a seller's goods or services,
announce delays or holds on a project, choose a competitor, or do
nothing and make no decision whatsoever. Options, prerogatives, or
the dreaded status quo are decisions used by buyers to leverage power
against sellers.

Buyers exercise the power of options with:

Options	Choosing a competitor
Prerogatives	Delays, postponements, rescheduling, putting the project on hold, starting the project over, etc.
Status Quo	Not purchasing the product or service, doing nothing, staying with the current product or service, not making a decision, etc.

Buyers often use the power of options as a last resort to secure price
concessions. By making the ultimate threat of not purchasing a product or starting the entire evaluation process over again, buyers often
intimidate sellers into offering discounts in order to maintain the life
of the sale.

Buyer Power: Sellers Beware

The most commonly used buyer power is TIME. Convincing sellers to invest time, money, and effort into a potential sale is not a difficult task. It's also the most dangerous buyer power because it's the most expensive. The most irreplaceable commodity known to man is time. You can replace money, but you can't buy back time. Actually, in a very real sense, time is money. When sellers invest time in a sale, it's like investing money in a sale. You can not recover it. There is nothing worse than investing excessive time and effort into a sale only to have a buyer not purchase. This is why qualifying leads and balancing power is so critical to negotiation.

> **Note**: Countering and balancing buyer power is addressed in Chapter 10.

Chapter 8

Buyer Types

—————⟶►◄⟵—————

In 783 A.D., a fury of "North men" began swarming the shores of England. The Scandinavian Vikings robbed, pillaged, and burned Saxon monasteries, villages, and townspeople. With no navy or standing army, the Anglo-Saxons were defenseless against these seafaring marauders. In 854, thousands of Vikings decided to winter in England, and it became obvious that something far more serious than plundering raids was yet to come. The Vikings were building an army and preparing to stay until they had drained England of its resources.

In 865, the Viking army struck. Driving south from modern day York, they leveled the various fiefdoms of North Umbria, Mercia, and East Anglica. By 870, they battled the powerful kingdom of Wessex, and although the Wessex Saxons fought bravely, they were defeated by the more warlike Vikings.

Into this moment of almost complete collapse stepped one of history's most renowned lead-ers—Alfred the Great. Alfred was the fifth son of King Ethelwulf of England and was the only monarch in the history of England to be called the Great. At the age of five, he was sent to Rome where he captivated Pope Leo IV. He learned to read and write. He was trained, not only in the art of war, but also in the skills of the mind. As the mantle of leadership fell upon him with the death of his father and brothers, Alfred studied his enemies. He became an astute student of the Viking culture, motivations, and methods. He ascertained that warfare alone would not protect his people from the ambitions of the Norsemen.

Because the Vikings were tribal, Alfred had to deal with multiple Viking leaders. He used spies and reconnaissance to learn specifics about their motivations and methods. Based on his acquired information, he formed strategies to combat each Scandinavian chief. With some Viking leaders, he knew that brute force was the only deterrent while with others, satisfying their greed would suffice.

During his kingship, Alfred successfully overpowered the Vikings with warfare, money, education, and religion. When warfare was the only viable solution, he defeated the Vikings using Roman infantry tactics he discovered in Latin history books. By concentrating his forces and building England's first navy, he drove the Vikings out of Southern England's capital, Wessex. When necessary, he used money and bribes (called the *danegelt*) to buy off his enemy. He even taught his enemies Anglish (later called English) in an attempt to Anglicize the Vikings. And in one of history's most extraordi-nary moves, he used the Christian ritual of baptism by immersion to befriend and reform his enemies.

By 896, Alfred had repelled the Viking invasions and secured southern England from Danish rule.

Unlike his predecessors who had failed to stop the Viking invasions, Alfred the Great used multiple strategies based on the characteristics of his enemies. Rather than using *only* generic, traditional means of warfare, he identified the individual methods and motivations of each Viking leader and dealt with each accordingly. He modified his approach based on the personality traits, strengths, and weaknesses of every Viking chief.

Buyer-Seller Relationships

Like Alfred the Great, sales-side negotiators cannot treat each negotiation counterpart the same way. Every buyer must be handled individually because each uses different tactics, motivations, and methods to obtain their objectives.

Of course, no two negotiations are exactly alike because no two buyers are exactly alike. However, skilled sellers have the ability to recognize and appropriately control multiple buyer-seller relationships. Skilled sellers recognize the kind of relationship they have with each client and adjust their negotiation strategies and approaches accordingly.

Buyer Profiling

In order to be an effective negotiator, sellers need to identify what type of buyer they are dealing with. Some negotiators are cordial and pleasant. Others are abrasive and offensive. Although it is impossible to encapsulate all buyers into one or two categories, placing buyers into a narrowed range of recognizable groups is extremely useful. Recognition of common negotiation tactics is easy when the tactics are labeled according to common negotiator types.

Identifying buyer types helps sellers categorize buyers into subgroups with common characteristics and behavioral tendencies. The rationale behind buyer profiling is simple: If you can identify the negotiator type with whom you are working and understand his or her motives and techniques, you can effectively position yourself to successfully negotiate. By mapping each type's characteristics, sellers can identify and predict attitudes, motives, and negotiation tactics.

Buyer Types

Recognizing buyer types is an important negotiation skill because it helps sellers establish appropriate relationships, identify buyer tactics, and close sales without unnecessary price-concessions or discounts.

There are four categories of buyers:

1. Hard Negotiators
2. Calculating Buyers
3. Soft Bargainers
4. Casual Shoppers

Buyer Types

Hard Negotiators
Merciless buyers who use adversarial negotiation tactics to dominate and intimidate sellers.

Calculating Buyers
Shrewd buyers who are intelligent, professional, "get down to business" negotiators.

Soft Bargainers
Friendly buyers who are highly relationship driven but still focused on ultimate buyer objectives.

Casual Shoppers
Buyers who are indifferent, unfocused, unpredictable and unqualified.

Figure 8.1

Hard Negotiators

Attitude	Confrontational, antagonistic
Mannerisms	Animated, loud, boisterous
Motivation	Win–Lose
Trust	Distrust others
Tactics	Used aggressively
Power	Maximized & exploited
Relationship	Treated as irrelevant
Goal	Victory

———>◦<———

In the years leading up to the Civil War, Congress could have easily been mistaken for a Western saloon. Senator James Hammond of South Carolina remarked, "Every man on the floor of both Houses was armed with a revolver, some with two revolvers and a Bowie knife." Senator Benjamin Wade of Ohio carried a sawed-off shotgun in open site. When a pistol concealed in one House member's desk accidentally discharged, there were instantly "fully thirty or forty pistols in the air," recalled Representative William Holman of Indiana.

During this raucous time, the brutal beating of Charles Sumner was one of the most violent episodes that resulted from the debates over slavery. On May 19, 1856, the abolitionist from Massachusetts delivered his famous "Crimes Against Kansas" speech in which he decried the efforts of Southerners to force slavery into the Kansas territory. Sumner's speech brimmed with inflammatory rhetoric, oratorical bombast, and personal digs against proslavery senator, Andrew Butler. Although Butler was not present to hear the speech, his kinsman and fellow Carolinian, Representative Preston Brooks was present. Brooks was outraged by Sumner's remarks and a few days later entered the Senate chamber to confront Sumner. "I have read your speech twice over carefully," Brooks announced. "It is a libel on South Carolina and Mr. Butler who is a relative of mine." Without warning, Brooks then started whacking Sumner with a wooden cane until it splintered and his victim fell from his chair in a bloody heap.

Northern reaction to the assault was one of horror. A debate soon raged in the House over whether or not to expel Brooks. After threats of expulsion, Brooks decided to resign, but his exile was brief. He ran for office and was sworn in just two weeks after his resignation.

———>◦<———

Although physical confrontations play no part in modern negotiations, unfortunately, oral confrontations and verbal "beatings" do. Some negotiators, especially hard negotiators, use personal attacks and verbal lashings to intimidate counterparts and dominate negotiations.

Hard negotiators are infamous for using merciless tactics, adversarial negotiation techniques, and any other available tactic (shy of a brutal beating) to dominate negotiations and advance their positions. Hard on both problems and people, they are high stress negotiators who use street fighting tactics to win negotiations. They like to apply pressure to sellers, making threats and often turning negotiations into a contest of wills. They are distrusting, stubborn, uncompromising, and downright belligerent. They view business with a "dog-eat-dog," "don't take any prisoners" mentality.

Hard negotiators are the most difficult negotiators to handle. They are too cold to reach emotionally and too arrogant to reach intellectually. They are abrasive, fixated on their interests, and care little about the feelings or interests of their counterparts. They act antagonistically towards sellers, exploit power at every opportunity, use tactics heavily, do not care only about winning, but also about seeing the adversary lose, and they cannot be trusted. They often raise their voices and attempt to intimidate sellers with physical and verbal outbursts such as slamming their fist down on a desk. In short, they are not pleasant people to deal with.

New York real estate tycoon Donald Trump is a well-known example of a hard negotiator. While being interviewed on CNN's *Larry King Live*, Trump illustrated his hard hitting negotiation prowess. As King began discussing Trump's business success, Trump paused and said, "Do you mind if I sit back a little because your breath is very bad? It really is. Has this been told to you before?"

King replied, "No."

"Okay, then I won't bother."

Perplexed, King continued, "That is how you get the edge isn't it?... That little thing you threw me right then—that no one has ever told me."

"Has no one ever told you that? You are kidding."

"Nobody."

After the show, a group of confused network producers approached Trump for an explanation. Trump shrugged off the incident and explained that he was simply demonstrating how he gets the edge in negotiations.

> **Note**: When dealing with hard negotiators, do not turn the negotiation into a contest of wills or make the process personal. Maintain your objectivity and professionalism.

Although most of us cringe at the thought of dealing with a personality like Donald Trump, when operating from a cerebral center, it can actually be fun—sometimes even amusing. It is one of those guilty pleasures. Seasoned negotiators find it humorous to observe the frustrations hard negotiators experience when their tactics fall flat.

My first joyous experience involving a hard negotiator came early in my sales career. I was selling a technical package to an information technology director who hated salespeople. He was rude, condescending, and used homemade technical acronyms and jargon he knew I wouldn't understand. He treated me like dirt. He was an existing customer who was looking to either upgrade to our most recent version of software or go with a competitor. He actually came right out and said, "Mr. Hansen, I don't particularly like your software. I think your technical support staff sucks, and I'm not going to pay for your software a second time. You have two choices. Upgrade our system at cost or lose us as a customer." He was the epitome of a hard negotiator. (See my response in the summary of Chapter 11).

When hard negotiators use verbal outbursts to intimidate, sellers must not give them the reaction they expect. Keep your cool, and maintain your poise. In Chapter 10, I will share specific strategies and counter actions that will neutralize hard negotiator tactics.[1]

---

1. See Chapter 14 in *Winning Sales Presentations* for more information regarding how to overcome "stump the chump" tactics.

Hard Negotiator Modification Strategies

Do	Do Not
Maintain your composure	Be defensive
Be professional	Be emotional
Focus on issues	Focus on personalities
Question assertions	Be intimidated into silence
Maintain your dignity	Be submissive
Be firm, but cordial	Reciprocate rudeness
Be cautious	Be trusting
Control the flow of information	Carelessly share information
Be willing to walk away	Show neediness

Calculating Buyers

Attitude	Businesslike, professional, serious
Mannerisms	Calm, poised, composed
Motivation	Win
Trust	Proceeds independent of trust
Tactics	Used deliberately
Power	Balanced
Relationship	Secondary to objectives
Goal	Resolution

Calculating buyers are shrewd negotiators. They are intelligent, astute, and make smart purchasing decisions. More often than not, they are cordial, professional, and sometimes even cooperative. However, they are not your "bud." They are known for being composed and in control, detached from any deep emotional connection with sellers. They purposely keep an arms-length relationship. They understand that becoming too close or too friendly with sellers could cloud their ability to negotiate.

Although they can be unsympathetic to the interests and feelings of sellers, they are not normally rude. In fact, they are characteristically professional. However, there is no doubt that the relationship is about business and business only.

Calculating buyers are typically good negotiators for two reasons: They are smart, and they make good business decisions. Calculating buyers are often (not always) executives. They are the cool heads in the crowd, and they are confident and comfortable with formal negotiations. They are commonly well educated, well dressed, and well versed in the business at hand. They do not hesitate to take charge of a situation or confront inconsistencies. They are easily frustrated with mundane conversations and have little tolerance for stupidity. They are usually very successful people who keep cooperative relationships with sellers as long as the relationship advances their agenda. They recognize power and exercise it. They use negotiation tactics strategically and intentionally. They are extremely business driven and their objective is to win, regardless if that means you win with them or you lose. Trust is not the motivating factor with calculating buyers because they don't make decisions based on trust. They make decisions based on logic, not emotion.

Although calculating buyers sometimes intimidate sellers, there are advantages in dealing with them. Because they are business and not relationship driven, they don't absorb substantial amounts of time on non-business related issues. They don't expect sellers to take them golfing or buy them lunch once a week.

> **Caution!** Back slapping relationships are completely taboo with calculating buyers. Do not try to become their "pal." They are uncomfortable with close buyer-seller relationships.

When dealing with calculating buyers, it's important to be professional and analytical. When making presentations, disseminating information, or negotiating, be specific. Provide detailed written proposals that include the strongest possible cost justification or risk reduction. A seller must be accurate with statements and projections. Provide facts, graphs, charts, and rationale to support your positions.

Calculating Buyer Negotiation Modification Strategies

Do	Do Not
Be businesslike	Be amateurish
Dress professionally	Dress casually
Avoid excessive small talk	Attempt to by chummy
Be organized and prepared	Be disorganized or unprepared
Be clear and specific	Be vague or ambiguous
Be brief and to the point	Be wordy or loquacious
Present accurate, factual data	Use guesswork or estimations
Provide reason and rationale	Express opinions
Be rational	Be emotional
Use professional closing tactics	Use closing gimmicks

Soft Bargainers

Attitude	Positive, friendly, sociable
Mannerisms	Talkative, conversational, enthusiastic
Motivation	Win–Win
Trust	Trust others
Tactics	Used reluctantly
Power	Shared
Relationship	Primary focus
Goal	Agreement

Soft bargainers are friendly buyers and are usually cheerful and optimistic. They like people, enjoy relationships, and look forward to social interaction. They view counterparts as friends. They typically yield to pressure, are soft on both problems and people, and normally have a good sense of humor. They are not easily offended, and they are almost entirely relationship driven. The type of relationship they have with the seller is often more important to them than the price of the good or service.

Soft bargainers are very trusting and more often than not give sellers the benefit of the doubt. They like sharing responsibility and want personal support, guarantees and assurances to limit risk.

When soft bargainers use tactics, they use them reluctantly because they are motivated by good relationships. Their objective is to win, but not at the expense of the seller. They are team players, so power is shared with soft bargainers. In other words, they don't exploit power. In fact, the concept of power is not part of their modus operandi. They think in terms of relationships, not power. Trust plays an implicit role with soft bargainers.

> **Note**: Although soft bargainers are extremely relationship driven, they are still focused on buyer objectives. They fully intend to meet their objectives. They just approach it more mildly than hard negotiators or calculating buyers.

Soft bargainers are the kind of buyers who send *you* "Thank you" cards. Once they trust you, you are their friend. As long as you perform as promised, they are fiercely loyal and won't change products or services just to save a few bucks.

One important characteristic of soft bargainers deserves notice. They are not good "table" negotiators. They don't like to sit across a table and negotiate. Instead, they like to discuss deals on the golf course or over lunch. They enjoy doing business in social settings, and they avoid "eye-to-eye," one-on-one negotiations.

Soft bargainers are easy people to negotiate with because they are not confrontational. Their friendliness, however, can be disarming and sometimes even dangerous because sellers may lower their guard. In this low-key environment, sellers can unnecessarily give away commissionable dollars and corporate profitability.

Even though soft bargainers use tactics reluctantly, they still use them. Soft bargainers leverage relationships with soft tactics to gently bargain and negotiate favorable terms.

Because soft bargainers are relationship driven, they often absorb a disproportionate amount of time and energy. This can be both reward-ing and draining. The more time and investment it takes to maintain the relationship, the less selling time is available for other clients.

Be cautious of jumping into time intensive relationships with soft bargainers. Getting too close to prospects can actually absorb inordi-nate amounts of non-sales related time, leading to building *relation-ships* instead of building *sales*.

Soft Bargainer Negotiation Modification Strategies

Do	Do Not
Focus on relationships	Focus strictly on business
Socialize, make small talk	Rush to negotiate
Use references and testimonials	Overuse facts and figures
Be thoughtful and friendly	Be demanding or threatening
Use stories and scenarios	Focus only on hard data
Negotiate informally	Be overly formal
Provide guarantees and limit risk	Concentrate on potential risks

Casual Shoppers

Attitude	Nonchalant, detached, indifferent
Mannerisms	Distant, standoffish, aloof
Motivation	Unidentified
Trust	Unestablished
Tactics	Used sporadically
Power	Exploited erratically
Relationships	Confusing and extraneous
Goal	Unidentified

Casual shoppers are amicable people but are totally unfocused. They don't have clear needs or identifiable objectives and do not use a predictable set of tactics.

Casual shoppers show interest in available goods and services, but they are both erratic, and more importantly, unqualified. This is the biggest danger when dealing with casual shoppers. They can siphon away large amounts of time without purchasing. They are "tire kickers" and "fence sitters."

Casual shoppers do not develop a defined relationship with sellers. They are vague, unclear, and usually leave an odd or confused feeling with sellers. They don't exercise power in any predictable pattern. They don't use consistent buyer tactics, their motives are unidentifiable, they don't have anything close to a precise objective, and they are too casual in their approach to be trusted.

> **Caution!** The casual shopper is the most dangerous of all buyers.

Because casual shoppers are impulse buyers, they *sometimes* purchase goods and services. That's the lure. That's the trap. Don't fall for it. Don't waste your time on twenty casual shoppers to hopefully, kind of, sort of, on a lucky day with a downhill wind, make a sale.

Casual Shopper Negotiation Modification Strategies

Do	Do Not
Ask stringent qualifying questions	Assume they are qualified
Identify critical needs	Presume matching needs
Be prepared to walk away	Be overly committed
Obtain firm commitments	Assume commitment
Limit TIME investment	Invest significant TIME

Elevating Buyer-Seller Relationships

One of the most accepted sales assertions is that *selling is about relationships*. There are dozens of books, tapes, and courses on relationship selling that stress the importance of having healthy, productive relationships with buyers. The reason behind the emphasis is that if a seller has a strong relationship, it is easier to sell. I would add to that assertion: the better the relationship, the easier it is to negotiate as well. The type of relationship a seller establishes with a buyer sets the tone and often determines the outcome of the negotiation.

The fundamental rule sellers should follow when dealing with buyers is to respond *in kind*. Even though sellers set the tone for the negotiation, it is buyers who typically set the tone of the relationship. They establish relationships based on comfort and convenience levels. Sellers should do their best to mirror the relationship buyers establish. If buyers have calculating, analytical personalities, sales professionals should adjust their approach and respond accordingly. For example, when working with calculating buyers, sellers should be analytical. They should emphasize results, be detailed oriented, and provide evidence for the proposed solution. On other hand, when working with soft bargainers, sellers should be friendly, engineer consensus, and emphasize good feelings.

If buyers are cordial and cooperative, sellers should mimic the relationship. *The exceptions are hard-negotiators and casual shoppers.* Sellers should do everything possible to elevate hard negotiators to a more productive relationship by exercising and balancing power. Casual shoppers need to be qualified to be considered a viable and worthwhile prospect. The key is to elevate hard negotiators and casual shoppers to soft bargainer and calculating buyer relationships.

Sales negotiations differ from other forms of negotiation because seller-negotiators develop and maintain long-term post-sale relationships *while simultaneously achieving aggressive profitability objectives.* This is why cerebral sellers attempt to elevate buyer relationships to the calculating buyer and soft bargainer categories.

Hard Negotiators = Exercise Power

Calculating Buyers

Sellers need to elevate relationships into these two categories

Soft Bargainers

Casual Shoppers = Qualify

Figure 8.2

The Point? For sellers interested in long-term relationships, it is necessary to progress buyers into relationships that are productive, profitable, and foster an atmosphere of mutual respect and implied trust.

In Summary

In our corporate trainings and executive retreats on negotiation, participants often ask, "How can we initially tell what buyer type we are dealing with?" Great question. There are two primary indicators. The first is the buyer's attitude. If it is open and cooperative, you know you are dealing with a soft bargainer. If a buyer is rude, controlling, or antagonistic, you are dealing with a hard negotiator. If the buyer is cordial, but strictly business-like, you are dealing with a calculating buyer. If a buyer is casual and indifferent, you are working with a casual shopper.

The second indicator is the nature of the tactics the buyer uses during the selling and negotiating process. Each buyer type uses different types of tactics (as addressed in Chapter 9). When sellers identify the types of tactics being used, they can determine the buyer type and prepare to deal with a predictable set of negotiation tactics.

part three III

NEGOTIATION TACTICS

Buyer Tactics

—————

J.P. Morgan Sr. was one of history's shrewdest businessmen. He once met with a jeweler in New York and expressed interest in buying a pearl scarf pin. The jeweler searched for weeks to find the most magnificent pearl available. He mounted the pearl in a beautiful setting and sent it to Morgan with an enclosed bill for $5,000. The next day the package was returned to the jeweler with a note that said, "I like the pin, but I don't like the price. If you will accept the enclosed check for $4,000 please send back the box with the seal unbroken." Enraged at Morgan's arrogance, the jeweler refused the offer, sent back the check, and dismissed the courier. He then opened the box to reclaim the pearl scarf pin. To his shock, he found that it had been removed. In its place was a check from Morgan for $5,000.

—————

Professional Buyers

Like J.P. Morgan, many businesses have figured out that the quickest way to put money on their bottom-line is to take it off the seller's. Buyers who attend professional seminars and negotiation workshops learn tactics designed to squeeze everything possible out of a sale. They are taught to be ruthless negotiators. I have learned to spot a trained, professional buyer within minutes of a conversation. They are easily identified, once you recognize their tactics.

> **Caution!** Buyer skills are devastating to unprepared sellers who are not trained to recognize and counter buyer negotiation tactics.

Buyer tactics are tools for influencing behavior and are used to gain discounts, price cuts, and other related seller concessions. When successfully executed, buyer tactics reduce profit margins and commissionable dollars.

There are nine buyer tactics associated with each buyer type. For example, soft bargainers do not normally use the same tactics to secure discounts that hard negotiators use. Once a seller identifies the buyer type, he or she can prepare to work with a predictable set of buyer tactics.

I name buyer tactics for the same reason that I name buyer types. It makes them easier to spot, and, therefore, easier to counter. Forewarned is forearmed. Recognizing traditional buyer negotiation tactics assists sellers in neutralizing attempts to obtain discounts and price concessions. *I will address how to deal with each tactic in the chapter on seller countertactics* (see Chapter 10).

> **Note**: Although each tactic is categorized by buyer type, no buyer has a monopoly on any one tactic.

Hard Negotiator Tactics

- The Price Pinch
- Competition
- Demands & Deadlines
- Control & Intimidation
- Cost Breakdown
- The Ridiculous Offer
- Pretended Anger
- Salt & Pepper
- Good Guy, Bad Guy

The Price Pinch

The Price Pinch uses price related statements to imply that the seller's price is too high, unreasonable, and/or unacceptable. Hard negotiators know that products and services almost always have some leeway in their price structure. They subscribe to the belief that everything is negotiable. *The Price Pinch* is one way to get to the bottom of it.

- "Your price is too high. You're 20 percent higher than the next highest bidder. I hope this is just your starting price and that you are prepared to talk about something reasonable."
- "The price in your proposal is completely unacceptable."
- "I don't have a lot of time to haggle over your initial offer. What's your rock bottom price?"

Hard negotiators commonly use *The Price Pinch* to persuade sellers to make additional offers. For instance, when buyers make statements such as, "Is that the best you can do?", or "You'll have to do better than that," they are attempting to lure sellers into bidding against themselves.

Competition

Competition minimizes unique solutions and competitive advantages by leveraging competing prices and/or competitive features against the seller. Buyers want the seller's quality, reputation, and benefits but at the competitor's price! This is a red herring approach. The seller's unique capability is swept aside by focusing on a competitor's price.

- "X competitor is 20 percent less expensive than you and includes training. You need to sharpen your pencil."
- "X product includes Y capability that you don't offer. How can you possibly justify being 20 percent more expensive?"
- "X competitor is offering a significant discount. Are you prepared to match it?"

Demands & Deadlines

———⟫◆⟨———

Near the end of his career with the Red Sox, Babe Ruth was in a bitter negotiation with owner Harry Frazee over his salary. Frazee professed amazement that Ruth would ask for so much money, claiming that not even the great actor John Barrymore made that amount. "I don't give a damn about any actors," Ruth retorted. "What good will John Barrymore do you with the bases loaded and two down in a tight ball game? Either I get the money or I don't play."

———⟫◆⟨———

Demands & Deadlines is a pressure tactic used to get sellers to make concessions based on pressure, threats, and intimidation. This is a favorite tactic used by hard negotiators, like Babe Ruth, because it makes them feel powerful and in control.

- "I don't want to talk about it again. Your failure to include the discounted price in the RFP put me in a bad situation. I want the corrected RFP on my desk by Monday. If you want the contract, you'll just have to figure out a way to get it done."
- "We won't purchase without a written guarantee that you can deliver within three weeks."
- "I'm not paying more than $1.00 a pound, and that's final."

Sometimes hard negotiators will push sellers to make a discount decision "on the spot" or lose the sale. Hard negotiators know that people are far more vulnerable when they are under time pressure. They are also aware that people who lack thinking time will make mistakes.

This technique was popularized by Niccolo Machiavelli. Machiavelli advised government officials to suddenly press aggressively for a decision during a negotiation. By making a demand or insisting on a dead-line, Machiavelli knew that the timing and patience of his adversary would be disrupted.

Control & Intimidation

This tactic attempts to control and intimidate sellers with extended waiting periods, delays for appointments, long periods on hold, inter-ruptions, receiving phone calls or visitors during negotiations, schedule control, etc.

- "Go ahead and sit down. I've got to make a couple of phone calls. I'll be with you shortly."
- "Ms. Thomas is in a meeting. Can we reschedule to meet some-time next week?"
- "Mr. Jones is on the phone right now. Please wait in the lobby. I will come to get you when he is ready to meet."

Making sellers wait is a powerful way of controlling and intimidating them. By controlling the clock, buyers can make sellers linger and fret. By making a seller wait in a lobby, or allowing interruptions to occur during the negotiation, buyers communicate that the meeting isn't really very important (power of options).

I flew a team of technicians to a client's headquarters to work out the technical details of a major product installation. The main techni-cian was a Novell fanatic and was angry that his organization decided on our Microsoft technology based product. When our technicians arrived, he told them to wait in the lobby until he "finished his coffee." Over an hour passed. When he finally emerged, he stated to our tech-nicians that he was out of time and that they would have to schedule another appointment. He was a hard negotiator who used control and intimidation to vie for position, influence, and power over the installa-tion process. Unfortunately, our technicians were technicians and not negotiators.

Hard negotiators often rely on intimidation factors to get what they want. If it suits their purposes, they will make rude statements, use abusive language, and/or engage in excessive talking in meetings and presentations. They will often make disparaging or humiliating remarks to intimidate sellers. (This tactic is often referred to as *Sticks and Stones*).

- "That's the stupidest thing I've heard from a sales rep in a long time."
- "You look terrible, John. Sales not going well for you?"

Non-verbal and other forms of bullying are also used to intimidate sellers. For example, rudely interrupting a seller in the middle of a sentence, ignoring the seller, reading while a salesperson is speaking, etc., are all tactics used to intimidate and control sellers.

Cost Breakdown

Joseph Duveen, who in later years became one of the world's foremost art dealers, was convinced that his uncle, Henry Duveen, was not getting as much for his art as he should from financial titan, J.P. Morgan. Accordingly, Joseph put before J.P. Morgan a collection of thirty miniatures, of which six were very rare, the rest unremarkable. Unbeknownst to Joseph, Morgan was as sharp an art collector as he was a banker. Morgan cast his eyes briefly over the collection and then asked what the thirty pieces cost. Duveen gave him the figure, upon which Morgan pocketed the six good miniatures, divided Duveen's figure by thirty, multiplied by six, and handed over that amount.

Cost Breakdown is intended to fool sellers into revealing price structures, cost breakdowns, and proposal architectures. The information is then used to chip away at available margins. The cost breakdown shows where and how much the profit is in order to cut into it. Similar to J.P. Morgan's tactic, it's an itemizing technique used to determine a seller's cost structure and profitability margins.

- "How did you line item your pricing?"
- "Explain to me how you came up with your price structure."
- "Your margins must be enormous with this pricing structure. What's your cost breakdown?"

The Ridiculous Offer

Buyers use *the Ridiculous Offer* to pinpoint how low a seller is willing to lower his or her price. This tactic is commonly referred to as "Lowballing." *The Ridiculous Offer* attempts to find the seller's lowest acceptable price by making a ridiculously low offer and seeing how the seller responds.

- "Heather, how about $1,000? That should be enough, shouldn't it?"
- "Chad, I can't imagine this being more than $5,000. How about $4,500?"
- "I'll make you an offer of $25,000. Take it or leave it."

As a boy, I collected and traded baseball cards. I was once showing my cards to a friend of mine when his father walked into the room. He looked at the cards and asked if I would be interested in selling them. "Sure," I replied. "How much?" He responded, "Five dollars." I replied, "Five dollars, no way! They are worth at least twenty dollars." By making an initial ridiculous offer, he lowered my aspiration level. I ended up selling thirty or forty dollars worth of baseball cards for twenty dollars.

Looking back, I learned a valuable lesson that day about the power of an initial low offer and the effect it can have on the human psyche.

Pretended Anger

This tactic is used almost exclusively by hard negotiators. A negotiator using *Pretended Anger* attempts to make the seller feel uncomfortable feigning anger or hostility at the seller or the seller's price. *Pretended Anger* is usually conveyed in verbal outbursts of frustration. For that reason, it is sometimes referred to as *Infantile* because the buyer approaches the negotiation with the maturity of a three year old, throwing a fit until he gets what he wants.

- "Jared, this is ridiculous. How can you expect us to do business with someone who gouges his customers with exorbitant prices? This really ticks me off."
- "I am shocked that you would offer such stringent terms. I would have expected more from you. I guess I thought wrong."

Sometimes anger or displeasure (real or pretended) is expressed in a theatrical, nonverbal manner. Examples might include raised eyebrows to show surprise, shifting in a chair to show discomfort, cringing to show irritation, or shaking one's head in shock, dismay, or disapproval. These physical gestures communicate displeasure and are used to affect and influence the thinking of sellers. As Sigmund Freud put it, "No mortal can keep a secret. If his lips are silent, he chatters with his fingertips; betrayal oozes out of him at every pore."

> **Note:** Body language is a powerful means of communication. Facial expressions and body movements communicate how a person is feeling.

Salt & Pepper

Deception is the oldest tactic in the book, beginning in the proverbial Garden of Eden. There, a snake deceived Eve with misleading statements and outright lies.

The Greeks used deception on the Trojans. They rolled their huge

Trojan Horse up to the gates of Troy and then pretended to head for their ships, returning home. When night fell, Greek soldiers emerged from the giant horse and lade waste to Troy.

Like "Greeks baring gifts," hard negotiators sometimes use less than forthright tactics to outmaneuver their counterparts. Using *Salt & Pepper,* hard negotiators attempt to confuse sellers. Rather than make an issue black *or* white, they confuse the issue by making it both black *and* white. *Salt & Pepper* is a deliberate attempt to complicate an issue, rather than simplify it.

Technical buyers are infamous for using this tactic on non-technical sellers. They use technical jargon to purposefully complicate an issue to confuse the seller. Confused, mentally flustered sellers are not good negotiators, and hard negotiators know it.

For the really dirty players, false statistics, intentional errors in arithmetic, and/or misleading information are used to deliberately deceive the seller and "muddy the water." It can be extremely challenging for even the best seller to decipher manipulated numbers and misleading information in order to make informed decisions and accurate proposals. Of course, once the deal is locked in place, duplicitous buyers attempt to hold sellers to the originally proposed price quotes, even though they were based on falsified numbers which were accepted by the seller in good faith. The double-standard is the standard of many hard negotiators. They don't bat an eye at using unethical tactics but act mortified when sellers question their calculations or intentions.

Good Guy, Bad Guy

The good guy, bad guy tactic is a popular bargaining ploy used by hard negotiators. Variations of this tactic have appeared in everything from Charles Dickens' *Great Expectations* to television police dramas that have popularized the "good cop, bad cop" routine.

Good Guy, Bad Guy is used as follows: A "bad guy" takes a strong stand on price. "I won't pay more than $1.00 a pound. Period." The good guy shifts in his shoes a bit, staring at the floor, and then says to the bad guy, "Look, don't be so unreasonable. Mr. Salesman is a good man. He's done a lot of good things for us and deserves to make a profit on this deal. Why don't we agree to $1.20 a pound?" The seller's aspiration level is supposed to have been diminished by the demeanor of the bad guy. When good guy is through speaking, the seller is supposed to think the good guy's offer is the best he's going to get.

Calculating Buyer Tactics

- Selective Memory
- The Maze
- Trophy Sale
- Budget
- Bloodhound
- Silence
- Lost Ground
- Done Deal
- What If...

Selective Memory

The buyer using the *Selective Memory* technique secures discounts, additional add-ons, and other seller concessions by selectively remembering and referencing previous conversations, statements, or agreements. *Selective Memory* can be used to remember things out of context, completely fabricate a conversation or agreement, or interpret a statement in the most liberal way possible. *Selective Memory* is a popular tactic with calculating buyers. They push the seller by testing his or her memory and will with statements such as:

- "I thought you said that feature was included in the original price?"
- "It seems like you mentioned the first year of support was included in this price. I remember your saying something like

that. I sure don't remember your saying it wasn't included in the initial price."
- "Maybe I misunderstood you, but I was certain you said delivery was included in your initial proposal."

Signatures, contracts, and agreements are for well-intentioned people with bad memories. To insure concrete communication, you should send a contract, letter of understanding, memorandum, or email that confirms agreement (save the email, of course). When dealing with calculating buyers, be careful not to rely on memory for details of an agreement.

The Maze

Calculating buyers love to utilize *The Maze* technique. These buyers strategically use maze tactics to exercise the power of TIME (Time, Investment, Money & Effort) in order to get sellers to invest significant amounts of energy into the sale. After completing a maze of work, sellers become married to the sale. Buyers then leverage the invested time and effort against the seller. Once sellers get too deep into the maze, they have too much invested to get out. It's actually one of the more subtle, yet cerebral, buyer tactics because the seller initially interprets being fully engaged and entrenched in the maze as a positive buying signal.

- "I need you to call Jim down in our I.T. department with an explanation of the database infrastructure. Also, please write up the ROI sheet we talked about and get that to our CFO, Dan Burton. Then, call Mary in purchasing and let her know when she can get that product comparison I know you are working on. I'm assuming we are still on for the presentation on the 15th?… Great. Oh, I almost forgot. Would you mind emailing an agenda of the presentation? In fact, while you're at it…"

Trophy Sale

The *Trophy Sale* tactic lures sellers into believing that the buyer's name, company, or brand commands such incredible market respect that other businesses will purchase the same good or service based solely on the fact that their company bought. In other words, the buyer would be a trophy sale. The buyer implies that by virtue of selecting the seller's services, other buyers will do likewise. Buyers use this potential market recognition and credibility as a reason to obtain discounts and price concessions.

- "If you get us, do you realize how much recognition and business is going to follow? I can't believe you would risk that over a measly 10 percent discount."
- "There are dozens of businesses watching our every move who mimic our decisions. In fact, we recently received a call from ABC Corporation asking how we currently handle X."
- "We are the largest widget distributor in the nation. Just saying you have us as a client will give you enormous credibility."

Budget

Budget is a popular price related negotiation tactic for one reason— it's effective. *Budget* attempts to use budgetary restraints to secure discounts and price concessions. The seller is faced with a fixed amount. That amount then becomes the focal point of the sale. Why? Because budgets have surface legitimacy. To many sellers, budgets are like unmovable pillars that must be maneuvered around and taken at face value.

In many cases, the budget tactic is perfectly legitimate, entirely ethical, and completely true. As we will address in Chapter 10, a budget can actually work to the advantage of the seller.

- "Mary, your proposal is exactly what we need. The problem is, our budget is only $250,000."

- "I've got $20,000 budgeted for this project. That's the absolute limit."
- "This is our department budget, and I have no authority to deviate from it. I'm afraid your prices need to fit within our budgeted brackets, or we may have to look somewhere else."

Bloodhound

Bloodhound is a simple but effective buyer tactic. It attempts to get sellers married to the sale by making them chase after it. Buyers purposefully string the process out and make it difficult for the seller to communicate with them. Calculating buyers adhere to Emerson's axiom, "That which is easily obtained is lightly esteemed." *Bloodhound* is nothing more than a buyer "playing hard to get" to make the seller desire the sale even more. The harder the seller works, and the more the seller wants the sale, the more willing he or she will be to do whatever it takes to get the sale—even discount. Examples of *Bloodhound* include:

- Unavailability for phone calls or appointments
- Unreturned emails
- Unreturned phone calls
- Missed appointments
- Delayed presentations

Silence

Buyers use *Silence* so that sellers will talk, specifically about discounts. People in general (not just salespeople) are uncomfortable with conversational silence. Because most salespeople are extroverts, they respond to silence by talking. By making sellers feel uncomfortable, buyers know that many sellers will start offering discounts, just to end the silence. It's an amazing phenomenon. Sellers sometimes start rattling off a list of what they will do for the buyer simply to end the discomfort of silence. It is one of the simplest, yet most effective buyer techniques used.

I worked with a corporation whose president participated in our training on negotiation. Ironically, he had worked with a salesperson who, that very week, fell into this trap. The salesperson quoted the president a price. The president said nothing. There was a long pause. The seller then said, "Of course, I would be willing to sell that to you at a 15 percent discount." When the president heard us discussing this tactic, he broke out laughing and stated, "I didn't know I was such a good negotiator. Honestly, I was just thinking about his quote." This story illustrates that it doesn't matter if tactics are used purposefully or inadvertently. In the end, if a salesperson is not careful, it will lead to the same result—unnecessary discounts.

Seller: Mr. Jensen, our price for that particular server is $6,000.
Buyer: Silence
Seller: Uhhh, of course, that price is negotiable Uhhh, in fact, we would be willing to offer you that particular server at a 10 percent discount.

Lost Ground

A buyer who utilizes the *Lost Ground* technique threatens to start the process over again if certain demands aren't met. The buyer makes demands on the seller. When the seller resists, the buyer threatens to go back to the beginning of the process and start over. Of course, if the process starts over, the seller loses all of the invested time and effort he or she has already put into the sale.

- "If you can't do a little better than that, we might just have to go back to the drawing board and start this entire process over."
- "Ryan, I'm afraid that if you don't meet these price specifications, we're going to have to go back and hammer this out again."
- "I know there are other vendors out there that would love to have our business. If you're not willing to sharpen your pencil, we might just have to start the bidding process over again."

Done Deal

Although subtle, the *Done Deal* can be one of the most difficult tactics to deal with. The *Done Deal* attempts to use public pressure to obtain seller concessions. It's similar to the *Assumptive Assertion* tactic except that the buyer goes public with assumptions that were not necessarily agreed upon or approved by the seller. Typically, those assumptions deal with price discounts, added products, or services such as training or delivery. When the buyer talks to the seller, he or she says, "We can't go back now. It's a done deal."

This tactic is tricky to deal with because if the buyer goes beyond just a verbal "done deal," and instead puts it in writing, it can be problematic to reject the contract. All sellers find it difficult to return a check, signed contract, faxed purchase order, or submitted order form.

- "This is a done deal, Forrest. I already went public with this to the executive team. They fully expect this to be delivered in the next thirty days with the additional server included."
- "This is a done deal. I've already submitted the authorization form, and it's signed and ready to send."
- "Ted, did you receive our faxed agreement?"

What If...

What If... is a tactic buyers use to obtain more information about the seller's pricing structure. Specifically, it's used to determine which bulk prices and volume discounts are available. The tactic exercises the power of information to learn more about costs, pricing structures, and profits. Once a buyer determines bulk rates or volume discounts, he or she can ascertain the seller's profit margins.

When a buyer uses the words "What if ..." and then follows with a non-binding, hypothetical situation that includes a bulk purchase, he or she is implementing the *What if...* tactic. The assumption is that the seller will reduce the price in return for a volume purchase. The value this tactic holds for the buyer is that there is no commitment. It is a hypothetical situation. Even if the seller gives the reduced price, the buyer is under no obligation to make the volume purchase. *What If...* is simply a test.

Buyer: How much is it if I purchase one license?
Seller: $1,000.
Buyer: *What if* I agree to purchase a license for five locations instead of just one? Then what would the price be?
Seller: $4,000.
Buyer: *What if* I decided to purchase a license for every facility in the U.S., all twenty-five of them? How much then?
Seller: Twenty-five licenses? That would be $15,000.
Buyer: So if I purchase twenty-five licenses, I'm basically getting each license for $600. Is that right?

The buyer now knows that the seller can sell licenses at $600 and still make a profit. Armed with this knowledge, the buyer can negotiate from a position of strength based on the acquired information.

Soft Bargainer Tactics

- Fairness
- Sympathy
- Third Party
- Assumptive Assertions
- Baiting
- Ambiguous Authority
- Nibbling
- Sunshine
- No John Hancock

Fairness

The Fairness tactic is just what is sounds like. A buyer attempts to exploit a seller's sense of fairness. Most human beings have a sense of fairness and justice. It's a basic human emotion that is extremely powerful. No one likes to hear that they are being unfair. Buyers use *Fairness* to get sellers to feel uncomfortable about their cost structure and/or to question the ethics of their price. They attempt to reach a seller's higher ideals by getting him or her to question the fairness of the proposal.

- "All I ask is that you be fair about this, Mary."
- "Kathy, we've known each other a long time, and I've always found you to be a fair and accommodating person, but your quote to automate the Charlotte facility without training just doesn't seem like a fair offer."
- "Come on Jared, we've known each other for a long time. $10,000 isn't a fair price. That would tank my entire budget."

Sympathy

Sympathy attempts to get sellers to make concessions based on difficult personal and/or corporate circumstances. Similar to the *Fairness* tactic, buyers use a basic human emotion (sympathy) to advance their agenda. In essence, buyers attempt to leverage the relationship and the sympathy of the seller in order to get a better price or other related discounts.

- "As you know Bill, this has been a difficult year for us. With the slow down in the economy, they slashed our budget… I'm getting a lot of pressure to cut costs… sales are down… my dog died… my aunt Peg was recently hospitalized… I would really appreciate it if you would work with me on bringing your price down."

Third Party

When a buyer uses the *Third Party* tactic, he or she is trying to pass the buck. It's always easier to make sellers think somebody else said "No" or that somebody else is applying pressure. Buyers utilize *Third Party* by dropping the names of executives, vice presidents, managers, purchasers, or some "third party" to whom the seller has no direct access. This creates FUD (fear, uncertainty, and doubt) in the mind of the seller and applies pressure to discount.

- "Jacob, I told our vice president about your proposal, and he didn't like it."
- "I reviewed your proposal with the H.R. manager. She didn't go for it."
- "I'm really catching some heat from the CEO to cut costs. Our CIO also asked me to review your proposal again. They're really sticklers on this stuff."

Assumptive Assertions

This tactic uses assumptive assertions to gain add-ons, throw-ins, or additional items. The buyer makes assumptions about the willingness of the seller to bend on certain issues. He or she just assumes that particular items are included in the price or package with statements such as:

- "Of course, training is included in that, right?"
- "I told management I was sure you would be willing to give us a 90 day trial license as a pilot site before we decide whether or not to purchase."
- "You mean the warranty isn't included in this package? I just assumed that was part of the price."

Baiting

Baiting is a tactic used by buyers to string out sellers. Like bait on a hook drawing a fish closer and closer to shore, *Baiting* uses a seller's desire to close the sale against him or her. Buyers bait and tease sellers with promising statements aimed at obtaining lower prices and eventual discounts.

- "I think we're going to be a big account for you, Sharon. You may need to bend a little on maintenance renewal pricing, but

I'm sure it will pay off for you in the long run. If you'll get me that revised proposal we talked about, I'll try to get with management later next week to finalize the deal. Call me the week after next. We'll go play a round of golf or grab some lunch."

- "We're close, Mark, really close. The board has approved funding to automate our facilities in the U.S. and China. If we can just wrap up the price and installation issues, I think we've got ourselves a deal."

- "Riley, I'm really excited to get this project started. We are going to be a great account for you. I just need you to revise the proposal to reflect a better volume discount and we can get this ball rolling."

If there is one classic maneuver played by multinationals and large corporations to take advantage of anxious sellers, this is it. *Baiting* builds positive expectations with pie-in-the-sky numbers and, after the seller agrees to price or other related concessions, starts in with the "Ifs, Ands, and Buts."

Ambiguous Authority

Ambiguous Authority is used to imply that the buyer is no longer the ultimate decision maker and does not have the authority to approve the sale. *Ambiguous Authority* is similar to *Third Party* with one major difference: when buyers use *Third Party* they reference a specific person or title such as "John, our I.T. director," "the CEO," or "Vice President." When buyers use *Ambiguous Authority*, they reference a vague entity such as upper management, middle management, business development, engineering, legal, or human resources. Buyers use this tactic as a convenient way to communicate ambiguous messages of decision-making authority, postponing the process, or using a vague entity as a leveraging tool against the seller.

Buyers often lead sellers to believe they have full authority to make a decision. After the seller works out what he or she thinks is a firm agreement, the buyer claims ambiguous authority and says, "I have to take it to the purchasing committee for final approval." This gives the buyer another swing at concessions and opens the seller up for further negotiations.

- "I'm not in a position to accept your pricing. I need to run this past human resources. "
- "I can't approve your current price structure. My hands are tied. It's really not in my jurisdiction anymore."
- "I think I had better get the engineering department involved in this decision."

Ambiguous Authority can also be used to switch or add negotiators late in the process. Sometimes, buyers will bring in a department representative or higher executive when a negotiation reaches a deadlock or when a negotiation starts getting confrontational. This can be devastating to a seller. Sellers weary of the negotiation process are more willing to compromise just to end the negotiation. *Ambiguous Authority* basically gives the buyer (or the buyer's company) another shot at negotiating better terms.

Nibbling

Nibbling is commonly referred to as *Ex Post Facto,* Latin for "after the fact." It usually occurs either just before or just after a buyer makes a decision. It's like the man who won't purchase a suit without a free tie. He tries on a few suits and looks at a few brands in various colors. He tries the suits with various shirts and ties, but he never mentions the free tie until he has selected the suit. Then he springs it on the seller. "OK. I'll take the blue suit if you throw in the red tie." The *Nibbling* principle suggests that it is easier to request additional concessions after a person is psychologically committed to the agreement.

Nibbling attempts to persuade the seller into making small concessions just prior to or just after the agreement is made. The ink might not be dry on the agreement, but the buyer is still making *Nibbling* negotiation requests. *Nibbling* is a little push for something more, a last shot at something extra.

- "If you can include training at the price you've already quoted, we'll have a deal."
- "Rachel, would you mind throwing in a few extra licenses for our tech team? We forgot to include them in our bid. Also, could you Fed Ex some manuals for me to get a little head start on the installation? In fact, while you're at it..."
- "Brent, if you can get us that additional delivery at our Missouri plant without any additional charges, I think you've got yourself a deal."

Sunshine

Sunshine is a tactic used to gain concessions based on flattery and words of adulation. It's the ultimate relationship leveraging technique. Soft bargainers sprinkle sunshine all over the salesperson. Using the sunshine tactic, buyers attempt to use flattery and complimentary statements to get the seller to bend on discount related issues.

- "We've really enjoyed working with you, Alexis. You've been very flexible and accommodating. We would like nothing more than to do business with you. Unfortunately, if you don't throw in the training, I'm just not sure this is going to fly."
- "Matt, you've been terrific. You are one of the best salespeople I've ever worked with, and I want to do business with you. If you can get us that 10 percent discount and a game of golf for the two of us, I think we've got a deal."
- "Linda, you've done a great job. Everyone has noticed the effort you've put into this. I know the counter offer to your proposal came as a surprise, but I'm confident we will reach an agreement."

No John Hancock

John Hancock was the first signer of *The Declaration of Independence*. His signature became the most recognizable name in America. Not getting a "John Hancock" means, of course, not getting the appropriate or required signature(s). *No John Hancock* tactics attempt to persuade sellers that the person responsible for sign off will never approve the current price or proposal structure. The buyer seeks to get the seller to make price allowances or concessions in order to get the appropriate authority to sign off.

- "There is no way management will sign this agreement at this price."
- "I could never get this signed."
- "I just know our vice president will not sign this proposed contract the way it stands right now. Now, if you could just be a little less restrictive on your return policy, I'm pretty sure we'll get the required signatures."

Casual Shoppers

Casual shoppers do not use a consistent or predictable set of buyer tactics. Because casual shoppers are impulse buyers, they use tactics similar to those used by the other buyer types, but they use them in a way that is sporadic and unpredictable.

In Summary

Many sellers unwittingly play into the hands of skilled buyers by not recognizing the tactics being used to secure discounts and price concessions. This is why recognizing buyer tactics is critically important.

> **Note:** Simply identifying buyer tactics, *as tactics*, limits their impact. Sometimes a tactic recognized is a tactic neutralized.

Visit www.patrickhenryinc.com to download a free negotiation podcast and other negotiation tools.

CHAPTER 10

Seller Countertactics

During the Second Punic War (219-202 B.C.), the great Carthaginian general Hannibal Barca wreaked havoc during his march toward Rome. Although his army was outnumbered, he was able to outmaneuver the Romans with clever battle tactics and duplicitous military strategies. On one occasion, though, Hannibal's scouts made a terrible blunder and led the Carthaginian army into marshy terrain with nothing but the sea at their backs. The Romans realized Hannibal's mistake and quickly maneuvered their troops to trap the Carthaginian army. Posting their best sentries at the only escape routes available, the Romans intended to destroy Hannibal and his invading army the next morning. However, in the middle of the night, something strange happened. As the sentries looked down the passes, they saw a huge procession of lights moving up the mountain toward them. Alarmed at the number of lights, the sentries concluded that Hannibal must have received reinforcements under the cover of darkness. It seemed as though his army had grown a hundred fold. As the sentries looked on, an almost magical scene took place. Fires broke out all over the mountain and a horrible noise filled the air, as if hundreds of horns were blowing simultaneously. The sentries, the bravest and most experienced soldiers in the Roman Army, panicked and abandoned their posts.

By morning, Hannibal's troops had escaped the marshland.

How did Hannibal's army escape? What caused the Roman guards to flee? At sundown, Hannibal had commanded his troops to fasten bundles of twigs to the horns of the thousands of oxen that traveled with his army. He then set the twigs on fire and sent the oxen up the passes, giving the impression of a vast army moving up a mountain. When the flames of the twigs burned down to the oxen's skin, the oxen bellowed and stampeded in all directions, setting fires all over the mountainside.

Confronted with seemingly insurmountable odds, Hannibal's simple, yet brilliant, countertactic confused the Roman sentries and allowed the trapped army to escape.

⟶⟫●⟨⟵

Like Hannibal, sometimes sellers feel trapped by clever buyer tactics. Nevertheless, armed with intelligent countertactics, sellers can not only escape from negotiation traps, they can also reverse the pressure onto buyers.

Small Units of Speech Can Yield Large Quantities of Power

Out of clutter, find simplicity.

From discord, find harmony.

In the middle of difficulty lies opportunity.

—Albert Einstein

When we hear *scientist* or *physicist*, we immediately think of Albert Einstein. Einstein cracked the cosmic code. He discovered that the smallest unit of matter yielded the largest quantity of energy. Similarly, the smallest units of speech often yield the largest quantity of power. Small phrases and simple rejoinders can create vast amounts of power in buyer-seller negotiations.

We've all been warned, "Buyer beware." If we've not been burned personally in previous purchases, we know someone who has. Buyers are justifiably suspect of the intentions and character of sellers. Unfortunately, honest sellers are stigmatized because of dishonest sellers who have put buyers "on guard."

Sellers rarely view buyers with an equal level of suspicion and often sell with their negotiation guards down. This is a big mistake. Because buyers use negotiation tactics to secure discounts and concessions, it is important for sellers to anticipate and counter those tactics to maintain profitability and commissionable dollars.

> **Note**: Well-timed, intelligent countertactics disarm and neutralize buyer tactics without defeating the person using the tactic.

Counter Measures Versus Countertactics

One way to counter buyer tactics is with seller countertactics. Countertactics are strategic words, phrases, and responses used to counteract the impact of buyer tactics. Although indispensable for successful negotiation, countertactics are reactionary by nature. They are what you do *during* the negotiation in response to tactics used by buyers.

In addition to countertactics, sellers have other means of neutralizing buyer tactics. Instead of simply responding with countertactics, sellers can use counter measures early in the sales cycle to prevent certain tactics from surfacing in the first place. Counter measures are what you do *prior* to the negotiation. Instead of relying solely on "head-to-head" negotiation countertactics, sellers can actually prevent certain tactics from developing by qualifying prospects prior to the negotiation.

A qualified opportunity in any market has three general characteristics:

1. Ultimate Decision Maker(s)
2. Available Funding
3. Acceptable Timeframe(s)

Pre-qualification is considered a seller counter measure because it prevents buyers from using a number of popular negotiation tactics. The better a seller qualifies a buyer, the fewer tactics will be available to use against the seller. For example, if a seller asks a qualifying questions such as, "Melissa, if this proposal meets your needs, is there any reason you wouldn't be able to make a decision this quarter?" a buyer will have a hard time using *Ambiguous Authority, No John Hancock,* or *Budget* tactics. By asking simple qualifying questions, sellers remove potential buyer tactics.[1]

The following are buyer tactics that can be prevented with appropriate qualification:

Buyer Tactics	Counter Measures
Third Party	Ultimate Decision Maker(s)
No John Hancock	Ultimate Decision Maker(s)
Ambiguous Authority	Ultimate Decision Maker(s)
The Price Pinch	Available Funding
Budget	Available Funding
Deadlines	Timeframe(s)

Successful sellers pick winnable battles. Even sellers with polished communication skills, extensive product knowledge, and powerful personalities, cannot be successful unless they concentrate on prospects with the greatest purchasing potential. If any one of the qualifying components is missing, the probability of successfully negotiating or closing a sale is diminished.

Qualifying buyers early in the sales cycle is an effective way to exercise the power of information. Information allows a seller to assess the close probability and determine the time required to make the sale. By probing for qualifying information in the areas of needs, decision makers, budget, and timeframe, sellers gain knowledge and insight that can be used to prevent buyers from using traditional discount tactics.

---

1. For a comprehensive list of qualifying questions see *The DNA Selling Method.*

The Point? Qualifying opportunities early in the sales process preemptively counters multiple buyer tactics and is an effective means for building and exercising the power of information.

Countertactics

Obviously, not all buyer tactics can be prevented by simply qualifying a prospect. Although counter measures are powerful tools, they are not enough. Sellers also need to use countertactics.

Sellers have a laundry list of countertactics to choose from in order to manage buyer tactics. I have identified twelve specific countertactics to balance and check buyer tactics:

1. Surprise
2. Policy & Procedure
3. Limited Authority
4. Third Party
5. Question & Clarify
6. Reason & Rationale
7. Deadline
8. Fairness
9. Quid Pro Quo
10. High Demand
11. Silence
12. Differentiation

Surprise

A fundamental rule in negotiation is to always respond with surprise. When buyers make a demand, they are watching and listening for your reaction. Regardless of the demand, react surprised at the buyer's proposal. This countertactic is used to "freeze frame" the negotiation and help buyers realize and reflect on the seriousness of their demand(s). Simply acting surprised about a situation can sometimes neutralize buyers. It's one of the simplest, yet most effective seller countertactics available.

> **Note**: A fundamental rule in negotiation is to always respond with surprise. When buyers make a demand, they are watching and listening for your reaction. Regardless of the demand, react surprised at the buyer's request.

Examples include:

- "Wow! That really surprises me. Help me understand what changed since we last spoke?"
- "Frankly, I'm a little disappointed. I thought we came to an agreement on that weeks ago."
- "I must admit, you've caught me a bit off guard. I didn't realize we were still discussing price."

Do not dismiss *Surprise* as a sophomoric negotiation tactic. It is an extremely effective technique that should be used by all sellers. When negotiating over the phone, use verbal means of showing surprise, maybe even shock. When negotiation face-to-face, use physical means of showing surprise. This tactic is commonly referred to as *Flinching*. *Flinching* is important because most people believe more in what they see than what they hear.

> **Note**: *Surprise* is a great way to "tee up" other seller countertactics. Use *Surprise* to introduce (and use in conjunction with) other seller tactics.

Policy & Procedure

Policy & Procedure tactics (sometimes called *Rule Book)* use company rules, regulations, policies, and procedures to counter buyer demands. It's like a stop sign on the road. People stop. We all do it. We go through life obeying signs, laws, and regulations without question. Price tags and published price sheets often have the same mystical effect. Have you ever tried to bargain over the price of a car battery at Wal-Mart? Not likely. The reason is simple. Wal-Mart has a policy of not negotiating price, and customers know it. The company's price tag communicates that it's nonnegotiable. (Making an issue nonnegotiable is a tactic that is often referred to as *Exclusion*).

> **Note**: *Policy & Procedure* helps to establish a nonnegotiable status for products, services, or issues that a seller deems necessary to exclude from a negotiation.

Examples of *Policy & Procedure* statements include:

- "Our standard policy and procedure is to adhere to our published price list, which means I'm not in a position to make a price allowance."
- "I'm sorry. Our corporate policy and procedure is to adhere to our price list."
- "Kenneth, our policies and procedures prevent any of our salespeople from deviating from the published price list. Corporate policy makes our prices about as negotiable as the law of gravity."

Published price sheets are extremely effective negotiation tools as are other published rules of engagement that sellers can show buyers. They are effective because it's easier for a piece of paper say "No" than for the seller to say it. Published price sheets, standard terms and conditions, policies and procedures—all give sellers legitimate reasons *not* to negotiate price.

In any negotiation, there is usually a little "give and take." Most negotiations involve multiple attempts to reach agreement and involve more than one buyer tactic. Although *Policy & Procedure* is a good countertactic to start with, it should usually be followed up with other seller countertactics.

Limited Authority

Limited Authority is used to imply that the seller doesn't possess the power to authorize a requested discount or price concession. *Limited Authority* can be communicated by simply stating, "I am not authorized to approve a discount" or can reference a vague entity such as middle management, a department, board of directors, committee, or corporate office. It is an effective seller countertactic because it applies pressure without confrontation or specifically identifying an ultimate decision maker.

This tactic is sometimes referred to as *Escalated Approval* or *Higher Authority*. Examples include:

- "I don't have the authority to authorize a price allowance."
- "I'm not in a position to offer a discount. I will have to review your proposal with our board of directors."
- "I have no authority from our corporate office to make an adjusted offer."

People don't expect to negotiate a can of beans with a cashier at a supermarket because they know the cashier has no authority to change the price. Sellers can often convey the same message with the *Limited Authority* tactic.

I once had a buyer request a discount, so I told him I would check with management to see if they would approve his request. When I informed the buyer that his request had been declined, he responded, "Oh well, I at least had to try." Had I not tested the seriousness of his request with this simple countertactic, I would have unnecessarily provided him with a discount. This illustrates the power of using *Limited Authority* to cordially neutralize buyer attempts to obtain discounts.

> **Caution!** Sellers who present themselves as ultimate decision-makers often put themselves at a severe bargaining disadvantage.

Third Party

For sellers, *Third Party* techniques are used the same way buyers use them. The seller uses the names of vice presidents, managers, executives, departments, "Corporate" or some third party to be the "bad guy" to let the buyer know that the requested demands were not or will not be approved. For situations that demand a specific authority, *Third Party* references an exact name or title.

- "I spoke with the (CEO, vice president, director, manager, etc.), and she won't authorize a price allowance."
- "Mr. Day, our executive vice president, declined the request for a 10 percent discount."
- "I will need to speak with 'Corporate' about this."

The downside to using this tactic is that it implies someone in your organization *does* have the authority to authorize a discount. When possible, use *Limited Authority* (a vague entity) rather than *Third Party* (a specific person) to negate buyer attempts to gain discounts or concessions.

Question & Clarify

Sellers use the *Question & Clarify* method to question an objection or demand and clarify the unique benefits associated with the proposed good or service. The *Question & Clarify* tactic reestablishes the need and then clarifies the value of the proposed solution.

- "Anna, help me understand why X has become an issue recently?... You mentioned that having Y was important. What happens if you don't have that capability?"
- "Our product is obviously the best solution for your needs. Help me understand what we can do to get this approved."

Asking questions equips sellers with information that can be used to counter negotiation tactics. For example, if a buyer uses the *Ambiguous Authority* tactic to secure a discount, a seller might respond with *Question & Clarify* by asking, "Who has the authority to increase the budget?" or "Who can authorize a change to the RFP?"

If a buyer uses the *Budget* tactic by saying, "I can only afford $2,000 for a computer system," a smart negotiator will respond with a question. "Karl, let me ask you this. If I can show you a computer system that is faster, includes Microsoft Office, and a companion printer, but the cost is $3,000 is there any point in showing it to you, or would I be wasting my time?" By questioning the *Budget* tactic, the seller not only tests the validity of the supposed financial restriction, he also clarifies the value of the proposed solution.

> **Note**: Questioning is a powerful selling and negotiating tool and is an extremely effective countertactic. Simply questioning buyer demands can neutralize attempts to gain seller concessions.

Reason & Rationale

At the height of the Civil War, Abraham Lincoln delivered a speech referring to Southerners as fellow human beings who were simply in error. An elderly woman in the audience verbally chastised him for not calling them irreconcilable enemies who must be destroyed. President Lincoln replied, "Why, madam, do I not destroy my enemies when I make them my friends?"

The power of President Lincoln's response was the logic that supported it.

While living in exile in London, a time when anti-French sentiment was at its highest, Voltaire used reason and rationale to get himself out of a potentially deadly situation. While walking down a London street, Voltaire suddenly found himself surrounded by an angry mob. "Hang him. Hang the Frenchman," they yelled. Voltaire calmly addressed the mob saying,

"Men of England! You wish to kill me because I am a Frenchman. Am I not punished enough in not being born an Englishman?"

The crowed cheered his thoughtful words and escorted him safely back to his lodgings.

Reason & Rationale is a favorite countertactic used by experienced negotiators. It's popular because it's a two edged tactic. On one hand, it offers reason and rationale, and on the other hand, it demands the same in return.

The first edge is offering reason and rationale. Your rationale is the logic and reason that supports your position. Buyers like explanations and rationale with proposals for two reasons. First, they like rational explanations themselves. Second, they like being armed with reason and rationale to convince others of their decision to purchase the good or service.

> **Note**: When proposing a price, provide rationale for your proposal. Give a clear reason why the price is what it is. That does not mean offering a cost breakdown. It means using product capabilities, differentiators or benefits as rationale for your price.

The second edge of this tactic is requiring reason and rationale in return. By asking buyers to offer reason and rationale for their demands, sellers reverse the pressure onto the buyer to justify the requested demand or concession. Requiring reason and rationale forces the buyer to articulate and verbally justify his or her position. It prevents random requests for discounts based on nothing but a desire to receive it. As a seller, refusal to yield except in response to sound reason is an easy position to defend.

Reason and Rationale is a kind of reverse "cost breakdown" tactic. Sellers basically ask buyers to itemize demands and calculations.

Examples include:

Buyer: $25,000 is just too high.

Seller: Too high? Andrew, help me understand the reason you feel like $25,000 is too high.

Seller: How did you arrive at that conclusion?

Seller: Help me understand the rationale behind that.

Seller: Why is it you feel that way?

Seller: Compared to what or whom?

I recall sitting down with two buyers who were business partners. One of them saw the value in the product I was selling and was, in essence, "sold." His partner was not sold and strongly asserted, "This is too expensive." I asked him, "Compared to what?" There was momentary silence. He paused, and then said, "I don't know." The assertion that it was too expensive never came up again, and they purchased the product at full price.

When requesting reason and rationale from buyers, you should be as soft and gentle as possible. Avoid sounding harsh or making buyers feel like they are being attacked. Use a tone that is non-threatening and language that is as mild as possible.

Fairness

This tactic attempts to appeal to a buyer's sense of fairness in explaining that the requested demands and discounts are not fair, reasonable, or practical. *Fairness* is a powerful human emotion that can be used to your advantage. When buyers make heavy demands that are unreasonable or manipulative, you can use *Fairness* to bring them back to a more acceptable position.

- "All I'm asking is that you be fair about this, Steve."
- "This is the same price we charge all of our customers. In order to be fair and equitable to all of our clients, we provide the best price right from the start."

- "John, be reasonable. You and I both know that X demand is not a fair solution."

What often angers a buyer is the feeling that someone else is getting a better deal than she is. When this issue arises, assure prospects that they are getting the best price anyone will get. Treating all customers fairly and equitably is an easy position to defend.

Quid Pro Quo

This tactic attempts to balance buyer demands by making counter demands. *Quid Pro Quo* is latin for *this for that.* When buyers demand that certain criteria be met before moving forward or making a decision, sellers should make counter demands to balance power and test the seriousness of the buyer's request. Preferably, counter demands should be of equivalent value.

- "Joseph, I would be happy to send you another proposal with the adjusted licensing agreement. In return, I am going to adjust the compensation schedule to reflect full payment within thirty instead of sixty days."

One of the more popular ways of implementing the counter demand is using the "If X, Then Y" model. *If* is the key word because the seller does not actually commit to anything unless the buyer responds favorably (See Chapter 13 for more information concerning the "If X, Then Y" model). For example,

- "Bill, if I agree to the licensing changes, then will you agree to a net-thirty instead of a net-sixty day payment plan?"
- "Ms. Jones, if we agree to deliver the shipment by your specified date, then are you prepared to sign the contract?"
- "Bruce, if I reduce the price by 10 percent, then will you commit to a full instead of partial order?"

The "If X, Then Y" model fulfills the *Quid Pro Quo* principle of negotiation and is action oriented. It forces a buyer's hand. If you agree to a buyer's demand, make a counter demand in the form of an agreement. It might be a down payment, signed contract, or memorandum of agreement. Whatever it is, get it signed as quickly as possible. The longer the delay, the greater the chance the buyer will back out of the agreement or forget (*Selective Memory*) what was agreed to.

By making counter demands, sellers balance power by creating an atmosphere of reciprocity. By demanding reciprocity, sellers trade concessions, and, in many cases, force buyers to give up on their efforts to obtain unilateral concessions from the seller.

Counter demands not only balance power, they also utilize the power of TIME (Time, Investment, Money & Effort). By making counter demands that require buyers to either match effort or give something in return for the concession, sellers convince buyers to invest TIME into the sale.

> **Note**: Don't give without getting. Avoid giving concessions without getting something in return. Make concessions conditional.

High Demand

High Demand is a seller countertactic that seeks to build the power of options. This excellent, but rarely used, tactic helps balance power by firmly establishing that the proposed solution is in high demand. By articulating a busy schedule and mentioning other demanding clients and selling engagements, sellers communicate to buyers that other options are available and that they are not desperate for business.

- "Ms. Hicks, I'm afraid flying out to give another presentation to the committee next week just isn't possible. As I'm sure you are aware, our product is in extremely high demand. I not only made implementation commitments to recent clients, but I'm also scheduled over the next three weeks to meet with multiple pending accounts."

- "Mitch, this is the third voice mail I've left in the last three weeks. I'd love to do business with you and am eager to demonstrate how our products will help your manufacturing process. However, since our product is in extremely high demand, I just don't have time to keep leaving voice mails. In fact, ABC Company recently selected our product. Please call me back. I look forward to hearing from you."

In economics the law of scarcity states: anything perceived as being scarce is also perceived as being more valuable. Communicating to buyers that your time and products are in high demand makes you and your product more scarce, and thus, more valuable.

Deadline

This countertactic uses price, proposal and delivery deadlines to increase buyer decisiveness, end stalled or "eternal negotiations," and counteract buyer delay tactics. Deadline balances power, accelerates decisions and puts pressure on buyers to take action to avoid the consequences of delayed decisions. Additionally, deadlines put a timeframe on the proposal and encourage buyers to take your offer more seriously.

- "As we've discussed, our proposal expires on June 1st. Additionally, we have an incremental price change that begins with our new fiscal year, so we will need to have a firm decision by the end of May to avoid a price increase."
- "As previously mentioned, this option expires at the end of the quarter."
- "In order to get delivery on X date, orders must be placed before Y date."
- "To ensure we hit your implementation date, we will need to finalize this agreement before X date."

Silence

Silence is a true friend who never betrays.

—Anonymous

In 1825, a new czar ascended the throne of Russia—Nicholas I. A rebellion ensued demanding modernization of Russia. Nicholas I brutally suppressed the uprising and sentenced its leader, Kondraty Ryleyev, to hang. Ryleyev stood on the gallows, the noose tight against his neck, but as the trapdoor opened, something unexpected happened. The rope snapped, dashing Kondraty to the ground. As Kondraty stood up he yelled to the crowd, "You see! In Russia they don't know how to do anything properly, not even how to make a rope!"

A guard entered the Winter Palace with the news of the failed hanging. Vexed by the situation and viewing the botched hanging as a possible sign of heavenly intervention, Nicholas I began drafting a pardon. Just before signing the pardon, however, he asked, "Did Kondraty say anything after this miracle?" The guard replied, "He said that in Russia they don't even know how to make a rope." "In that case," said the czar, "let us prove the contrary." Kondraty was then hanged a second time, successfully.

The moral of the story is to know when to be silent.

One of my recent negotiations demonstrates the benefits derived from knowing when to be silent. I arrived at a hotel in Miami at which I had a guaranteed reservation. The clerk informed me that the hotel had a number of holdovers that had not departed as scheduled and offered to relocate me to another hotel. Tired from a full day of travel, I did not want the hassle of relocating, so I asked the clerk if they had *any* rooms available. She said they had an executive suite available, but that the price was $350. I suggested that the price was excessive considering the circumstance. I was then silent and awaited a response. I expected a reasonable price reduction and was willing to pay up to $250 for the room. I was surprised when, after an awkward pause, the clerk offered me the executive suite on a complimentary basis. Had I kept speaking or made an initial offer, I would have talked my way out of a complimentary room.

When buyers (or anyone else) make demands on me, I sometimes say nothing in return. Uncomfortable silence induces many buyers to spew information. I've actually had buyers lessen the demands they had made in a previous sentence. Seller silence forces a buyer's hand. Because people are often uncomfortable with silence, they will typically continue to talk or make explanations.

Silence is especially important after you have made an offer. Once you have provided an offer or counter offer, be silent—it's the other side's turn to respond.

Silence is also used to counter strongly worded buyer demands. When buyers become heated or verbally abusive, sometimes saying nothing speaks volumes.

Differentiation

Differentiation builds power, justifies higher prices, and establishes value. *Differentiation* neutralizes buyer attempts to lump sellers, products, and companies into the same category by throwing competing parties into the same basket and attempting to diminish unique solutions and product benefits. *Differentiation* positions the seller as a consultative authority figure by establishing him or herself as an industry expert rather than a biased seller.

> Buyer: You're all basically the same. The only real difference is that you are more expensive.

> Seller: I am familiar with X and Y competitors. I am also aware of their limitations in fulfilling standard client demands such as… We, on the other hand, address those needs with unique offerings such as… As you can see, there are serious and significant differences between the products. In short, your needs are best served by the unique capabilities that only we provide.

Differentiation positions the seller at the top of the pyramid with competing vendors at the lower corners of the model. Differentiation identifies sellers as consultative authority figures. When a seller conveys an expertise about competitors, the seller establishes him or her self as an industry expert rather than a biased seller. *Differentiation* is an effort to counter buyer attempts to undermine seller solutions and discount unique selling points. Differentiation places sellers above the fray and helps separate them from competitors.

Figure 10.1

Be careful not to categorically dismiss competitors with off hand criticisms and name calling. Your buyer may have developed relationships with your competitors. Speak of them respectfully—in a straightforward, clear, and substantive manner.[2]

Over time, it is common for competitors to cross paths. Try not to make the competition personal or burn bridges. "I've met Tom (the competitor), and he's a great guy, but that's not the issue. You (the buyer) are seeking to make the best business decision for your organization. In order to help you do that, let's review this spread sheet. It provides a detailed side-by-side comparison of what we both have to offer you."

In Summary

Seller countermeasures and countertactics are effective negotiation tools that help sellers protect price margins, ensure profitability, and avoid giving away unnecessary discounts and unwarranted concessions.

---

2. See Chapter 13 in *Winning Sales Presentations* to learn how to "slam competition with grace."

Chapter 11

Overcoming Buyer Tactics with Seller Countertactics

In 1588, Spain was a thriving empire. Since the glory days of Rome, no country had claimed more territory than Spain. Spain controlled much of Europe, North Africa, parts of Asia, and most of Latin America.

Standing in the shadows of this enormous empire was feeble little England. In 1588, England was a tiny country, strong in courage and ambition, but weak in territory, allies, and military strength. With the exception of the Dutch, she had no foreign power as an ally. Scotland was a separate kingdom, and Ireland was in the throes of revolt. It was David against Goliath—a tiny island defying a world empire.

Spain was ruled by Phillip II, a fervent Catholic and leader of the Counter Reformation. He hated Protestants, especially English Protestants so much that he authorized the burning of heretics in a ceremony called *acto-de-fe* (act of faith).

Against this personification of Spanish pride stood one of history's shrewdest leaders—Queen Elizabeth of England, daughter of Henry VIII and Ann Boleyn.

Enmity between the two countries had been building up to a climax. Tired of English raids on Spanish commerce, and eager to convert England to Catholicism, Phillip II sent a powerful armada consisting of over 130 ships carrying an army of close to 20,000 men to conquer England. Seeking divine favor, the seaman of the armada were forbidden from swearing, gambling, or associating with loose women. Their ships bore the names of saints and apostles.

Sir Francis Drake, England's most feared privateer, was playing a game of bowls on the greens at Plymouth Hoe when a messenger dashed up to the grounds with news that the Spanish Armada was approaching. Not to be interrupted, Drake turned to his fellow officers and said, "First, we will finish the game and then we will beat the Spaniards."

The British Royal Navy numbered only 39 ships, but they were armed with something much more powerful than galleys and guns—an angry English populace aroused by the boasting of the Spaniards.

The "invincible" Spanish Armada was crushed. Armed with smaller, more versatile ships, and using clever navigational tactics to counteract the attacks of the larger Spanish ships, the English "sea dogs" repelled one of the largest maritime invasions in history. This victory marked the beginning of the British Empire. After the destruction of the armada, Spain slid downward into decadence.

The tiny British navy defeated the giant Spanish Armada for two reasons: First, the British maintained their composure. They did not panic at the site of overwhelming opposition. Second, they used unconventional naval strategies to counteract the Spanish warship's tactics.

———◦⟫●⟨◦———

Managing Buyer Tactics

We confide in our strength, without boasting of it; we respect that of others, without fearing it.

—Thomas Jefferson

Like the "sea dogs" of England in 1588, strategic negotiators maintain their confidence and composure when facing buyer tactics. They recognize tactics and skillfully neutralize them with strategic countertactics of their own.

One of the primary differences between cerebral sellers and average sellers is the ability to manage buyer tactics. Sellers who implement intelligent negotiation principles and master effective countertactics sell at higher margins, increase profitability, and avoid giving away commissionable dollars. The more countertactics sellers have at their disposal, the more effectively (and rapidly) they can close favorable agreements.

Successful negotiators follow a three-step process to manage buyer tactics:

Prevent — Adequately qualifying opportunities prior to negotiating (Countermeasures).

Identify — Recognizing buyer types and tactics.

Counteract — Implementing seller countertactics to neutralize buyer tactics.

Figure 11.1

The first step in managing buyer tactics is to prevent buyers from using tactics in the first place. A seller accomplishes this by building power, establishing product or service value, and adequately qualifying accounts in the early stages of the selling process (see Chapter 10).

The second step is recognizing the buyer type (hard negotiator, calculating buyer, soft bargainer, and casual shopper), and their corresponding tactics. Because a seller recognizes the negotiator *type*, he or she can prepare to handle predictable attitudes, behaviors, and tactics. Identifying tactics is an equally important part of managing buyer-seller negotiations. As I mentioned previously, simply recognizing a tactic *as a tactic* severely diminishes its impact.

Although recognizing buyer tactics is important, it is not wise to announce to a buyer, "I'm on to you. I spotted that tactic a mile away. Using the ol' *Third Party* technique, huh?" I've seen negotiators who, in an attempt to demonstrate their negotiation savvy, blatantly broadcast their recognition of tactics—a mistake tantamount to an under cover officer announcing to a bank robber "Hey! You with the gun! I'm on to you, man. I'm an undercover police officer. I have a pistol in my shoulder holster. And, if that doesn't work, I have a smaller gun strapped around my ankle." Not smart.

A strategic negotiator must implement the third step, which is utilizing seller countertactics that neutralize buyer attempts to secure discounts and price concessions.

Using Tactics Without Defeating Buyers

The aim of argument, or of discussion, should not be victory, but progress.

—Joseph Joubert

⸺⸳⸼⸳⸺

Alexander Hamilton was notoriously critical of his fellow Founding Fathers. During the Constitutional Convention in Philadelphia, he departed in a fit of self-righteous disgust. As a member of the cabinet during the presidency of George Washington, he constantly battled Thomas Jefferson. During the reelection campaign for the presidency in 1800, he wrote scathing attacks on fellow Federalist, President John Adams. He also had an active dislike for the primary framer of the Constitution, James Madison. Out of all his personal and political rivalries, his hatred for Aaron Burr bordered pathological.

Although Hamilton and Burr maintained a superficial friendship—socializing together and occasionally teaming up as co-counsel on a number of civil and criminal cases in New York—Hamilton seemed determined to destroy his "friend" politically. Whatever the cause for Hamilton's animosity, his criticisms of Burr were relentless. He was particularly venomous during the presidential election of 1800. Due in large part to his attacks, Burr lost the presidential election by a hair to Thomas Jefferson in one of the most contested elections in U.S. history. In 1804, when Burr was running for Governor of New York, he lost miserably, thanks in no small part to the efforts of

Hamilton.

Letters and communication between Hamilton and Burr became increasingly vitriolic until in July of 1804 when Burr challenged Hamilton to settle their dispute the way gentlemen had for centuries—in ritualized, mortal combat—the duel.

On July 11, 1804, Hamilton arrived at the appointed location and stood, ironically, on the same spot in which his beloved son Philip had been killed in a duel several years before. Holding the same pistol his son had used, Hamilton awaited the confrontation. As Burr approached, each man removed his hat and saluted politely. The seconds measured the distance between combatants and carefully loaded the pistols in each other's presence. Then Burr and Hamilton took their assigned places. The instant the agreed-upon second called "Present!" Burr pulled his trigger, hitting Hamilton in the chest. Hamilton's pistol discharged, clipping a twig off a branch high above Burr's head.

Hamilton lay mortally wounded and died the next day.

Burr survived the encounter, satisfied he had justifiably defeated his opponent, regained his dignity, and restored his reputation—a reputation he felt Hamilton had destroyed. On the contrary, just the opposite occurred. When news of Hamilton's death surfaced, Burr faced the scorn of a nation. Horrified by Hamilton's violent demise, Americans rallied to his defense. Burr's political career was ruined, giving Hamilton in death that which he had spent his life trying to accomplish.

Like Aaron Burr, negotiators who attempt to defeat their opponents almost always lose more than they gain.

In buyer-seller negotiations, countertactics are not designed to defeat buyers. *They are designed to build, balance, and maintain power—and ultimately reach an agreement that is beneficial and acceptable to both parties.* Sellers cannot conduct successful negotiations if buyers resent what is accomplished in the negotiation. A successful negotiation is benchmarked when the other side feels good about the agreement.

> **Caution!** The purpose of using countertactics is not to defeat a buyer or "win" a negotiation. The purpose of using countertactics is to neutralize buyer tactics aimed at securing discounts—without defeating the buyer.

Seller Countertactics

At the height of military conflict between England and Germany during WW II, British intelligence discovered that German spies were using carrier pigeons to send messages to bases across the English Channel. S.S. leader Heinrich Himmler, a pigeon fancier and holder of the prestigious title of President of the German National Pigeon Society, used the birds as a clandestine means of communicating with his undercover agents. The Nazis confiscated thousands of pigeons from their owners to use for the war effort and smuggled them into England.

To counter the menace, the British MI5 spy agency tamed its own crack force of ballistic birds—peregrine falcons. The falcons were trained to conduct search and destroy missions over the English Channel by patrolling the air over the British coasts in two-hour shifts and taking down any pigeons flying off toward the mainland.

Similar to British counter espionage efforts, successful sellers use whatever countertactics are available to neutralize buyer efforts to drive prices down and secure unwarranted discounts.

As I addressed in Chapter 10, there are numerous countertactics that sellers can choose from to mitigate buyer tactics. The following countertactics are recommendations and should not be interpreted as being the only possible countertactic solutions. Each countertactic can and should be used in conjunction with other countertactics. Many of them work hand-in-hand and compliment each other.

The Price Pinch

Buyer Type:	Hard Negotiator
Definition:	*The Price Pinch* uses price related statements intended to imply the seller's price is too high, unreasonable and/or unacceptable.
Prevention:	Available Funding
Buyer:	Your price is too high. You are 20 percent more expensive than the next highest bidder. I hope this is just your starting price and that you are prepared to talk about something reasonable.
Traditional Response:	We really want your business, Bill. I'll work this bid over one more time and see what I can do to lower that price for you. Where exactly do we need to be?
Countertactics:	*Surprise, Fairness, Policy & Procedure, Question & Clarify*
Cerebral Response:	Frankly, that surprises me . . . In order to be fair and consistent, our policy and procedure is to offer a fair and competitive price right from the start. When you say our price is too high, what exactly to you mean? With regard to competitive proposals or budgetary restrictions?

One way sellers can counter price related tactics is to shift the discussion's focus to value related issues and away from price related issues (see Chapter 14). A seller can effectively respond to *The Price Pinch* by asking the buyer, "If price were not an issue, what product would you choose and why?" If the buyer has determined that your product best meets his or her needs, and the haggling is simply over price, this question forces the buyer to articulate the reasons for the selection. In other words, the buyer will spout off the benefits and value of your proposed solution. His or her reasons for choosing your solutions can then be used to justify your proposed price.

Hard negotiators often ask, "What's your rock bottom price?" Be careful how you respond to this question. One way to counter this request is by asking the buyer, "What's the most you are willing to pay?" The key to responding to the "rock bottom" request is to avoid giving a quick answer. Ask questions about quantity, quality, or timeframes. Answer the buyer's question by saying, "To give you a rock bottom price, I need to know how many widgets you will be purchasing?… Are you looking to purchase the X or Y version?… Will you be purchasing in quarter one or quarter two?"

Competition

Buyer Type:	Hard Negotiator
Definition:	*Competition* seeks to take away a seller's unique solutions and competitive advantages by leveraging competing prices and competitive features against the seller.
Buyer:	X product is 20 percent less expensive than yours and includes training. How can you justify being 20 percent more expensive? You need to sharpen your pencil.
Traditional Response:	Well, O.K. I'm sure we can work this out. If I can match X competitor's price, plus throw in training, will that do it for you?
Countertactics:	*Question & Clarify*
Cerebral Response:	Nathan, help me understand why pricing has become an issue recently?… You mentioned that having X capability was important. What happens if you don't have that capability?

Demands & Deadlines

Buyer Type:	Hard Negotiator
Definition:	*Demands & Deadlines* threaten sellers into making concessions.
Prevention:	Timeframe
Buyer:	I don't want to talk about it again. Your failure to include your discounted price in the RFP put me in a bad situation. I want the corrected RFP on my desk by Monday. If you want the contract, you'll just have to figure out a way to get it done.
Traditional Response:	I didn't realize you needed the discounted price in the RFP. I'll get to work on this right away. I'll hammer it out over the weekend and have it emailed to you Monday morning.
Countertactics:	*Surprise, Question & Clarify, Reason & Rationale*
Cerebral Response:	Frankly, that surprises me. What reason did you have for believing I was going to include a discounted rate in the RFP? Help me understand the rationale for the Monday deadline.

Control & Intimidation

Buyer Type:	Hard Negotiator
Definition:	*Control & Intimidation* attempts to control and intimidate sellers with extended waiting periods, delays for appointments, long periods on hold, deliberate interruptions, schedule control, rude or condescending remarks, abusive language, and excessive talking in meetings and presentations.
Buyer:	That's the stupidest thing I've heard from a sales rep in a long time.

Traditional Response:	Well, I'm just trying to make everybody happy, Mr. Guzzy. If we discount this price by 10 percent, will that take care of it?
Countertactics:	*Silence, Surprise, Question & Clarify*
Cerebral Response:	*Silence,* or "Frankly, I'm a little disappointed. I recognize that if we are not a good fit, we are not a good fit. But, that is not the case here. Our products meet your needs for increased performance. What's the next best step to move this program forward?"

If buyers attempt to intimidate you with verbal outbursts, humiliating or derogatory remarks, remember that no deal is better than a bad deal. There comes a time when it's best to take a stand, end the abuse, and exercise the power of options by walking out. State to the buyer, "I came here to reach an agreement. I did not come here to be verbally abused."

Cost Breakdown

Buyer Type:	Hard Negotiator
Definition:	*Cost Breakdown* bombards sellers with questions designed to get them to reveal price structures, cost breakdowns, commission amounts and proposal architectures.
Buyer:	Your margins must be enormous. How did you line item your price structure? What's your cost breakdown?
Traditional Response:	Well, as you can see on the proposal, we offer both wireless and Web licenses. To be honest with you, where we really come out ahead is with our Web licensing. Each Web license…
Countertactics:	*Question & Clarify, Limited Authority*
Cerebral Response:	Help me understand why this information is critical to your decision… I am not authorized

to reveal the proprietary structure of our pricing model.

Be careful when and how much information is divulged to prospects. Volunteering important data will create an information imbalance favoring the buyer.

I cannot think of a single reason a seller should divulge price structures or cost breakdowns. Simply respond to any request to do so with a smile and state, "Nice try Danielle, but you know I can't give you that information. However, I can assure you that we will provide you with quality work at a fair cost."

> **The Point?** Information is a powerful weapon. While deliberate deception has no place in professional negotiations, good faith negotiation does not demand that parties volunteer everything they know.

The Ridiculous Offer

Buyer Type:	Hard Negotiator
Definition:	*The Ridiculous Offer* is a tactic used to find out how low a seller is willing to go by making a ridiculously low offer and seeing how the seller responds.
Buyer:	Gavin, how about $10,000? That should be enough, shouldn't it?
Traditional Response:	A $10,000 discount? I don't know. Of course, I'm willing to offer a discount but $10,000— that might be a little much.
Countertactics:	*Surprise, Fairness*
Cerebral Response:	That really surprises me you think X would sell for Y amount. Although I appreciate your offer, we aren't even in the same ballpark. For both your benefit and mine, it's important that we discuss numbers that are fair and reasonable.

Sometimes it's best to counter *The Ridiculous Offer* with simple humor and a chuckle. You might cordially laugh and say something like, "Nice try, Steve. Come on, you know that's not even close." Remember, the buyer might think his offer is as ridiculous as you do. He might just be testing the water to see how far he can *Lowball* you. I've heard of a seller who carried a laughing doll in his briefcase. When buyers would lowball, he'd set the doll on the desk, pull the string and listen to maniacal laughter fill the air.

Humor can also be used to counter *The Ridiculous Offer* and related tactics. I recall the story of an unusually acrimonious negotiation between a labor union and a group of business owners. After an intense argument, the parties stared at one another across the bargaining table. The leader of the labor union suddenly rose from his seat and walked slowly around the table toward the business owners. The room became dead silent. As he approached the chief negotiator for the business owners, he squatted next to his chair, looked across the table at his colleagues and said, "You know, he's right. From here, you guys do look like sons of #!@%'s." Everyone laughed, and a short time later, an agreement was made.

In face-to-face negotiations, a warm smile is one of the most powerful countertactics you can use. Smiles have been known to derail even the most difficult negotiators. Smiling communicates confidence, and makes a statement about the relationship. It's difficult to feel hostility toward someone who is smiling.

Caution! Do not respond to *The Ridiculous Offer* with anger. Keep anger and hostility out of the negotiation, regardless of the circumstance. Anger and hostility cloud thinking, replace intelligence with emotion, and cripple negotiating skills.

Pretended Anger

Buyer Type:	Hard Negotiator
Definition:	*Pretended Anger* attempts to make the seller feel uncomfortable using feigned anger or hostility directed at the seller or the price.
Buyer:	This is ridiculous. How can you expect us to do business with someone who gouges her customers with such exorbitant prices? This really makes me angry.
Traditional Response:	I'm sorry. I didn't mean to make you angry. I'll tell you what. Because you are a valued customer, I'll talk to my manager about getting that price down.
Countertactics:	*Surprise, Question & Clarify*
Cerebral Response:	I'm surprised you are so angry. Help me understand what the real issue is behind your frustration.

When buyers express anger or surprise (real or pretended) by "flinching," simply ignore their expressions or other means of non-verbal communication.

Salt & Pepper

Buyer Type:	Hard Negotiator
Definition:	*Salt & Pepper* is a buyer's deliberate attempt to complicate an issue in order to mentally confuse a seller.
Buyer:	Deliberately attempts to confuse the seller with misleading information, intentional errors in arithmetic, or false statistics.
Traditional Response:	I guess this looks alright. So if we sign it as is, have we got ourselves a deal?
Countertactics:	*Surprise, Question & Clarify*
Cerebral Response:	Bill, I'll be frank. These numbers look confusing. The last thing I want for you or for

me is to make a decision based on numbers we either don't understand or that are inaccurate. How do you recommend that we ensure we're working with data that is both accurate and understandable?

Sometimes hard negotiators use *Salt & Pepper* to confuse sellers by forcing them to address multiple issues simultaneously. To counteract this tactic, break the discussion into manageable segments. Then address each segment individually, beginning with the less significant topics. Addressing less significant topics first is important for two reasons: First, you want to generate quick agreement on less controversial issues. Second, you wan to create a psychological commitment to the negotiation process.

Good Guy, Bad Guy

Buyer Type:	Hard Negotiator
Definition:	A "tag team" approach wherein one buyer takes the uncompromising "bad guy" role. The second buyer takes the reasonable, compromising "good guy" role. The "good guy's" goal is inviting the seller to compromise by settling somewhere between the initial offer and the "bad guy's" counter offer.
Bad Guy:	I won't pay more than $1.00 a pound. Period. End of story.
Good Guy:	Come on Mark. Mr. Salesman is a good man and has done some nice things for us. He deserves to make a profit. Why don't we agree to $1.20 a pound?
Traditional Response:	$1.20 is a little bit lower than we normally go, but O.K. I guess that's what I have to do to get your business.
Countertactics:	*Surprise, Policy & Procedure*
Cerebral Response:	While I appreciate your offer of $1.20 a

pound, I can't accept it. Our standard policy and procedure is to give all of our customers the best price from the start and not deviate from our published price list. Help me understand, aside from dropping our price, what we can do to move this project forward?

Simply identifying this tactic as a tactic can sometimes take the wind out of a buyer's sail. Many buyers become embarrassed when caught using this tactic. If the buyer shows up with an attorney or executive that is obviously there to play "bad guy," a seller might interrupt their game plan and say, "I'm sure you are here to play bad guy, but let's not go down that road. I'm as anxious to find a solution as you are."

> **Note**: One way to counter the *Good Guy, Bad Guy* tactic is to create a bad guy of your own. Use *Limited Authority* or *Third Party* and make your boss or manager the bad guy.

Selective Memory

Buyer Type:	Calculating Buyer
Definition:	This tactic is used to secure discounts, additional add-ons, or other concessions by selectively remembering previous conversations, statements or agreements.
Buyer:	It seems like you said the first year of support was included in this price. I remember you saying something like that. I sure don't remember you saying it wasn't included in the initial price.
Traditional Response:	I might have said that, but I don't really remember. I guess if that's what you remember me saying, we can include support in the first year.

Countertactics: *Surprise, Limited Authority*
Cerebral Response: I'm surprised you thought support was
                         included in the initial price. Our price
                         structure doesn't include support in the cost
                         of the software, which means I'm not in a
                         position to include it in the proposal price.

This can be an extremely subtle tactic, causing sellers to second guess
their own memory and question inwardly, "Did I say that?" The best
way you can combat *Selective Memory* is by keeping detailed notes.
Notes protect sellers from having to rely on their own memory to combat the selective memory of a buyer.

The Maze

Buyer Type: Calculating Buyer
Definition: A buyer tactic that exercises the power of
                         TIME by getting sellers to complete a "maze"
                         of work by investing time, money and effort
                         into the sale. Buyers then leverage invested
                         TIME against the seller.
Buyer: Cindy, I need you to call Jim down in our
                         I.T. department with an explanation of the
                         productivity calculator. Also, please write up
                         the ROI sheet we talked about and get that
                         to our CFO, Dan Burton. Then, call Mary
                         in purchasing and let her know when she can
                         get that product comparison I know you are
                         working on. I'm assuming we are still on for
                         the presentation on the 15th?... Great. Oh, I
                         almost forgot. Would you mind emailing to
                         me an agenda of the presentation? In fact,
                         while you're at it...
Traditional Response: Excellent! I'll get right on it and call you
                         tomorrow with an update.
Countertactics: *Quid Pro Quo*

Cerebral Response:	In order for me to send the results from the productivity calculator, I need you to email me your average annual supply expense per employee. To give you an accurate R.O.I., I need you to let me know how many employees you will be supplying. The product comparison sheet is not complete. I am still waiting for your email with a list of the final vendors in the sale. Oh, I almost forgot…

Trophy Sale

Buyer Type:	Calculating Buyer
Definition:	The buyer implies that by virtue of his or her selecting the seller's services, other buyers will do likewise.
Buyer:	If you get us, do you realize how much recognition and business is going to follow? I can't believe you would risk that for a measly 10 percent discount.
Traditional Response:	Well, I can't argue with that. I'll talk to my manager and see if I can't get that discount approved today.
Countertactics:	*Policy & Procedure, Limited Authority*
Cerebral Response:	There is no doubt you are an important account to us. However, our policy is to be fair and equitable to all of our customers by providing the best price right from the start, which means I'm not in a position to offer a price allowance.

Budget

Buyer Type:	Calculating Buyer
Definition:	*Budget* uses budgetary restraints to secure discounts and price concessions.

Prevention:	Funding
Buyer:	I've been given a budget and I have no authority to deviate from it. I'm afraid your prices need to fit within our budgeted brackets or we may have to look somewhere else.
Traditional Response:	I'm certain we can work within your budget. If I reduce the cost of X, does that fit within your budget?
Countertactics:	*Surprise, Question & Clarify, Third Party*
Cerebral Response:	I'm surprised that such aggressive growth goals are being met with such limited budget constraints. What budget parameters are you working with?... I will need to discuss your situation with Corporate.

Budget is a popular tactic taught in buyer seminars and courses. Budgetary tactics are tough to deal with because it can be difficult to tell whether a buyer is making a legitimate statement of fact or bluffing to get a price concession.

An effective way to test the seriousness of the budgetary restraint is to state, "Let's do as much under your present budget as possible and leave the remainder until next quarter." This forces a buyer's hand. I can't tell you how many times I've experienced people, initially stating budgetary restrictions, who amazingly found more funding to secure the purchase. Most budgets are far more flexible than it first appears.

> **Note**: Challenge any form of "bracketed" restrictions introduced to the negotiation by buyers. Don't just accept the stated budget at face value.

Policy & Procedure is another great countertactic to *Budget*. In a sense, a seller's published price list is a seller's version of *Budget*. It establishes a set boundary of prices with which a buyer has to deal.

Be cautious in the initial stages of the sales cycle when buyers ask, "Can you give me an approximate or projected cost of this project?" Sellers sometimes unwittingly box themselves into brackets they later have to re-negotiate because they quote price ranges that buyers use to establish a budget in the first place. To avoid this situation, don't just blurt out "approximate" prices. Probe to ensure you offer numbers that you won't have to re-negotiate later.

Bloodhound

Buyer Type:	Calculating Buyer
Definition:	*Bloodhound* attempts to get sellers married to the project by making them chase after the sale. It's a sales version of "playing hard to get" in which buyers purposefully string the process out and don't make it easy for sellers to communicate.
Buyer:	Unreturned messages, unreturned emails, unavailable for calls, missed appointments, etc.
Traditional Response:	[Voicemail] Hi Shannon, this is Mary again with ABC Corporation. Sorry I missed you yesterday. I'm really looking forward to meeting with you. I'll try calling again tomorrow. Have a great day!
Countertactics:	*High Demand, Quid Pro Quo*
Cerebral Response:	[Voicemail] Hi Shannon, this is Nathaniel again with ABC Corporation. As we've discussed, X product is currently in extremely high demand. Consequently, so is my schedule. I do think we're a great match, and I look forward to doing business with you, but I am really crunched for time. Please call me back with your design specifications to move this project forward. I look forward to hearing from you.[1]

---

1. For more information on leaving effective voice messages, see Chapter 15 in *Power Prospecting.*

Bloodhound can be a difficult tactic to deal with, especially if a seller really wants a buyer's business. The key is to find a way to balance power. When sellers chase buyers, the power scale is out of balance in the buyer's favor. To balance the scale, exercise the power of TIME and the power of options.

Silence

Buyer Type:	Calculating Buyer
Definition:	*Silence* is used to get sellers to talk about price concessions and discounts. When sellers offer a price, many buyers are trained to remain completely silent. Sellers, uncomfortable with the silence, often start backing down from the price they quoted in previous statements or discussions.
Seller:	Mr. Jensen, our price for that particular server is $6,000.
Buyer:	[Silence].
Traditional Response:	Uh, of course, we would be willing to discount that particular server by 10 percent.
Countertactics:	*Silence, Question & Clarify*
Cerebral Response:	*Silence* or, "Take as much time as you need to think that over."

Silence is often the catalyst for one of the most famous negotiation statements ever made: *"The next person to talk loses."* If you offer a price and a buyer is silent, the theory is that if you speak next, you lose. While this is obviously an oversimplification, it certainly has merit. To safeguard against this scenario, always respond to silence with reciprocated silence or with a question—never a statement.

Lost Ground

Buyer Type:	Calculating Buyer
Definition:	*Lost Ground* threatens to start the sales process over again if certain demands aren't met.

Buyer: I'm afraid that if you don't meet our requirements we're going to have to go back to the drawing board and start this process over again.

Traditional Response: Robert, we have too much history for this to go out for RFP. What do I need to do to earn your business?

Countertactics: *Surprise, Fairness, Reason & Rationale, Question & Clarify*

Cerebral Response: Wow! That's surprising. I thought we resolved that proposal point weeks ago. As I mentioned before, we are adhering to our proposed price and feel it is fair and equitable. What would be your rationale for potentially starting the process over again? Have you considered the hard and opportunity costs associated with starting this process over?

Done Deal

Buyer Type: Calculating Buyer

Definition: *Done Deal* (sometimes called *Fait Accompli*) uses public pressure to obtain seller concessions by going public with assumptive decisions that were not agreed upon or approved by the seller.

Buyer: Sandy, this is a done deal. I already went public with this to the Vice President. He not only approved it, he expects this to be delivered in the next thirty days with the training included.

Traditional Response: The Vice President already approved it? Well, I guess there isn't anything I can do. I'll check with my regional manager this afternoon and make sure we get it delivered on time.

Countertactics: *Policy & Procedure, Limited Authority*

Cerebral Response:	I'm excited your Vice President has approved this. Unfortunately, training is not part of our agreement. Our policy is to adhere to our published price, which means I'm not authorized to include the training. However, I'll work up a proposal for the additional training and email it to you tomorrow morning.

What if...

Buyer Type:	Calculating Buyer
Definition:	*What If...* seeks to obtain information about a seller's pricing structure, margins, profits, and volume purchase breakdowns. That information is then used to secure minimum orders at volume prices.
Buyer:	How much is it if I purchase one software license?
Seller:	It's $1,000.
Buyer:	What if I agree to purchase a license for five locations instead of just one?
Seller:	That would be $4,000.
Buyer:	What if I decided to purchase a license for every facility in the U.S., all twenty-five of them? How much then?
Seller:	Twenty-five licenses? Let me check our volume rate sheet. That would be $15,000.
Buyer:	So if I purchase twenty-five licenses, I'm basically getting each license for $600 instead of $1,000. Is that right?
Seller:	Correct. Will you be purchasing for all twenty-five locations?
Buyer:	No, we don't have the funding for all twenty five facilities. But at $600 a license, I think I'll go ahead and order at least ten of them.

Traditional Response: John, I don't know if I can sell you ten licenses at $600, but I'm sure we can work out some sort of discount.

Countertactics: *Question & Clarify, Policy & Procedure*

Cerebral Response: I'm glad to hear you've decided on our product. However, corporate policy does not allow me to deviate from our published rate sheet, which means I'm not in a position to offer you the ten licenses at $600. However, the volume rate sheet does provide you with significant savings. Ten licenses would be $7,500.

Fairness

Buyer Type: Soft Bargainer

Definition: Buyers use *Fairness* to get sellers to feel uncomfortable about their cost structure and/or to question the ethics of their price. They attempt to reach a seller's higher motives by having them question the fairness of their proposal.

Buyer: Come on. That's not a fair price. That would tank my entire budget. All I'm asking is that you be *fair and reasonable* about this.

Traditional Response: Well, I suppose providing a discount isn't unreasonable. Would taking 10 percent off the proposal price be sufficient?

Countertactics: *Surprise, Question & Clarify*

Cerebral Response: Ken, I'm surprised you don't find our prices fair. When you say it would tank your entire budget, what exactly do you mean?

Sympathy

Buyer Type:	Soft Bargainer
Definition:	*Sympathy* is an attempt to leverage the buyer-seller relationship and the sympathy of the seller.
Buyer:	As you know Debbie, this has been a difficult year for us. With the slow down in the economy, they slashed our budget. I'm getting a lot of pressure to cut costs… sales are down… my dog died… my Aunt Peg was recently hospitalized… I would really appreciate it if you would work with me on bringing your price down.
Traditional Response:	Wow, that's terrible. I'm sure we can do something to bring the price down.
Countertactics:	*Limited Authority, Fairness*
Cerebral Response:	Gosh Bill, it sounds like you've had a rough year. Unfortunately, I don't have the authority to deviate from our current price. In order to be fair to all of our customers, we offer the best price, up front, from the start.

> **Caution!** Sometimes it's best to simply ignore problems that are not germane to the sale or negotiation. If it's not relevant to the agreement, sympathize with the buyer, but don't try to fix their problems.

Third Party

Buyer Type:	Soft Bargainer
Definition:	Buyers implement this tactic by using the names of executives, vice presidents, managers, purchasing agents or some third party (to whom you do not have direct access) to apply additional negotiation pressure.

Prevention:	Ultimate Decision Maker
Buyer:	Tim, I'm really catching heat to cut costs. They reviewed your proposal with the V.P. of operations and he didn't like it. They're really sticklers on this stuff.
Traditional Response:	Where do we need to be to earn your business?
Countertactics:	*Surprise, Question & Clarify*
Cerebral Response:	They apparently do not see the value of our proposed solution. Would it help if I spoke to them directly?… I checked with my manager, and his hands are tied. Obviously, we are the best solution for your needs. Aside from price, what can we do to resolve this issue?

Assumptive Assertions

Buyer Type:	Soft Bargainer
Definition:	Buyers use *Assumptive Assertions* to imply that certain items are included in the proposal.
Buyer:	So X is included in that price, right?
Seller:	No, I'm afraid it's not.
Buyer:	You mean to tell me X isn't included in this proposal? I just assumed that was part of the price.
Traditional Response:	I apologize for the misunderstanding. I guess we can include X as part of the proposal.
Countertactics:	*Surprise, Limited Authority*
Cerebral Response:	I'm surprised you assumed we included X. That is a significant add-on. I wish I could help, but including X in the existing package just isn't something I am authorized to offer without a volume purchase or longer contract.

Baiting

Buyer Type:	Soft Bargainer
Definition:	Baiting strings the selling process out. Buyers bait sellers with half-truths, somewhat misleading commitments, and statements aimed at obtaining lower prices and eventual discounts.
Buyer:	We're close Sharon, really close. If we can just wrap up the remaining few issues and drop that yearly renewal price, I think we've got ourselves a deal.
Traditional Response:	Excellent! I'm sure we can wrap up those remaining issues. Don't worry about the yearly renewal price. I'll drop that down to $399 a year instead of $599.
Countertactics:	*Question & Clarify*
Cerebral Response:	It sounds to me like we are not as close to wrapping this up as I had thought. What steps remain for us to reach agreement?... What remaining issues are you aware of?… Help me understand where you don't see the value in the yearly renewal.

Ambiguous Authority

Buyer Type:	Soft Bargainer
Definition:	*Ambiguous Authority* implies the buyer is no longer the ultimate decision maker and does not have the authority to approve the agreement. The counterpart communicates ambiguous messages of decision-making authority and references vague entities such as "management," "committees," or

	"departments" to delay the process or pass negotiating responsibilities to someone else.
Prevention:	Ultimate Decision Maker
Buyer:	I can't approve your current proposal. It's really not in my jurisdiction anymore. I'm going to need to get the procurement department involved.
Traditional Response:	Going through procurement always slows things down. What do you need for us to get this deal done?
Countertactics:	*Surprise, Question & Clarify*
Cerebral Response:	Frankly, I'm a little surprised. Help me understand what's changed since we last spoke? Aside from yourself, who *is* making the final decision?

Nibbling

Buyer Type:	Calculating Buyer
Definition:	*Nibbling* attempts to obtain small concessions just prior to or just after the agreement is made. It's that little push for something more, that last shot at something extra.
Buyer:	Would you mind throwing in a few extra pieces for in-store distribution? We forgot to include them in our RFP. And, if you could just Fed Ex those to each store for me to get a little head start on each promotion. In fact, while you're at it...
Traditional Response:	That shouldn't be too hard to accommodate. Anything else?
Countertactics:	*Policy & Procedure, Limited Authority*
Cerebral Response:	Unfortunately, our policy is that X requires an incremental charge. I am not authorized to modify that policy, which means I cannot offer any discounts.

Nibbling attempts and last minute demands that magically appear after a negotiation has been largely completed are not always what they seem. Most of the time, buyers use the *Nibbling* tactic to ensure that the negotiation is the best possible agreement. Sellers must help buyers recognize that they are getting the best deal. The correct response, therefore, is to hold firm to your position. In most cases, the buyer will be relieved that the negotiated agreement is indeed the best possible arrangement.

> **Note:** One way to counter Nibbling is to make counter demands (see Chapter 13). Requesting reciprocal concessions is an effective way to stop Nibbling attempts.

Sunshine

Buyer Type:	Soft Bargainer
Definition:	*Sunshine* is a tactic used to gain concessions based on flattery and words of adulation. It's the ultimate relationship-leveraging technique. Soft bargainers sprinkle sunshine all over the sales person.
Buyer:	Matt, you've been terrific. You're one of the best sales people I've ever worked with. If you can get us that 10 percent discount and a game of golf I think we've got a deal!
Traditional Response:	Consider it done! I'll get the golf tickets and call you with a tee time in the morning.
Countertactics:	*Limited Authority, Third Party*
Cerebral Response:	It's been great working with you as well. Unfortunately, I'm not authorized to offer such a significant discount without a volume purchase. I'm certain I won't get signoff at Corporate to authorize a discount without it.

However, I can accommodate you on a game of golf!

In Summary

Although the above examples are role-play scenarios, they represent common tactics, demands, and responses from buyers. In fact, it's quite common for multiple buyer tactics to be used in a single buyer-seller interaction.

My rookie year in sales, I had an existing customer call me and demand a significant discount. The conversation went something like this. "Hi, Mr. Hansen. My name is Steve, and I'm the technical coordinator for my school district. Our district is currently using your software. We recently purchased an entirely new network for our school district and want to upgrade your system in each library. But, I'll be damned if I'm going to pay at full price." (*The Price Pinch*) I responded, "Steve, I'm happy to hear you are going to upgrade. How many schools will you be upgrading?"

"All eight of them."

"Great, the cost will be X dollars."

"Didn't you hear me? I refuse to pay full price! (*Pretended Anger, Control & Intimidation*) At minimum, we want whatever your discount rate is for existing customers. (*Assumptive Assertion*) We are the most advanced school district in this state with the most cutting edge technology. When we make a decision, every surrounding school district follows. (*Trophy Sale*) If you lose us, you will lose a lot more than just us. In fact, I'm not even terribly happy with your product or your customer service, and I'm seriously considering going with X competitor. (*Competition*)"

In less than two minutes, this guy rattled off (what I later determined to be) six buyer tactics. He caught me off guard. I wasn't sure how to respond and my instincts took over. In the heat of the moment, I stated back to him, "So pricing isn't an issue?"

Frustrated with my response, he replied, "What? Your price is the reason I'm calling."

"No. Price must not be an issue or you wouldn't have mentioned going with X competitor. They will charge you full price instead of an upgrade price. Your cost will double by migrating your district to X competitor than it will by upgrading with us. So if price really isn't the issue, what is? *(Triangulation, Question & Clarify)"*

He didn't know what to say. Every tactic he used was focused on securing a discount. He was dumbfounded. I then said to him, "Not only will you be spending more if you choose X competitor, but our prices are going up June 1st (which was absolutely true). If you want to get this implemented before the end of the school year and avoid the price increase, you will need to fax that order to me within the next two weeks."

I received the order at full price.

> **The Point?** Buyer tactics are neutralized with effective seller countertactics. One simple rejoinder can counter a half dozen tactics and save you from making unnecessary discounts.

Visit www.patrickhenryinc.com to download a sample podcast and other sales and negotiation tools.

part four IV

NEGOTIATION STRATEGY

CHAPTER 12

Negotiation 101

In 1863, Prussian premier Otto von Bismarck assessed the European chessboard of power. England, France, and Austria were the dominant players while his own country, Prussia, consisted of loosely associated German states called The German Federation. As Bismarck surveyed the geopolitical landscape, he was determined to make Prussia a dominant European power.

First, he neutralized his most ominous opponent, Austria. Austria had made sure that the independent German states remained weak and divided—and in the case of Prussia, subservient. As Bismarck evaluated his military and political options, he chose to make war on Denmark to recover a former Prussian province called Schleswig-Holstein. However, in his declaration of war, there was a bizarre twist that shocked Europe: he was invading Schleswig-Holstein on behalf of Austria! This forced Austria to enlist in the war as an ally of Prussia, but after the war, Bismarck demanded that the lands be turned over to Prussia.

This infuriated the Austrians, but they complied. First they turned over Schleswig and one-year later, Holstein. With this bold and calculated move, Bismarck cleverly announced to the world that Austria was weakening and Prussia was strengthening.

Bismarck's next move was to draw Austria into a military conflict with Prussia. Although the other German states were vehemently opposed to the war, Bismarck succeeded in forcing the conflict. He went on to defeat the Austrians in what history named The Seven Weeks War. After the crushing defeat of the Austrians, The German Federation wanted to claim as much land from Austria as possible. Bismarck refused, and instead positioned himself to the European community as an arbiter of peace. The result was a treaty with Austria that granted total autonomy and positioned Prussia as the dominant power in Germany and in Europe.

The English and the French began comparing Bismarck to Attila the Hun and publicly referred to him as the "Iron Chancellor." Bismarck ignored these distractions and continued to focus on his ultimate objective—making Prussia the most powerful state in Europe. Using cat-and-mouse political and diplomatic tactics, he provoked the French into war in 1870 and in less than three months destroyed the entire French army. The English recognized that they were dealing with an extremely shrewd and calculating leader, so they chose to settle through negotiation what they feared they would not be able to accomplish with war. A year later Bismarck founded the German Empire, an empire Hitler later referred to as The Second Reich.

Bismarck's planning and preparations were demonstrated in his military and political strategies. Rather than rushing headlong into battle with Austria, France, and England, he dismantled them one at a time. He studied his strengths and weaknesses and those of his enemies. Most importantly, he never lost site of his goal: an independent German state led by his beloved Prussia.

Negotiators can learn a great deal from Bismarck's approach to politics and war. First, negotiators need to think, plan, and prepare strategies prior to the actual negotiation (see The Pre-Negotiation Planner at the end of this chapter). Second, negotiators need to survey the political and power landscape of their counterparts. What are *their* strengths and weaknesses? What potential strategies might *they* implement? What demands might they make? Third, negotiators need to stay focused on the primary objective: a profitable agreement.

Negotiation Defined

Strategy without tactics is the slowest route to victory. Tactics without strategy is the noise before defeat.

—Sun Tzu

Thus far, I have addressed the *tactical* side of negotiation. We've analyzed the primary components of buyer-seller negotiations including power, tactics, and countertactics. I will now focus on the *strategic* side of sales-side negotiation.

Developing successful negotiation strategies requires that sellers understand the meanings and definitions of the words I use to create negotiation strategies.

A strategy is an overall process of plan execution. It consists of a premeditated objective with multiple tasks involved in fulfilling the objective. A tactic, on the other hand, is a means of achieving the objective. It's the action required to implement the strategy. For example, in warfare a strategy is defined as the planning of conduct for a large-scale combat operation. A tactic is defined as the military art of deploying and directing troops, ships, and aircraft to secure the objectives of the plan. In negotiation, the strategy is the overall game plan. Tactics are then used to implement the strategy and achieve the objective.

> **Note**: Negotiation is a process of communication for the purpose of reaching a joint decision. The objective is to achieve agreement. In successful negotiations, both parties gain. Nevertheless, more often than not, one side gains more than the other.

Negotiation: Expect It

Let us never negotiate out of fear, but let us never fear to negotiate.

—John F. Kennedy

Many sellers do not recognize their role as negotiators. This is a big mistake because selling is negotiating. It is critical for sales professionals to know how to negotiate because it directly affects how much money they earn. Sellers who know how to negotiate maintain higher margins, increase personal and corporate profitability, are better performers, earn higher commissions, and are more successful in general.

I frequently visit my local Barnes and Noble bookstore and browse the business section. On one occasion, I picked up multiple books on negotiation and found an interesting pattern. Skim the chapter headings of most negotiation books and guess what you'll find? The majority of negotiation books teach buyers how to negotiate against sellers! Traditional negotiation books instruct buyers how to acquire what they want from sellers, not the other way around.

> **Note**: Very few professions negotiate as much as the sales profession.

Unfortunately, negotiation is a neglected area of sales training, and, as a result, a neglected area of sales performance. Since most sellers are not excellent negotiators, they believe that discounting is a necessary component of selling. They think price reductions are fundamental to the selling process. Regrettably, this status quo exists for two reasons:

1. Most sellers do not view themselves as professional negotiators.
2. Most sellers have not been trained to professionally negotiate.

This creates an interesting dynamic because most buyers expect to negotiate with sellers. They expect to bargain when they buy, especially when purchasing large ticket or high value items. They walk into the sale anticipating negotiating a better deal than the published price tag. Many buyers come prepared to do just that.

The opposite is not true for sellers. Most sellers do not anticipate or adequately plan to negotiate with prospects. Research indicates that many sellers neglect to adequately prepare for negotiation because they feel threatened or intimidated by the negotiation process. They find it stressful or difficult to deal with buyer-negotiator tactics that attempt to adjust product prices, delivery dates, or other specifications.

Sales-Side Negotiation Rules

If a seller understands fundamental rules of negotiation and follows simple guidelines, it will help alleviate many of the stresses associated with negotiating.

Sales-side negotiators utilize three primary negotiation rules:

1. Sell first. Negotiate second.
2. Trade. Never donate concessions (see Chapter 13).
3. Negotiate prepared.

Sell First. Negotiate Second.

The most common negotiating mistake sellers make is negotiating too soon. Sellers who are not proficient or who are not confident in their selling abilities often start negotiating at the beginning of the sale by offering discounts. They do this to initiate interest or compensate for poor selling skills. *Discounting* becomes a substitute for selling.

Negotiating early in the sale is a mistake for multiple reasons:

1. It detracts from the purpose of selling—building value.
2. It lessens the impact of the negotiated concession.
3. It sets a precedent and encourages buyers to negotiate additional concessions.

One of the most fundamental skills of selling is building value. If sellers begin the sales process by offering discounts and concessions, they are selling price instead of value. The problem with selling price is that there is nothing unique about price. There is no inherent value in price. *If value is not established, price has no meaning.* Without understanding the value of a product or service, buyers have no way of determining the meaning of the price.

Negotiating early in the sales process also diminishes the impact of the negotiated concession. If a seller offers discounts early in the sale in an effort to generate interest, prior to establishing and building value, the discount has little or no meaning. If nothing is valued, nothing is gained in the exchange.

Discounts lose their impact if salespeople offer them without first establishing and building value. For instance, if I'm selling corporate sales training, and I begin the sales presentation with a statement such as, "Hi, it's good to be here. Before we begin, I want to let you know that I'm offering a 10 percent discount on all of my trainings." What meaning will 10 percent have if it's not, in some way, compared to the worth of the good or service being offered? If I offer a discount without first establishing what exactly it is I'm discounting, then what meaning can the discount possibly have?

In order for concessions to have an impact, they need to be negotiated at the end of the selling process after needs and pains have been identified, solutions have been presented, and the value of the good or service has been firmly established. Ideally, negotiation should be the last step of the sales cycle. (See *figure 12.1*).

> **Caution!** Negotiations inherently focus on price, not value. By negotiating early in the sale, sellers distract buyers from focusing on solutions and benefits. Don't distract buyers by introducing negotiation issues early in the sales process.

Many sellers compensate for a lack of selling skill by offering discounts at the beginning of the sale. I've observed sellers who, unwittingly, gave away almost their entire profit margin by offering a discount as a means of generating interest. They didn't realize it, but they weren't selling. They were negotiating. They were giving away commissionable dollars when they should have been selling.

Unskilled sellers broadcast their willingness to offer discounts with statements such as, "Of course, this price is negotiable," or "By the way, there is a discount schedule." These statements scream to buyers, "I'm a sucker. I have no set pricing structure. I'm inviting you to come and take advantage of me."

Negotiating early in the sales process also establishes a precedent for future negotiations. When sellers begin the selling process with a discount, or offer concessions early in the sales cycle, they "tee" them-

The DNA Selling System[1]

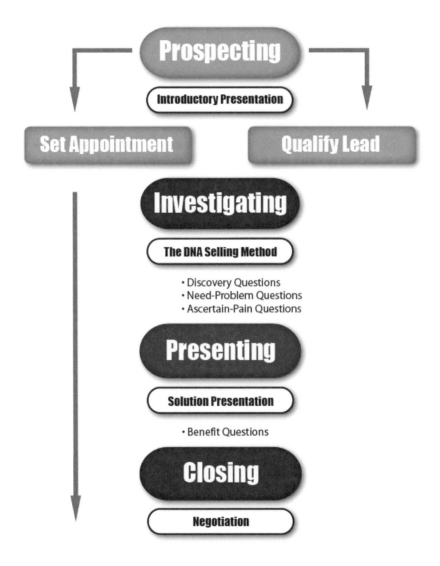

---

1. For more information regarding *The DNA Selling System* see, Part 2 in *The DNA Selling Method*. For information regarding prospecting see *Power Prospecting*. For information regarding presentations see, *Winning Sales Presentations*.

selves up for future negotiation expectations. Buyers rightfully assume, if sellers offer discounts or concessions early in the sale that the sellers don't have a firm price structure and they are open to future negotiations. When they offer discounts and concessions, sellers communicate that they are open game for future negotiation.

After conducting a fifteen-year study, VASS Training Group reported that 67 percent of sellers needlessly volunteered price reductions without a request from buyers. If sellers offer price discounts without being asked, they're not negotiating. They're just being plain stupid.

> **The Point?** Negotiating is a poor substitute for selling. Don't negotiate until you have to. Avoid modifying your price or altering terms until you have no alternative. Negotiate as little and as late as possible. Sell first. Negotiate second.

Ask Questions (Lots of Them!)

During harsh financial battles between financial titan J.P. Morgan and steel magnate Andrew Carnegie, Morgan made a bold and daring proposition. After months of competitive maneuvering, Morgan concluded that the only way to financially overpower Carnegie was to buy him out. Morgan personally approached Carnegie in 1901 and brusquely asked him what he would take for his steel empire. Carnegie suggested the sum of $300 million. Desperate to counter the exponential growth of Carnegie's industrial enterprise, Morgan considered the proposal and consented to make the purchase. Carnegie immediately accepted Morgan's offer.

Months later, Morgan and Carnegie were on the same Atlantic liner bound for recreation in foreign lands. Coming down late to their morning coffee, the men found a few minutes for reminiscence between them. "Do you know, Mr. Morgan" said Carnegie, "I have been thinking it over, and I find I made a mistake. I should have asked you for another hundred million for those Carnegie properties." "If you had," responded Morgan in his frank, unfeeling truthfulness, "I would have paid it."[2]

The mistake that Carnegie made, which is a common negotiation mistake, was hastily agreeing to the offer without questioning the need for the purchase. Had Carnegie asked a few questions instead of immediately consenting to the deal, he more than likely would have sensed the urgency Morgan was feeling to buy his business. Had Carnegie simply asked, "Mr. Morgan, help me understand why you want to purchase my business," or "Mr. Morgan, what motivated you to offer to buy my steel enterprise?" Carnegie would have equipped himself with the necessary insight to determine the real value of his business. Had he asked Morgan a few questions rather than immediately consenting to the offer, he would have avoided the mistake of undervaluing his business by a hundred million dollars!

Many negotiation experts believe asking questions is not just one of the most important negotiation skills, but *the* most important negotiation skill.

As addressed in great detail in *The DNA Selling Method*, a primary component of successful selling is questioning.[3] Questions help extract buyer needs, identify problems, and unearth pain. Sellers who don't ask questions don't discover pain. This impacts negotiation because buyers in pain have less room to negotiate.

The seller's most important job is to uncover buyer problems to solve. Once buyers have a clear picture of the seriousness of their problems, and how a seller's goods or services resolve those problems, they associate value with the proposal.

---

2. The *Wall Street Journal*, August 3, 1909.
3. See *The DNA Selling Method*.

Questions also divulge critical account information and equip sellers with the data needed to negotiate. Very often, when negotiations reach what is referred to as *deadlock*, asking questions is the only way out. For example, if a buyer digs in on a particular item of negotiation, such as a delivery date that can't be met, a seller will get nowhere explaining all of the reasons for not being able to deliver. Skilled negotiators overcome these kinds of dilemmas by asking questions. "Chad, tell me why early delivery is so important?" "Help me understand what's driving that particular date." For all the seller knows, Chad is pushing for an early delivery date because he has to make the payment during his fiscal year budget or he will lose his funding, and the delivery is scheduled after the end of the fiscal year.

Questions reveal information that can help end deadlocks and resolve other uncomfortable negotiation dilemmas.

Remember that negotiation is an art of persuasion. Persuading a counterpart to a *mutually beneficial agreement* is the purpose of negotiation. People are persuaded much more by effective questions than they are by statements. Regardless of how well a person talks or presents, questions have the greatest impact on the success or failure of a negotiation.

> **The Point?** Successful negotiators focus on what to ask, not what to say.

The Sales-Side Negotiation Planner

In forming the plan of a campaign, it is requisite to foresee everything the enemy may do and to be prepared with the necessary means to counteract it.

—Napoleon Bonaparte

Like trial attorneys anticipating the tactics, questions, and motives of opposing lawyers, strategic negotiators don't walk into negotiation meetings blindly. Rather, they insulate themselves from making poor decisions by establishing strategies prior to the negotiation. They determine such issues as *bottom line* concessions prior to the negotiation. Potential questions, concerns, demands, and objections are anticipated. Rationale for anticipated buyer demands, counter demands, and positions are identified. In short, they create a blueprint for the negotiation.

Nearing the end of a hard-fought presidential election in 1912, Theodore Roosevelt scheduled a final whistle-stop campaign across America. At each stop, Roosevelt planned to deliver a stirring speech and distribute an elegant pamphlet with a presidential portrait on the cover and a copy of the speech inside. Over three million copies of the pamphlet had been printed when a campaign worker discovered that the photograph on the a stirring speech and distribute an elegant pamphlet with a presidential portrait on the cover and a copy of the speech inside. Over three million copies of the pamphlet had been printed when a campaign worker discovered that the photograph on the brochure had been copyrighted by Moffett Studios in Chicago. Because Moffett Studios owned the copyright, any unauthorized use of the photo could cost the campaign millions of dollars and lead to a political scandal. On the other hand, not using the pamphlets would damage Roosevelt's election prospects. With no time to reprint the brochure, the dispirited campaign workers turned to Roosevelt's senior political advisor, George Perkins, a former partner of J.P. Morgan.

Perkins immediately contacted the campaign's Chicago operatives to learn more about Moffett Studios. What he learned was disheartening: Moffett was financially struggling and was hard up for money. Perkins reviewed the situation and evaluated his alternatives. After assessing his options, and those of his counterpart, he summoned a stenographer to dispatch a cable to Moffett Studios: "We are planning to distribute millions of pamphlets with Roosevelt's picture on the cover. It will be great publicity for the studio whose photograph we use. How much will you pay us to use yours? Respond immediately." Moffett replied, "We've never done this before, but under the circumstances we'd be pleased to offer you $250."

———————

Perkins' duplicitous approach raises ethical questions and is not a model negotiation on how to enhance long-term buyer-seller relationships. Yet his assessment of the situation is a textbook example of how to prepare for a negotiation. He evaluated power, anticipated Moffett's response, devised alternatives, and identified the value he could offer to his counterpart, *prior to the negotiation*. Based on his preparation, Perkins was able to develop a negotiation strategy that defused a potential financial and political disaster for the Roosevelt campaign.

Although many negotiations take place in informal settings (sometimes even over the phone), other negotiations come to a summit in formal, sit down meetings in which price, terms, delivery, service, training, and resources are determined over a "bargaining table." In such cases, it's prudent to plan negotiation strategies in advance.

Planning means doing your homework. Each sale is unique. Consequently, the dynamics in each sale will vary from simple to complex. Like Perkins, you must take the time to think through and visualize the upcoming negotiation, the players, the tactics, the strengths and weaknesses of various counterparts, proposals, and positions.

I recommend that sellers prepare for negotiations with *The Sales-Side Negotiation Planner*. This worksheet is a tool to create strategies prior to negotiating. Like Bismarck surveying the political chessboard of Europe, or a military general preparing for battle, cerebral sellers anticipate the strategies, tactics, and capabilities of their counterparts. They identify vulnerability: in their counterparts and themselves. They recognize their own strengths. By conducting pre-negotiation briefing sessions, sellers create both proactive and reactive negotiation strategies and avoid the stress that comes with feeling unprepared or being put on the spot, scrambling for an answer.

Negotiation Planner

NEGOTIATION AGENDA

-
-
-

QUALIFICATIONS

Decision Makers:

Funding:

Timeframe:

PRIMARY BUYER NEEDS

-
-
-

VALUE WE PROVIDE

-
-
-

COMPETITOR(S)

-
-
-

DIFFERENTIATORS

-
-
-

SELLER POWER

- ☐ TIME
- ☐ Information
- ☐ Options
- ☐ Differentiation
- ☐ Experience/Expertise
- ☐ People/Pressure

BUYER POWER

- ☐ TIME
- ☐ Information
- ☐ Options

CONCESSION PATTERN

1. Start with No
2. Concede Reluctantly
3. Respond Slowly

PRICE CONCESSION BOUNDARIES

Optimistic:

Pessimistic:

Rock bottom:

RATIONALE TO SUPPORT OUR POSITIONS:

What justifies our request(s)?

What rationale do we have to support our position(s)?

Why should our counterpart agree?

BUYER TACTICS

	HARD NEGOTIATOR		CALCULATING BUYER		SOFT BARGAINER
☐	The Price Pinch	☐	Selective Memory	☐	Fairness
☐	Competition	☐	The Maze	☐	Sympathy
☐	Demands & Deadlines	☐	Trophy Sale	☐	Third Party
☐	Control & Intimidation	☐	Budget	☐	Assumptive Assertions
☐	Cost Breakdown	☐	Bloodhound	☐	Baiting
☐	The Ridiculous Offer	☐	Silence	☐	Ambigious Authority
☐	Pretended Anger	☐	Lost Ground	☐	Nibbling
☐	Salt & Pepper	☐	Done Deal	☐	Sunshine
☐	Good Guy, Bad Guy	☐	What If...	☐	No John Hancock

COUNTERTACTICS

☐	Surprise	☐	Question & Clarify	☐	High Demand
☐	Policy & Procedure	☐	Reason & Rationale	☐	Deadline
☐	Limited Authority	☐	Fairness	☐	Silence
☐	Third Party	☐	Quid Pro Quo	☐	Differentiation

Tactic	Response

NOTES:

Visit www.patrickhenryinc.com to download a PDF version of the Negotiation Planner.

To win by strategy is no less the role of a general than to win by arms.

—Julius Caesar

An important component of sales-side negotiation is preparing questions. It's important to plan questions in advance. Ineffective negotiators spend most of their time conjuring up ways to explain their position to the other side, resulting in talking instead of probing. Good questions don't just flow off the top of a seller's head, especially in a negotiation. Asking good questions is not easy. Questions need to be planned in advance and rehearsed. Even the tone in which they are asked needs to be planned.[4]

> **The Point?** Preparation precedes power. Power comes from making informed decisions. Enter negotiations prepared with planned strategies, countertactics, and questions using The Sales-Side Negotiation Planner.

Focus on Solutions

Focusing on solutions seems like an obvious negotiation skill, but it isn't. In fact, my negotiation experience has been that focusing on solutions isn't as simple as it sounds. Why? Sellers are easily distracted. They are thrown off course by prospects who are focused on limitations and problems rather than solutions. Buyers center on what sellers *cannot* do. Their bargaining power comes from concentrating on seller weaknesses and limitations, not seller strengths or solutions.

I was involved in a negotiation in San Antonio, Texas, that demonstrates why focusing on solutions is so important. A committee composed of twenty plus members unanimously selected our product. It

---

4. For an extensive list of questions that reveal needs, problems, pains, and other related issues, see *The DNA Selling Method*.

was a huge sale. The only remaining details were the technical specifications for hardware, networking, and software installations. When the technical committee began grilling us on the "specs" of the project, they discovered a fairly serious oversight on their part. They had forgotten to include a vital implementation component in their RFP (request for proposal). We did not meet their overlooked specs but informed them that we had the development capabilities to meet their needs within a reasonably short timeframe. Amazingly, it didn't matter. They kept focusing on the fact that it wasn't available to implement that day. During the negotiation, they concentrated on this particular limitation, ignoring all of the other capabilities that led them to choose our product. They focused on problems, deficiencies, and limitations while we focused on solutions. No matter how hard they tried, we kept coming back to what we did, not what we couldn't do at that exact moment. Had we fallen into their trap and kept the negotiation centered on limitations, we would have lost the deal. Focusing on solutions salvaged the sale.

In sales related negotiations, seller strength flows from focusing on ways to benefit customers. By zeroing in on solutions and benefits, sellers keep limitations off the table, and value on the table.

> **The Point?** Keep negotiations focused on how to help the buyer. Center discussions on areas of maximum leverage. Focus on solutions.

The Role of Reason and Rationale in Negotiation

—————◦◦◦◦—————

In 1582, Protestants in the Netherlands were struggling to gain independence from their Catholic ruler, Spain. *Inquisition* executions and brutal torturing techniques rallied the Dutch Protestants to revolt. Seeking assistance from England, the Protestant rebels appealed to Queen Elizabeth I. Not wishing to engage in open warfare with Spain, the most powerful empire in the world at the time, Elizabeth resisted intervention. In 1585, however, she agreed to a treaty which bound her to send an army to assist the Dutch Protestants. Before committing English troops, though, she issued an extraordinary twenty-page pamphlet which was translated into French, Spanish, and Dutch, and distributed across England and the European continent. The pamphlet and its distribution was an unprecedented move—a sovereign ruler justifying her actions before the opinions of the world. In her political treatise, she provided the reason and rationale for her intervention. She discussed the tyrannical nature of Spanish governors and outlined the violation of "ancient laws of liberty." The pamphlet had the desired effect and rallied Protestants across Europe to support her decision.

Although sellers should never feel obliged to apologize for their actions, like Queen Elizabeth I, they should be prepared to explain and provide rationale for decisions that might be subject to misinterpretation or adverse interpretation.

Communicating reason and rationale is a method that generates wide support for difficult or potentially uncomfortable decisions. When a seller uses reason and rationale to support proposals, buyers don't feel like they are being personally attacked. Instead, the seller's position legitimately demands attention based on the merits being presented.

Using and requiring reason and rationale also ensures that solutions are reached based on *principles*, not *pressure*. For example, why not insist that a negotiated price be based on some objective standard such as solution value, return on investment, market value, precedent, replacement cost, or competitive pricing, instead of just random demands or desires?

A good principle to follow in a price negotiation is to be specific. Provide specific reasons for existing price structures. This is especially important when dealing with a calculating buyer. Offer rationale to support your position. This does not mean offering cost breakdowns or margin structures. It means supporting your prices with capability sheets and benefit statements. Having Competitive Differential Advantage (CDA) documents, Point of Difference (POD) comparisons, Unique Selling Points (USP), Most Valuable Proposition (MVP) statements, and Top Ten Reason lists will come in handy.

You might base your price position on specific issues such as:

- Better Products
- Better Service
- Better Quality
- Better Reputation

- Better Solutions
- Better Support
- Better Warranty
- Better Technology

Concrete details make price positions more credible. By providing buyers with reasons for your price and rationale for your proposal, you justify price structures and take price related bargaining power away from buyers.

CHAPTER 13

Trading Versus Donating Concessions

In 1934, Adolf Hitler repudiated the clauses of the Treaty of Versailles that limited Germany's armed forces and began a massive plan of rearmament. By 1936, he had strengthened the German army to unprecedented heights, so much so, that by the end of that year, he invaded and reoccupied the Rhineland. Hitler then turned east and began pressuring Czechoslovakia to make whatever concessions the Sudeten German subjects demanded. In September, 1938, the Prime Ministers of Britain and France, Neville Chamberlain and Edouard Daladier, flew to Munich to meet with the fascist dictators of Italy and Germany—Benito Mussolini and Adolf Hitler—to reach an agreement in the alleged interest of European peace.

Hitler immediately began making demands exacting huge concessions on the part of Czechoslovakia and other countries with German citizens. In one of the most infamous acts of negotiation history, Neville Chamberlain succumbed to Hitler's tactics by making unprecedented military and territory concessions *without making a single counter demand of Hitler.* In the absence of Czechoslovakian representation, Chamberlain agreed to Czechoslovakia's virtual dismemberment. When the meeting ended, Chamberlain thought he had a peace agreement. In reality, his concessions emboldened Hitler and led to even more demands by the Fuehrer. Within one year, World War II began, and Neville Chamberlain resigned a defeated man.

Had Chamberlain been a skilled negotiator, Europe might have taken another course. Had Chamberlain implemented even the most fundamental negotiation strategies, such as balancing power and making counter demands, Hitler's territorial ambitions might have been put in check. Instead, Hitler's success at the negotiation table only encouraged his mad obsession to expand the borders of Germany.

Trading instead of donating concessions is an elemental part of good negotiation. When a seller makes counter demands, he or she not only balances power but also prevents future demands.

Discounts, Concessions, and Relationships

Many sellers believe that discounting "makes friends" and strengthens buyer-seller relationships. Nothing could be further from the truth. In many cases, discounting has just the opposite effect and can hurt buyer-seller relationships. When a buyer makes price related objections and a seller immediately discounts, what is communicated to the buyer? The seller's concession suggests that the original price was inflated.

Discounting or making price concessions early in a sale can harm relationships by causing buyers to question the honesty of the seller. It also leads buyers to ask, "What's rock bottom?" It sets the seller up for further discounts and potential negotiation conflict. Undisciplined sellers, who are quick to discount, can damage the trust and credibility they need to maintain lasting buyer-seller relationships.

Sellers who fail to implement effective selling skills make up for it by discounting. Many sellers actually start the sale by offering a discount. "Just to let you know, if you choose our product, we will offer a 25 percent discount." Discounting becomes the weapon of choice for unskilled sellers.

> **Caution!** Don't jump to discount. Avoid immediate concessions. If a concession is made, make the buyer go through a process to obtain it. Offer concessions reluctantly and slowly.

Trade. Never Donate Concessions

He gives twice that gives soon, i.e., he will soon be called to give again.

—Benjamin Franklin

Of course, there are times when concessions are required, rational, and/or necessary to win a sale. In many cases, it makes sense to deviate from published price lists and provide discounts. However, when price concessions are necessary to win a sale, it is important sellers *trade* concessions, not *donate* concessions.

<hr />

In the early 1600's, Great Britain and Holland were vying for control of the Spice Islands in the East Indies. The Spice Islands were considered prized possessions because they produced nutmeg and cloves, spices found nowhere else in the known world. Although it was discovered by British explorers, the island of Run, which contained the world's only nutmeg forests, was overrun by a band of Dutch sailors in 1620. The Dutch valued the nutmeg, not only because of its taste, but also because it was believed to be a cure for the plague. They plotted to keep prices high and to prevent nutmeg plants from falling into British hands. Because of the value of spices, the British and Dutch battled for control of Run Island and the spice trade in the East Indies.

Years later, the two nations attempted to negotiate a treaty that would end the warring factions. During the negotiation, the issue of Run Island was a serious bone of contention because the Dutch refused to bequeath it in the settlement. Unwilling to simply donate their claims to Run Island, the British suggested a trade. They offered to accept another island in return for Run Island. The island's name: Manhattan, The Big Apple for a forest of nutmeg—not a bad trade.

<hr />

There is a fundamental negotiation rule sellers should follow: *don't give without getting.* Don't make the same mistake Neville Chamberlain made with Hitler. Instead, follow the example of the British when they traded their claims to Run Island for Manhattan.

A concession is not a donation. The only reason to offer a concession is to get something in return—if possible, something of comparable value.

Make Concessions Conditional

———◦————

History books are packed with examples of negotiation. No text, perhaps, has more examples of bargaining and arbitration than the Old Testament. The Old Testament is replete with stories and examples of negotiation including Abraham's bargaining with God to save the cities of Sodom and Gomorrah; the feud between Isaac's twins—Jacob and Esau—over the sale of Esau's birthright; Laban's disputed agreement with Jacob to marry his daughter, Rachel, whom Jacob preferred to Laban's older daughter, Leah; Moses's pleading with God at Mount Sinai to spare the Israelites after repeated incidence of idolatry; Esther's delicate negotiations with King Ahasuerus, linking Haman's conspiracy against the Jews to discredit Haman and orchestrate his demise.

Not one of all the negotiations in the Old Testament, however,

match the irony of Israelite spies negotiating with a Jericho prostitute named Rahab.

After the death of Moses, Joshua became leader of the Israelites and prepared for the occupation of Canaan by sending out spies to reconnoiter the country. "They came to the house of a harlot named Rahab and lodged there. The king of Jericho was told, 'Some men have come here tonight, Israelites, to spy out the country.' The king of Jericho thereupon sent orders to Rahab: 'Produce the men who came to you and entered your house, for they have come to spy out the whole country.'"[1] Aware of the fierce reputation of the God of Israel, Rahab admitted to seeing the spies but told the royal guards that they had already fled. Rahab then hid the spies on her roof among stalks of flax.

As a prostitute, Rahab was

---

1. Joshua 2: 1-3

certainly knowledgeable about the exchange of favors. Not intending to let her hiding of the spies go unrewarded, she made the following proposition: "Now, since I have shown loyalty to you, swear to me by the LORD that you in turn will show loyalty to my family."[2] Recognizing a good deal when they saw one, the spies willingly accepted the proposition but with a proviso of their own. To secure Rahab's affidavit, the spies told Rahab that their agreement was conditional on her continued loyalty and adherence to their instructions during the raid on Jericho.

As Jericho was captured, the Israelite spies led Rahab and her family to safety.

The Biblical story of Rahab's negotiation with Israelite spies is a textbook example of making concessions conditional. Both parties made bargaining agreements conditional on counter demands being fulfilled by the opposing party.

In sales, all concessions should be conditional and based on whether counter demands are met by buyers. If a buyer agrees to a counter demand, then a concession should be made. If a buyer does not agree to a counter demand (large or small), a concession should not be made.

The Sales-Side Negotiation Concession Pattern

When a seller concedes to provide a good or service at a discounted price, a simple concession pattern should be implemented.

---

2. *Ibid*: 2: 12

The Sales-Side Negotiation Concession Pattern:

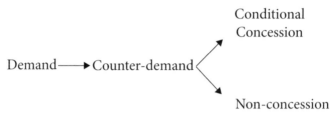

Figure 13.1

I learned this principle by studying the philosopher Friedrich Hegel. Georg Wilhelm Friedrich Hegel was born in Germany in 1770. His most notable contribution to philosophy is his celebrated dialectical method. The dialectical method works something like this:

1. In order to fully understand an issue, begin with a *thesis.*
2. Then contemplate its opposite, or *antithesis.*
3. Then merge the two opposites to create a *synthesis.*

For example, if our notion or thesis were "existence," we would contemplate its opposite, or antithesis, "non-existence." We would then merge the two opposites together to form a synthesis. If we were to merge the concept of existence with the notion of nonexistence, our synthesis would be "becoming."

It was actually Hegel's triadic method of contradiction that formulated my understanding of the importance of making counter demands. Hegel's method of thesis—antithesis—synthesis parallels *The Sales-Side Negotiation Concession Pattern.*

Demand →	Counter Demand →	Conditional Concession
(Thesis)	(Anti-thesis)	(Synthesis)

When a buyer makes a demand, and a seller concedes, one side wins the negotiation. Conversely, when a buyer makes a demand, and then makes a concession based on a counter demand, power is balanced and the seller gains a sense of synthesis or balance.

When buyers make demands, seller concessions should always be followed with counter demands. There are no exceptions to this rule. Asking for something in return is a cardinal rule of negotiation.

> **Note:** When making counter demands, concessions, or non-concessions, be sure to offer reason and rationale to soften and support your position.

The "If X, Then Y" Model

The best time to negotiate a counter concession is when you are offering a concession yourself. If a buyer demands a discount that you are willing to concede, ask for something in return. For example, before you make a price concession, get a commitment from the buyer using the "If X, Then Y" model.

- "*If* I'm able to get approval on a 5 percent discount, *then* will you submit your order before the end of the week?"
- "*If* I can guarantee delivery before the end of the quarter, *then* are you prepared to sign the agreement?"
- "*If* I concede to a discount, *then* will you pay in full, rather than in payments?"

I met with a Marriott Hotel events coordinator in Chicago. During our conversation, she expressed to me the frustrations her staff experiences when negotiating with aggressive clients who use negotiation tactics to secure discounts and concessions. Because of the amount of money her clients spend on ballrooms, catering, and event related services, they continually pressure her staff to discount normal event rates and "comp" sleeping rooms. The primary problem her staff encounters is agreeing to a discounted price and then having clients return with further demands. The clients are not content with an inch when they think they can take a mile. Her initial solution was discontinuing all discounts, but this created friction between her staff and her clients.

I pointed out that her problem was not that her staff made initial concessions. The problem was that they did not attach counter demands to the concessions. What her staff needed to do was to link the concession to a demand from the hotel. For example, when a client made a demand, I recommended that her employees respond with a counter demand. "*If* I agree to provide three complimentary rooms, *then* will you consent that this agreement is final?" By making the initial concession conditional, in this case meaning final, her problem was solved. She essentially traded a minimal discount for a finalized agreement and avoided straining relationships and eternally negotiating with her clients.

Why Make Counter Demands?

There are hosts of reasons counter demands should be a standard part of every negotiation. Here are four primary reasons:

1. Counter demands balance power.
2. Counter demands prevent future demands.
3. Counter demands add value to the concession.
4. Counter demands give sellers something of value in exchange for the concession.

Counter Demands Balance Power

The first and foremost reason to make counter demands is to balance power. Remember, power is the most important component in negotiation. When buyers make demands that sellers immediately grant, the power scale is out of balance. To balance power, sellers need to make the buyer act in some way or give something in return.

> **Note**: Counter demands don't always have to be of equal value. Sometimes, that's just not possible. Still, obtain something in return for a concession, even if it's small.

Counter Demands Prevent Future Demands

The second reason for making counter demands is to set a precedent of not caving to every whim or desire of the buyer. Too many sellers view salespeople as subservient to buyers. This false impression can hurt a person's ability to sell.

If a seller concedes without a counter demand, he loses the legitimacy to say "No" or make counter demands in the future. What rationale will she offer to make a counter demand in the future after having conceded without a counter demand in the past? I'm reminded of Patrick Henry's famous quote, "I have but one lamp by which my feet are guided, and that is the lamp of experience. *I know of no way of judging the future but by the past.*"

There is a popular saying in Japan: *Tada yori takai mono wa nai.* Translation: Nothing is more costly than something given free of charge.

A friend shared an experience he had while buying a new truck. He was not buying just any truck, but a big, massive diesel truck to pull his horse trailer. We called it a Christmas tree on wheels. It was forest green and had trucker lights all over it. He told me about the negotiation he had during the purchasing process. He repeatedly said to the seller, "I'm really close, but I'm just not totally sure. How about the warranty? Can you extend the warranty to thirty thousand miles?" (The *Baiting* tactic). The seller, anxious to close the deal, caved. Consequently, my friend upped his demands. "I don't know. I'm just not sure that does it for me. What about the pin stripes I saw on the other model? Can you put those on this baby?" The seller caved again, so my colleague just kept upping the ante. He asked for more. Amazingly, the seller kept conceding. My friend finally got to the point where he literally ran out of things to ask for. Finally, he told the guy, "You've got yourself a deal." But just before he signed the dotted line, he thought of one more thing to ask for—an extra spare tire. He asked for it (*Nibbling* tactic), and he got it.

Had the seller made a counter demand to check the initial demand for a better warranty, my colleague would have been less inclined to keep asking for more discounts and throw-ins.

> **The Point?** Counter demands prevent future demands. Buyers who obtain concessions without counter demands will return to make further demands and will be conditioned to expect exceptions whenever they apply pressure.

Counter Demands Add Value to the Concession

Counter demands also add value to the concession. When sellers make counter demands, buyers have to give something in return to receive the desired concession. They now have "skin in the game."

Counter demands also make concessions more valuable in the mind of the buyer. Why? Because something given for nothing has no value. The buyer has to give something of value in return for the demanded concession. It isn't free. In a sense, the buyer earns it.

Counter Demands Give Sellers Something in Exchange for the Concession

An obvious reason to make counter demands is to receive something in return. Counter demands give sellers something of value in exchange for the concession. Better terms, earlier payments, solidified deals, signed contracts, delayed delivery, references—whatever is of value to the seller.

How to Counter Demand

———⟫●⟨———

While negotiating the purchase of door handles for his Model T, Henry Ford was faced with a difficult situation. Late in the manufacturing and design process, the supplier of the door handles unexpectedly demanded a 5% increase in price. Ford, understandably, didn't want to pay the price. The two parties appeared to be at an impasse. The carmaker, however, thought of a way out and prepared a counter demand.

The door handle supplier shipped his supplies to Ford packed in wooden crates. Ford told the supplier that he would agree to the 5% increase if he would change the size and location of the bolt holes on the lids of the wooden crates. Shocked at the simplicity of the request, the supplier was happy to make the change. Ford was happy as well because the floorboards of the Model Ts were made from the same type of wood as the crate lids. With the modification, Ford was able to use the crate lids as floorboards. The trade did, of course, increase the cost of the handles, but that increase was far outweighed by the savings he realized by eliminating the cost of raw materials and the processing of the floorboards.

———⟫●⟨———

As Henry Ford's example illustrates, difficult negotiation situations can be overcome with creative solutions.

The key to making counter demands is two fold:

1. Be prepared
2. Be creative

Sellers who are prepared with premeditated trades usually concede less than sellers who enter negotiations unprepared. Unprepared sellers who negotiate by the seat of their pants or who invent options off the top of their heads usually concede far more than necessary to win sales. They give away too much, and because discounts go to the bottom line, they are unnecessarily giving away profitability.

To avoid making unnecessary concessions, use *The Sales Negotiation Planner* (Chapter 12) to prepare for potential negotiations. You should anticipate and prepare counter demands in advance.

In addition to being prepared, being creative is also vital to making counter demands. Creative sellers often devise options for buyers that are mutually beneficial and not one sided in favor of the buyer.

What to Counter Demand

George Lucas was vastly underpaid by Twentieth Century Fox for his work on *Star Wars*. As a writer he received $50,000; as director, $100,000. During contract negotiations, Lucas accepted the agreement on condition of one counter demand. He would accept the dismal writing and directing fees if he maintained the merchandizing and licensing rights—called "garbage" provisions—to his characters, a first in the film business. *Star Wars*, which was released in 1977, went on to become the most successful film up to that time in movie history and made George Lucas extremely rich, not from his film fees but from his merchandising and licensing rights. When the time came to do a sequel, *The Empire Strikes Back*, Lucas not only maintained his merchandising and licensing rights, he also demanded complete artistic control. So tough were his terms that his negotiator, Tom Pollack, presented the contract to the head of Twentieth Century Fox on Yom Kippur, saying, "This is your day of atonement."

The following are creative counter demands to use when dealing with demanding buyers.

- Accelerated payments (up front, 30 instead of 90 days, etc.)
- Increased volume (in exchange for a lower rate)
- Referrals
- References and endorsements
- Competitive intelligence
- Letters of recommendation
- Account sponsorship—"Would you call and introduce me to so-and-so?"
- Favorable quotes to be used in marketing collateral
- Statements in public forums such as internet "listservs"
- Attendance at presentations
- Making a presentation on the seller's behalf
- Conducting a workshop at a trade show
- Hosting a user group meeting
- Writing a positive article in a trade magazine
- Additional purchases (add other items to the order)
- Length of Contract—"We'll accept your figure if you make it a two-year contract instead of a one-year contract."

Any of the recommended counter demands can be used to create better agreements and strengthen buyer-seller relationships.

Protect Your Price

It is better to sell the wool than the sheep.

—Scottish Proverb

Buyers are motivated to acquire the best possible price they can from sellers. Sellers are charged with selling goods and services at maximum profit. These opposing agendas often lead to a collision course with sellers, more often than not, bearing the brunt of the accident.

One of the most fundamental pieces of advice I received as a young salesman was to protect my price. At all costs, protect profitability. I learned to make non-price concessions in order to protect my price. When buyers made acceptable demands, I would often concede. But I would attempt to concede something other than price, and to my surprise, people didn't mind. In fact, many buyers actually felt like they were getting a "bargain." I was amazed. In my limited thinking, I thought of bargains only in terms of price reductions.

There are numerous concessions that sellers can use in place of price discounts. When concessions are necessary to close a sale, sellers should attempt to use non-price related concessions to satisfy the interests of buyers. Potential non-price concessions include:

- Guaranteed prices for future purchases
- Extended warranties
- Return privileges
- Delayed payments
- Waived shipping charges
- Training
- Guaranteed upgrades
- Free upgrades
- Free trial period
- Early delivery
- No setup charges
- Free installation

The Point? Aggressively protect price and profitability. If you have to make concessions, concede something other than price.

Make Concessions in Small Increments

Sellers who plan their negotiations in advance anticipate making concessions to reach agreement. When planning negotiations determine what concessions you are willing to make. Start off with minor concessions and concede in small increments. Only give a little at a time.

Giving large concessions tells buyers that there is plenty of fat to be trimmed and that the price was inflated to begin with. Giving small concessions, on the other hand, communicates that margins are tight, prices are fair and reasonable, and there is not much wiggle room on price.

Studies repeatedly indicate that sellers tend to give away too much, far more than is necessary to close sales. Very often, buyers will bite on the first concession regardless of its size. By offering a small concession, many buyers have their bargaining "taste bud" satisfied. When sellers make concessions in small increments, they gradually work toward the buyer's level of comfort rather than offering the whole enchilada in one swooping concession.

The Power of a Bargain

In the end, what buyers want is not just a good price—they want satisfaction. A buyer's satisfaction comes from getting a great deal. Everyone loves a bargain. When buyers feel they "got a bargain," their level of satisfaction skyrockets, regardless of what they paid for the good or service. The opposite is also true. When people feel they didn't get a bargain, they are not satisfied, regardless of what they paid for the good or service.

In my early twenties, I spent two years of voluntary service in South Africa. I lived and traveled throughout South Africa, Botswana, Lesotho, and Swaziland. Because leather was less expensive in South Africa than in the United States, I wanted to purchase a leather jacket before returning home. The city of Johannesburg had a huge flea market that would take all day to get through. I went to multiple shops searching for a jacket. After looking at various jackets, I found one I really liked. It was the only one of its kind, and it was the last one on the rack. When I asked to buy it, the shop owner told me he had kept that particular jacket for a family member. It wasn't for sale. I was very disappointed. I left his shop and went looking for the same style of jacket in other shops with no luck. On the verge of abandoning my quest, I determined to give it one more shot. I returned to his store and asked if he would let me purchase it. He agreed to sell it to me. I made no attempt to negotiate the price. I don't remember exactly what I paid for that jacket, but I didn't care. I felt like I had "gotten a bargain." After all, I acquired the last one, and it was the one I wanted most. Neither of these conditions had anything to do with price. The feeling of getting a great deal was more important to me than the dollar amount I spent to get the deal.

> **The Point?** The feeling of getting a bargain is more important than the price spent to acquire the product or service.

Successful Sales-Side Negotiation

Let's briefly walk through the steps of a successful negotiation. (See Figure 13.2 for a graphic illustration of a successful sales-side negotiation). The first step to successful sales negotiation is focusing on effective selling skills. As I previously mentioned, how you sell is as important as how you negotiate. Everything you do as a seller impacts the negotiation—from the beginning stages of the sales cycle to the signed contract.

Throughout the sales process, cerebral sellers focus on two primary objectives: Building value and building power. Sellers build value in their product or service by implementing effective prospecting, investigating, presenting, and closing skills. Sellers build power by implementing intelligent sales strategies and tactics. When enough value is established, and enough power is built, sellers are in a position to successfully negotiate.

Armed with value and power, sellers are prepared to deal with buyer demands. When buyers make demands, the first thing cerebral sellers do is listen.

> **Note**: Many experts consider listening to be the most important skill in negotiation. Listening is the primary means for gaining information—and information is power.

When buyers make demands, avoid interrupting them. Be patient and hear them out. After a buyer clearly articulates a demand, respond with questions. Verify that you understand the demand with confirmation statements such as, "Let me make sure I understand what you are asking me. If I understand you correctly you are asking me to..." Acknowledging and understanding the buyer's demand fulfills a fundamental human need for recognition—a need to be heard and understood.

When the buyer demand is thoroughly understood, assess the firmness of the demand by making a counter demand. Because buyers often send out trial balloons to test the willingness of a seller to make concessions, seller counter demands should always be linked with buyer demands. Many buyers will back off once they realize that they might have to give something in return for the requested demand.

Based on the buyer's response to the counter demand, a seller is faced with a decision. The seller must decide whether or not to make a concession. Any concession—even a relatively minor one—should be carefully considered. Thoughtfully considering concessions is important because easily won concessions are rarely valued. Remember the saying, "What costs nothing is worth nothing."

Whether a concession is granted or not, it is critical that sellers provide rationale to support the decision. Rationale provides justification for the decision and lessens potential buyer resentment toward the seller.

> **Note**: Sellers should provide rationale for both concessions and non-concessions. Rationale provides justification and softens the impact of the decision.

In Summary

Never concede without making counter demands. Without reciprocal demands, concessions have little to no perceived value. Always make concessions contingent upon clients returning something in exchange for the concession. Do your best to protect your price by offering non-price related concessions.

The Sales-Side Negotiation Framework

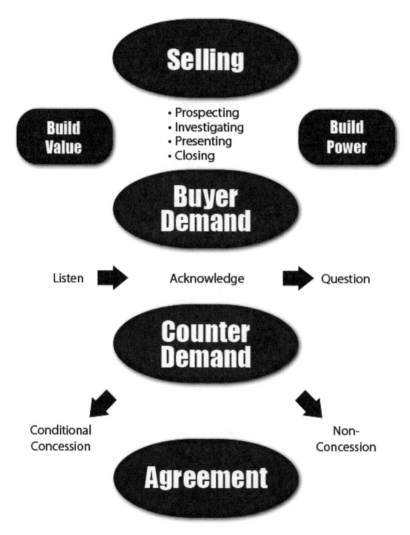

Figure 13.2

CHAPTER 14

Overcoming Price Specific Objections

———⟫●⟨———

Ambroise Vollard was a famous late nineteenth-century art dealer who specialized in expensive, fine art. Customers would visit Vollard's gallery to review and purchase the latest in contemporary art. Vollard used a totally unique approach to making sales. He would bring out three of his finest paintings for customers to review. Then, while customers were examining the paintings, Vollard would purposefully go to sleep. The customer would then be forced to return the next day. The next day, Vollard would repeat this same tactic with one variation—he would display paintings of lesser value. The baffled customers would review the paintings, leave to consider the offering, and then return again. Upon their return, Vollard would repeat the same pattern. By the third visit, buyers realized what was happening and would quickly purchase the displayed paintings knowing that the next day they would have to settle for something of less quality.

Vollard's bizarre sales strategy worked for one reason: he knew that people didn't purchase price, they purchased *value*. Vollard's sales approach did not focus on the price of the paintings. Instead, he focused exclusively on the value and availability of the paintings. He knew that the more scarce he made the paintings, the more valuable they became.

Vollard sold value, not price.

———⟫●⟨———

Price, Price, Price?

Learning how to overcome price-specific objections is an invaluable selling and negotiating skill. Sellers who know how to effectively handle price related concerns overcome more objections, give away fewer discounts, and win more sales.

The most consistently negotiated topic in sales is price. It seems as if it is always on the table. In fact, sometimes it seems as if it's the only issue on the table. Rarely, however, is that truly the case. Price is like a giant iceberg. The tip (price) is always what you see, but below is a mountain of unseen ice.

Unskilled negotiators typically overreact to price concerns. The concern over a price reduction tends to dominate their thinking. They worry that, if they don't cave to price related demands, they will lose the sale. They believe price is the only concession that will have an impact on customers.

But is price really what people buy? Is price really the most important issue to buyers? Should it be the sole negotiation focus of sellers? What about the role of cost? Is cost the same as price? What about value? Can value outweigh the importance of price?

Answers to these important questions will help sellers overcome price specific objections.

Price, Cost, and Value

The value of a thing sometimes lies not in what one attains with it, but in what one pays for it—what it costs us.

—Friedrich Nietzsche

Price, cost, and value are the triad of sales. They are an everyday part of a seller's life and ultimately dictate a seller's success or failure. They are linked to each other and have a symbiotic relationship, one affecting the others.

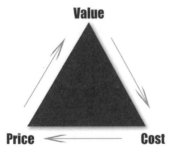

Figure 14.1

Of course, there are no exact definitions to any of these words. Buyers define them differently than sellers. Sellers define them differently from each other. Even dictionaries define them differently. Rather than give a dictionary definition of price, cost, or value, I will define them within the context of their relationship to selling and negotiating. The better sellers understand the impact that this triad has on sales, the more prepared they will be to negotiate from a position of strength.

Price is the amount of money it takes to purchase a good or service. It represents the dollar amount on the price tag. Price is typically a fixed amount asked in exchange for something of value.

Cost represents the risks and results of a purchase, positive or negative. The cost is the consequence of paying the price. It is the amount of money it takes to do business over the lifetime usage of a product or service. Cost is typically calculated, in contrast to price, which is just a fixed amount on a price tag. Cost is calculated by determining the risks and results of paying the price. In other words, the purchase price is not the same as the cost of ownership. The purchase price is only part of the cost. For example, an inexpensive car (price) that gets poor gas mileage may *cost* more than a more expensive car with good gas mileage.

> **Note**: When sellers understand the difference between price and cost, they can help buyers see and understand that a lower price is not always a lower cost.

Value represents the benefits gained in an exchange. In other words, the positive costs. You pay the price. You calculate the cost. You determine the value after the purchase. Value is often determined by the amount of pain eliminated, increased pleasure or productivity, or some other positive benefit.

Many marketing books differentiate price, cost, and value with various equations. For example:

$$C - P = V$$ (Cost minus Price equals Value)

$$V = B / I$$ (Value equals total Benefits minus total Investment)

$$B = V / C$$ (Benefits equals Value divided by Cost)

The Role of Value in Sales and Negotiation

The real price of every thing, what every thing really costs to the man who wants to acquire it, is the toil and trouble of acquiring it.

—Adam Smith, *The Wealth of Nations*, 1776

All of the previous definitions and equations point to value. Value is the key, the objective. There is an inverse relationship between value and price. The more value sellers build, the less relevant price becomes. This is why cerebral sellers do not engage in pricing debates with buyers. Instead, they focus on building and selling value.

If a seller has done a poor job in developing value, it won't matter how skilled he or she is at overcoming price objections. Fancy price objection techniques simply address the symptoms of either poor selling skills or buyers who don't perceive the value associated with the good or service.

> **Note**: The root of price objections is not price. Price objections are simply a result of not perceiving value. When prospects perceive value, they are less resistant to price. The key to overcoming price objections, therefore, is to build value.

Buyers often telegraph their concerns regarding value with questions, such as, "Am I getting the best possible deal here?" Many sellers interpret that to be a price related question, but this question has more to do with value than it does price. The buyer already knows the price of the good or service and is simply weighing and comparing the price to the value. To adequately answer the question, a seller needs to point out the value of the exchange, rather than focus on the reasons for the price.

It is critical to differentiate the proposed solution at all levels of the sale in order to justify price and illustrate value. Why? Buyers typically don't purchase until they have mentally and emotionally balanced the price with the value of the good or service. Value puts price in the context of what is gained in exchange for dollars.

It takes a problem-solver mentality to emphasize the value of a solution versus the price of the sale. *Remember, people buy solutions, not products and not prices.* The best solution is to move negotiation discussions from price, to cost, to value.

$$\text{Price} \rightarrow \text{Cost} \rightarrow \text{Value}$$

In some cases, price is a legitimate concern. However, in almost every selling situation, price is a miserable place to sell. If the difference between gaining and losing a commitment is based solely on price, sellers may not have effectively identified the costs or communicated the value of the products and services.

> **The Point?** All things being equal, most people will buy strictly on the best price. The salesperson's job is to help buyers see that things are not equal by emphasizing the value of the proposed product or service.

Profit Value

On a visit as mayor of West Berlin, Willy Brandt was invited to view the great new Mann auditorium in Tel Aviv. Having expressed his appreciation of Israel's naming the concert hall for the German writer, Thomas Mann, Brandt was politely corrected by his host. The hall was actually named for a certain Frederic Mann of Philadelphia. "What did he ever write?" exclaimed Brandt. "A check," the host replied.

The bottom line in business-to-business sales is the bottom line. Executives and managers are not interested in product features or service capabilities. They are interested in increased performance, return-on-investment, decreased costs, and profitability. After all, they are accountable for these things. The product or service is just a means to an end. The ultimate objective is increased profitability. This is why, if you are negotiating with high-level decision makers, you need to speak their language. And the language of executives is not price, features, or capabilities. It is performance, profitability, return-on-investment, increased revenue, decreased costs, volume, margins, and savings.

As seasoned business executives know, and as mentioned in Chapter 1, there are only three ways to increase profitability:

1. Increase Sales
2. Increase Sales Margins
3. Decrease Costs

That's it. To increase profitability, a business can increase sales, increase sales margins, or decrease costs. Or, they can do a combination of the three. If a salesperson can improve any one of these categories, he or she can sell and negotiate on the basis of return-on-investment (R.O.I.) instead of the price of the good or service.

I delivered a presentation to a large corporation and provided them with an R.O.I. sheet. I gave them an educated projection of the increased sales they would experience if they implemented our training and consultation programs. One of the committee members questioned my projections. Instead of becoming defensive, I simply said to the man, "Let's assume you are right and that my projections are overly optimistic. Let's instead just use the number one. What if each of your sales reps makes one more sale every day? What if overall sales increases by only one percent? What if we cut your average sales cycle by only one week? What if corporate profitability improves only one percentage point? What will be your return-on-investment by investing in our sales and negotiation training program?"

They purchased the training.

Far too often, salespeople focus on *products* instead of *profitability*. In business-to-business negotiations, cerebral sellers do not focus on products—they focus on value. *Instead of asking for money, they offer money in the form of a return on the buyer's investment.* They specify the profit value they can add in terms of cost savings or increased revenue. They relate the price of the product or service to the value of the R.O.I. and emphasize that the value is not in providing a product or service. The product or service is providing the value.

The Point? Successful negotiators focus on financial benefits, not product features. They concentrate on the financial value their product provides in the form of increased volume, better margins, decreased costs, and overall profitability.

Cognitive Dissonance

A well-known theory in psychology is the theory of cognitive dissonance. This theory holds that people instinctively dislike inconsistency and will act to eliminate it. For example, what's wrong with this picture?

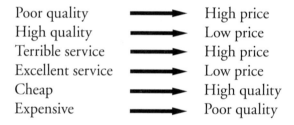

Poor quality	→	High price
High quality	→	Low price
Terrible service	→	High price
Excellent service	→	Low price
Cheap	→	High quality
Expensive	→	Poor quality

People recognize inconsistencies. The inverse, that people recognize consistencies, is also true. Establishing consistency between the value of the solution and the price of the product is a powerful factor in selling. The more value you build, the more buyers expect to pay because buyers instinctively match value to price. Price is simply a number. Value, however, is what the number represents.

If you build higher value, buyers will expect higher prices. The more value you build, the less relevant price becomes. The less relevant price becomes, the less you will ever need to negotiate.

Building value reduces price sensitivity.

The Role of Price in Sales and Negotiation

What we obtain too cheap, we esteem too lightly.

—Thomas Paine

Price is always at the forefront of sales negotiations. How seller-negotiators deal with price discussions often determines the amount of commission and profitability they can expect from the sale. More importantly, how a person sells prior to the price discussion determines the level of power a seller has when discussing price related issues.

Rarely, if ever, should sales professionals sell price. Unless you are the owner of *All a Dollar* or a retail store having an "End of year blowout sale," price should not be the vanguard of your sales vernacular. Imagine a seller who starts a sales conversation by saying, "Hi, we're the least expensive product on the market. Buy from us!" What would immediately go through the mind of a buyer? What message would be communicated? One word comes to mind: cheap. People don't normally buy "cheap."

Astronaut Neil Armstrong responded to a reporter who asked him to relate his feelings as Apollo 11 approached the moon. Armstrong replied, "How do you think you'd feel if you knew you were on top of two million parts built by the lowest bidder in a government contract?"

Price communicates the quality and value purchasers can expect to receive from goods and services. As we pointed out in our analysis of cognitive dissonance, the higher the price, the higher the expected quality and value of a good or service. When sellers immediately concede to price objections, they communicate to buyers that the proposed good or service wasn't (and isn't) worth the original price.

———⪼⪻———

A classic example of the role of price is Callaway's Big Bertha golf club. Ely Callaway intentionally jacked up the price of this club when he introduced it to the golf industry. He purposefully set the price far above the industry standard and far above what he needed to make a profit. Ely Callaway understood that at a lower price the Big Bertha would have been just another golf club. Because of the inflated price, the Big Bertha caught the attention of golfers worldwide who then searched for value—and found it.

As Ely Callaway's example illustrates, sellers need to be careful what they communicate with price.

> **Note**: Remember this rule: If they come for price, they will leave for price.

It must be admitted that there are buyers who make purchasing decisions based solely on price. But, herein lies the problem; customers who make purchases based strictly on price will always find a lower price and better discount than yours. Not only that, but discount buyers are the worst possible customers to win. They do not refer you to other clients, nor do they remain long-term customers. They have no product or brand loyalty, and they don't care about quality or service. If a buyer refuses to purchase without a discount, do yourself a favor and refer him or her to your competitor.

If at all possible, avoid answering price related questions until after you have identified needs and problems and communicated how you intend to solve those problems. Without first communicating value, your product or service has little meaning to the buyer. Without understanding the value of your good or service, the client will almost always believe its too expensive. To avoid this situation, try to ask at least one qualifying question and then quickly build the value of your product or service before offering a price. For instance, if a buyer says, "What's your bottom line? Just give me your price." You might respond by saying:

- "That depends. What is it you need?"
- "I'll be glad to answer that. But first, what do you know about what I'm offering?"
- "I'd be glad to quote our prices, but unless you understand what I'm offering, it won't make much sense. Would you mind answering a few short questions first?"

If the buyer refuses to receive a product presentation, answer questions, or if he insists on a price, quote your least expensive price. You might say, "Our entry-level product, which includes X, costs Y dollars."

The Cost of Doing Nothing

━━━⟫●⟪━━━

French control of the region west of the Mississippi River dated from 1682, when French explorer Sieur de La Salla claimed, on behalf of King Louis IX, a vaguely defined area he named Louisiana. Rather than lose the colony to Britain as a result of its defeat in the Seven Years War, France ceded Louisiana to Spain in 1762.

With the military conquests of Napoleon Bonaparte in Europe, Spain transferred Louisiana back to France in 1801. Fearful that the French would restrict American trade on the Mississippi River and disrupt American naviga-tion rights in the Gulf of Mexico, President Thomas Jefferson dispatched Robert Livingston of New York to negotiate the purchase of New Orleans from the French. Direct negotiations, however, appeared to be all but impossible. For months, Livingston was faced with tantalizing hints of a potential deal, but every time the discussions faded into diplomatic chatter. Livingston finally deployed a cunning tactic to get the attention of the French. He let it be known that a rapprochement with Great Britain might best serve his country. With the imminence of a renewed war with

Great Britain, Napoleon wanted no talk of an Anglo-American alliance.

Livingston's threat prompted Napoleon to offer the United States the entire Louisiana Territory. At this juncture, James Monroe arrived in Paris as Jefferson's minister to France. Hearing the news that Napoleon wanted to sell the entire Louisiana Territory, Monroe was placed in a constitutional quandary. Thomas Jefferson, a strict construction-ist, had only authorized Monroe to negotiate the purchase of New Orleans. The Constitution did not empower a minister to make territorial acquisitions without specific instructions and authorization from Congress. Because communication between the U.S. and France could take months, Monroe had no choice but to make a unilateral decision. As he weighed the significance of his decision, he balanced the legality of his predicament with the consequence of not making the purchase. The *price* of the purchase was $11,250,000. The *cost* was of much greater significance. If he did not make the purchase, the outcome of European wars would dictate the ownership of half of the American continent and limit the westward expansion of the United States. After serious deliberation, Monroe decided that the cost of doing nothing far outweighed the price of the purchase. On April 30, 1803, the American nego-tiators signed a treaty transferring the Louisiana Territory to the United States. The United States Senate later ratified the treaty by a vote of 24 to 7.

Like the Louisiana Purchase, sometimes the cost of doing nothing can be more than the price of the proposed good or service.

Similar to James Monroe, when buyers make a purchase, they must balance two opposing factors. First, they must weigh the seriousness of their needs or problems. Second, they must examine the seriousness of their needs or problems versus the cost of the solution. In sales, needs, problems, and dissatisfactions drive buyers to act. The cost of an exist-ing need or problem is the catalyst that accelerates the sales cycle. The more pain a prospect feels, the greater the need for the purchase. The more problems a prospect experiences, the more justification he or she has to procure the good or service to resolve the problems. This is why *The DNA Selling Method* is such an effective negotiation tool. It builds the seriousness of the problem and helps the buyer understand the costs associated with leaving the problem unresolved.[1]

> **The Point?** For prospects with pressing needs, failure to purchase the proposed product or service may be the higher cost.

Advanced Price Objection Questions

Skilled sellers respond to price objections with questions—specific, conditional, commitment questions that gain agreement and some sense of closure to the objection. Advanced objection questions narrow the issue to the specific objection and then identify the benefits of resolving the concern.

Examples include:

Buyer: You're still too high. This is going nowhere.
Seller: Suppose we are able to resolve that issue. Are there any other issues standing in the way of us doing business?

Buyer: Without including training in this price, I'm just not sure this makes sense.
Seller: Suppose we are able to resolve that issue, I know it's not resolved right now, but just suppose we could. Are there any other issues preventing us from reaching an agreement?

Advanced price objection questions are non-manipulative, non-pressure questions aimed at pinpointing the exact objection and gain-

---

1. To learn more about using *The DNA Selling Method* to identify and develop needs, problems, and pains, see *The DNA Selling Method.*

ing agreement without having to eternally negotiate a deal. Advanced price objection questions also counter *Nibbling* negotiation tactics and prevent buyers from "piling on" after an agreement is reached.

Temporarily Set the Objection Aside

One of the best strategies for overcoming an objection is to temporarily set the objection aside. Rather than rushing in and immediately solving the objection, sellers should simply set it aside and focus on other aspects of the sale, such as the benefits of the proposed product or service.

I trained a team of corporate sales professionals how to overcome objections. I started the training by asking how they were currently dealing with objections. Predictably, they were rushing in and immediately addressing buyer concerns. I asked them to brainstorm as a team and come up with the top three objections they regularly faced. After writing their top three objections on a white board, I began role-playing with the participants regarding how to overcome each objection. As part of the strategy, I initially set each objection aside and helped refocus the buyer on the value of the proposed product.

Buyer: I'm just not sure we have enough in our budget to justify the purchase.
Seller: (Sets the objection a side) Jason, let's just set that aside for a moment. What is it you like most about our product?

Buyer: I need more time to think about this.
Seller: (Sets the objection aside) Kim, let's just set that aside for a minute. You mentioned to me earlier the bottleneck your current program creates for your office staff. What benefits, if any, would you anticipate from implementing our solutions?

Skilled negotiators are strategic. They don't rush in and answer every objection. They set objections aside and help buyers focus on the benefits of the proposed product or service rather than the stated concern.[2]

Shelving the objection also communicates confidence that the objection is not serious enough to kill the deal.

Dealing With Unreasonable Price Demands

Buyers are sometimes unreasonable in their price demands and expectations. Regardless of the skills or logic used by sellers, some buyers will not relinquish unreasonable demands. When you are the recipient of unreasonable buyer demands, the best counter method is to decline the demand, explain why (provide rationale), and make a counter offer. For example:

Buyer: I won't purchase this unless you include the extended warranty and drop your price to X amount.

Seller: Ms. Jones, let me explain why your requested changes, taken together, take me further than I can go. Our policy and procedure is to adhere to our published price list, which means I'm not in a position to extend the warranty or make a price allowance. Would you like to discuss what I think might work?

> **Caution!** Be sure not to argue with buyers. If you argue, the buyer has a personal stake in proving you wrong. The more you argue, the more you will force the buyer to defend his or her position. Win an argument, lose a sale.

---

2. See *The DNA Selling Method* for an in-depth analysis of the *Set Aside* strategy.

Specific Price Related Responses

Sometimes sellers have to be blunt with buyers. In those cases, it is useful to have a few memorized responses ready for unreasonable price demands. Here is a collection of potential responses:

Buyer: I like your product, but the difference in pricing between you and your competitor is significant.

Seller: Other than pricing, is there any other reason why you wouldn't use our product over the competitor's, given the significant advantages our product offers?

Buyer: I can buy this product, or one just like it, for a lot less money.

Seller: I've learned over the years that people look for three things when they make purchases: They look for quality, service, and the lowest investment. It's been my experience that no company can offer all three. We choose not to lower our quality or service so that the long term happiness and satisfaction of our clients are not jeopardized.

Buyer: Your product is too expensive.

Seller: When you say too expensive, in what sense do you mean? Do you mean too expensive compared to competitors or budgetary restraints?

> **Note:** When dealing with competitive price comparisons, it's helpful to deal with the difference in cost and not the full amount. For example, if your price is $20,000 and your competitor is $15,000, the problem is not $20,000, it's $5,000.

Buyer: Your price is too high.

Potential seller responses:

- I've learned over the years that people look for three things when they make purchases: They look for quality, service, and the lowest investment. It's also been my experience that no company can offer all three. We choose not to focus exclusively on price so that the long-term satisfaction of our clients is not jeopardized.

- Is it the price or the cost that concerns you? Let me share with you what I mean by that: you pay the price only once, when you purchase. Cost, however, is of concern for as long as you own the product. You might find a lower price but I don't believe you will find a lower cost.

- Is price your primary consideration? Are you going to make your decision based solely on price?... If you are looking exclusively for the lowest price, we're probably not the best option for you.

- In order to be fair and equitable to all of our customers, we offer competitive pricing right from the start.

- Let me explain why your requests, taken together, take me further than I can go. Our policy is to adhere to our proposed pricing model, which means I'm not in a position to make a price allowance. Would you like to discuss what I think might work?

- We may not be able to offer the lowest price. But, we do guarantee the best product with the best service.

- How important is quality in your evaluation? Sometimes sacrificing quality can end up being very costly.

- Other than pricing, is there any other reason why you wouldn't choose our product over the competitor's?

- Is it price or cost that you are evaluating?... Have you considered the total cost of ownership?

- A year from now price won't be of concern if the product lives up to your expectations. If you pay a lower price, you're likely to deal with the long-term cost of poor performance, inferior service, and lack of quality.

Caution! Most of the previous responses are reactionary. No response, regardless of how clever or well worded, can replace effectively building value prior to a price discussion or negotiation.

In Summary

All salespeople are ultimately measured by their ability to close sales. Successful sellers are professionals who can end negotiations with signed contracts, purchase orders, or checks. But that's not all. The terms of the negotiated agreements are of equal importance. Favorable terms determine the profitability of the agreement.

In some cases, price is a legitimate selling and negotiating concern. However, in almost every selling situation, price is a depressing place to sell and negotiate. In many cases, when the difference between gaining or losing commitment is based solely on price, the seller may have failed to communicate the value of the product or service. In that situation, the seller should do everything in his or her power to get value back on the table and make it the primary topic of discussion.

The Point? Don't sell price. Sell value.

CHAPTER 15

The Ten Commandments of Sales-Side Negotiation

⸺⫸●⫷⸺

As a child in Egypt, Moses was saved from the slaughter of all male Israelite children by being hidden in the bulrushes in the Nile. He was found by one of Pharaoh's daughters and raised in the Egyptian court. He later became the prophet and lawgiver of the Israelites and led them out of Egypt. After wandering in the wilderness for forty years, the Israelites approached the promised land of Canaan.

To communicate with God, Moses climbed Mount Sinai. There, Jehovah gave him Ten Commandments for the Israelites to abide by in order to retain their favored status with God. Throughout their history, when the Israelites obeyed the Ten Commandments, they flourished. When they disobeyed the Ten Commandments, they floundered.

⸺⫸●⫷⸺

By comparison, The Ten Commandments of Sales-Side Negotiation are rules of engagement. They are proven success formulas and tested negotiation principles that lead to success. By following The Ten Commandments of Sales-Side Negotiation, sellers achieve predictable negotiation results. By violating The Ten Commandments of Sales-Side Negotiation, sellers proceed at their own risk.

Commandment 1: Negotiate Prepared

Every battle is won before it's ever fought… Carefully compare the opposing army with your own so that you may know where strength is exceedingly abundant and where it is deficient.

—Sun Tzu

Roman senator, Marcus Crassus, was rich and powerful. By 60 B.C. he had financially muscled himself into the first Triumvirate with Pompey and Caesar. Crassus, though, lacked the honor reserved for generals who had been victorious over Roman enemies. Pompey had defeated the Mithradates and cleared the Mediterranean of piracy. Caesar had been awarded civic honors for his valor as a young man and was earning military laurels with his campaigns in Gaul.

Crassus' failure to achieve comparable honors weighed heavily on his colossal ego. He determined to redress the situation by invading Syria. He schemed of following in the footsteps of Alexander the Great, conquering Parthia, and marching on India. In the spring of 54 B.C., he arrived in Syria with an army of seven legions, more than forty thousand soldiers. He had little cavalry, but hoped the neighboring Armenians would provide the necessary horses to combat the famed Parthian horsemen.

Crassus, who had never led troops, crossed the Euphrates River and burned the bridge behind him, signaling to his troops that there would be no retreat. Although short on supplies, horses, and moral, Crassus was eager for glory. He marched his troops across the desert at double pace to face the Parthians. Parthian archers struck first and then carefully retreated. Crassus ordered his exhausted troops to pursue the archers, forcing his infantry to keep up with his cavalry. The Romans suddenly found themselves facing the main Parthian army. Confused, exhausted, disorganized, and ill prepared, the Parthians crushed the Romans at the battle of Carrhae. Crassus' defeat cost Rome thirty thousand casualties. Crassus attempted to escape but was captured and publicly executed by the Parthians.

Crassus' lack of pre-battle planning and logistical preparation led to the single worst defeat in the annals of Rome. His thrashing at the battle of Carrhae was emblazoned in the minds of Romans and earned him the reputation as the worst military fool their nation ever produced.

Negotiation is commonly referred to as a game of *mental jousting.* I agree. It takes brainpower to be a successful negotiator. Being mentally prepared gives a negotiator an edge. In most endeavors, preparation precedes power. In negotiation, preparation plays an especially important role.

For informal negotiations that don't take place over a bargaining table, a negotiator is best prepared when he or she can recognize buyer-negotiator tactics and strategically implement effective seller-negotiator countertactics. It takes time to memorize and rehearse buyer and seller negotiation tactics.

For formal negotiations I recommend *The Sales-Side Negotiation Planner.* (See Chapter 12). This worksheet is designed for the seller-negotiator dedicated to successful negotiation. *The Sales-Side Negotiation Planner* gives sellers a strategic framework to anticipate buyer-negotiator types and tactics. It helps identify and anticipate buyer demands, questions, and objections. It also helps sellers predetermine concession boundaries so that they don't make regrettable decisions in the heat of the moment. It helps sellers prepare potential counter demands and non-price concessions and provides sellers a chance to develop rationale to justify and explain principles and positions. In short, *The Sales-Side Negotiation Planner* helps sellers develop negotiation strategies to ensure negotiation success.

> **The Point?** Good negotiators are prepared negotiators.

Commandment 2: Focus On Value, Not Price

Skilled negotiators build power and develop negotiating strength by keeping discussions focused on problem resolution. The more problems a seller resolves, the more power he or she has to negotiate from a position of strength.

By concentrating on problem resolution, sellers center on the issue that gives them the most power: value. The more problems a seller resolves, the more value a seller establishes. The more value a seller provides the less relevant price becomes.

By keeping discussions centered on problem resolution, sellers prevent buyers from focusing on limitations and potential product or service inadequacies. Buyer-negotiator power is gained when sellers are put on the defensive. Additionally, unless price is the seller's primary sales point (which should rarely if ever be the case), price discussions divert attention away from the issue that matters the most: value. Remember, buyer-negotiator power comes from concentrating on seller weaknesses and limitations (not strengths and solutions) that can be used as leverage to gain price reductions.

Effective seller-negotiators center negotiations on ways they can benefit customers. They focus discussions on areas of maximum leverage. They concentrate on value, not price.

> **Note**: Without first establishing value, price is completely meaningless. Price and value are not synonymous. When sellers focus on price instead of value, they voluntarily place themselves in a position of weakness.

Commandment 3: Avoid Making the First Concession

In the spring of 1870, Thomas Edison put on a suit and top hat and headed to New York City to sell his new stock-ticker. His new device solved a problem all tickers had at the time: Tickers sometimes printed sporadically, throwing the entire ticker system out of line. He approached the president of Gold & Stock, Marshall Lefferts, to sell his new invention. Lefferts was obviously interested in what was an important improvement. When he asked for the price, Edison hedged. Desperate for cash, (the most Edison had ever made in a year was $1,480), he had hoped to sell the new device for $5,000 but was willing to sell it for as low as $3,000. "I hadn't the nerve to ask for such a large sum, so I said, 'Well sir, suppose you make me an offer?'" Lefferts responded, "How would $40,000 strike you?" Edison agreed, shook hands, and walked away with a $40,000 check.

———⟫●⟪———

There are very few negotiation rules that are universally agreed upon by negotiation authors and scholars, but this is one of them. *Avoid making the first concession.* There are numerous negotiation studies that confirm a predictable and consistent pattern. Less successful negotiators tend to make the first compromise. Put differently, successful negotiators force their counterparts to make the first offer. Had Edison made the first offer or concession, he would have lost thousands of dollars.

In sales-side negotiations, it is especially important to avoid leading off sales discussions with discounts or price reductions. It lessens the value of the concession and empowers the buyer. When sellers make the first concession, they inadvertently give the appearance that they are either desperate for business or overly eager to make the sale, both of which diminish power.

Of course, as the sale progresses to the point of negotiation, *not* offering the first concession is not always possible. In the real world of sales, sometimes sellers have to make the first concession. When sales grow stagnant, sometimes it makes sense to use price as a means of enticing and reengaging buyers. When buyers and sellers "deadlock," sometimes it pays to make the first concession instead of losing a deal. When this happens, follow a simple guideline: if you are forced to make the first concession, offer a minor or small concession.

The Point? As a general rule, avoid making the first concession. Don't start off sales by offering discounts or making price an initial topic of discussion.

Commandment 4: Concede Reluctantly

In buyer-seller negotiations, *how you concede can be as important as what you concede.* When making concessions, don't make it a trivial or trifling process. "Okie dokie," does not carry the same impact as, "Let's work out some figures on paper and then make a decision." When sellers make concessions seem inconsequential, they communicate to buyers that the conceded item wasn't terribly important to begin with.

When sellers make concessions, it should be done reluctantly. Reluctantly doesn't mean grudgingly or with the attitude of a sore loser. It means *conceding with calculation.* You might express a little pain as you do it, but make it a cerebral decision. Pull out a calculator and carefully weigh the cost. Let buyers see the thoughtful contemplation given to the decision before agreeing to the concession.

> **Note**: One way to create the impression that you have done your homework in calculating a discounted price is to avoid using round numbers. Use odd numbers and decimal fractions such as 5.2 percent or 11.9 percent.

I was once involved in a negotiation that caught me off guard. I made an introductory presentation to a company expecting an elongated sales process before a decision would be reached. Instead, the decision was made at the conclusion of the presentation. The only remaining matter was price. They hit me. "What's the price?" I was shocked. It took me by such surprise that I honestly hadn't determined the price. Because of the impact of the presentation, I knew I had momentum in my corner, so I didn't want to reply, "I'll get back to you with a proposal." The decision makers were in the room, and they were ready to move forward. I asked them a few questions (always the best stall maneuver to gather your thoughts and formulate a plan). They then pressed me again. They had a fairly aggressive CEO, and I expected him to negotiate with me regardless of the price I offered. I gave them an inflated initial price offer (Commandment 5). They balked a bit, asked me a few questions and then countered. Their counter price was still higher than my normal price. I felt like screaming, "Fantastic! When do we start?" Instead, I was silent. I took my glasses off, slowly shook my head, shifted in my chair a few times, and asked them more questions. In other words, I made it a thoughtful, trepid decision. After we went back and forth for a bit, I reluctantly agreed to the deal if they agreed to a few stipulations, which they did.

When concessions are offered too quickly, buyers question whether or not they are getting the best price. For example, if a car salesperson proposes a price of $30,000 and a buyer counters with $28,000, what happens when the seller immediately agrees to the counter offer? The buyer, of course, wonders if he should have made a lower counter offer. *Rather than feeling good about the price, he now questions whether or not he is making a good decision.* If the salesperson deliberately hesitates, visibly cringes a bit (a sales negotiation countertactic called *Surprise*—see Chapter 10), checks with his manager, and reluctantly concedes to the counter offer, the buyer feels like he won the sale and that he received the best possible price.

Make buyers earn concessions. It adds value to the concession, gives meaning to the compromise, and builds power for future negotiations and business interactions.

> **The Point?** Even when concessions are completely agreeable, don't concede quickly. Don't jump to discount or immediately bend to buyer pressure. Be thoughtful. Give reluctantly and slowly.

Commandment 5: Inflate Your Initial Demand

Effectiveness at the conference table depends upon overstating one's demands.

—Henry Kissinger

During the campaign of 1844, presidential candidate James Polk ran on a nationalistic platform that stressed the procurement of Oregon Territory as far north as latitude 54 degrees 40 minutes. At the time, this was the southern boundary of Russian-owned Alaska. One of Polk's campaign slogans was, "Fifty-four Forty or Fight!" After elected, however, it became apparent that compromise would be necessary.

Through skilled negotiation, Polk was able to reach a favorable agreement with the British that established the national boundary at 49 degrees north. This was the precise border that Polk had pushed for in earlier negotiations, only to encounter British refusal. By inflating his initial demand, Polk was able to reach a permanent settlement that favored the United States.

Inflating your initial demand is a very popular negotiation strategy. It is especially popular with buyers who make high initial demands of sellers (a tactic referred to in Chapter 9 as *The Ridiculous Offer*). Buyers are trained in professional negotiation seminars to inflate their initial demands. Inflated initial demands lower the aspiration levels of negotiation counterparts and improve the probability of success.

Adolf Hitler used this strategy in his negotiations with British Prime Minister Neville Chamberlain. Hitler initially made extremely high demands (that he did not believe the British would accept) in an attempt to win a smaller territory he desperately desired. By making an inflated initial demand, Hitler succeeded in annexing all of Czechoslovakia instead of the smaller territory he had originally coveted.

Inflated or exaggerated initial demands can also work for sellers. If a seller is serious about achieving the minimum concession possible, he or she would be crazy to start off with a maximum concession figure. The obvious reason is that offering a minimum concession gives sellers negotiating flexibility. By making a high initial proposal, sellers give both themselves and their counterparts negotiating room. Sellers can always come down, but they can rarely go up on price.

There is another important reason to inflate your initial demand. It creates a climate in which the buyer feels that he or she won the negotiation. If a seller makes his best offer up front, there's no way the buyer can negotiate and feel they "won" because they never gained a compromise from the seller. The only person who compromised was the buyer. For example, if a seller is willing to compromise or concede 10 percent of his total price, he will not initially offer a full 10 percent discount. He will offer a 5 percent discount. Let's say the buyer counters by asking for a 10 percent discount. If the seller concedes to the full 10 percent, the buyer feels he won the negotiation because the seller increased the initial discount by 5 percent and agreed to *his* offer.

Win-win negotiation is more than just a trendy phrase; it is a concept that is indispensable to strategic negotiators. *Allowing a buyer to feel that he or she has succeeded in a negotiation is beyond being ethically correct. It is pragmatically sound.* It is virtually impossible for a seller to "win" a negotiation if the customer feels that he or she "lost." Ideal sales-side negotiations leave buyers feeling like they won the negotiation.

Don't start a negotiation by offering your maximum discount. Offer your minimum discount. When offering either demands or concessions, make the demands smaller or larger than the targeted objective. In other words, exaggerate the demand in whichever direction suits your purpose.

Inexperienced negotiators always want to start with their best offer. Avoid this mistake by inflating your initial demand.

> **The Point?** Offering minimum concessions improves the probability of negotiation success and increases the likelihood of making the buyer feel like he or she won the negotiation.

Commandment 6: Concentrate on Areas of Maximum Leverage

The best strategy is always to be very strong; first in general, then at the decisive point... There is no higher and simpler law of strategy than that of keeping one's forces concentrated... In short, the first principle is: act with utmost concentration.

—Carl von Clausewitz

Skilled negotiators focus on areas of maximum leverage. Areas of maximum leverage are negotiation topics that give sellers an edge.

I managed a salesperson who continually pressured me to approve discounts. He could not seem to negotiate without caving on price. He would panic. He acted as though price was the only concession that would impact the sale. As the vice president of sales, I would often intervene on his behalf. As an outsider walking fresh into the sale/negotiation, I would ask the buyers numerous questions about their situation, the problems they were experiencing, how they thought we resolved those problems, what would happen if those problems weren't resolved, etc. In other words, I would determine what issues gave us maximum leverage. I would ascertain what was crucial and what was not. Once I identified the primary issue driving the sale, I would hammer it. I would focus on it. I wouldn't leave it alone. I would concentrate on the issue(s) that gave me the most power. As the negotiation would progress, inevitably we either did not need to offer a discount to close the deal, or we would offer a concession far less than the salesperson had initially intended.

With depressing frequency, many sellers let price dominate negotiations. They allow price to continually emerge as the most important issue.

> **Note**: Unless your good or service is the least expensive product on the market, price is an issue that gives buyers maximum leverage, not sellers.

You've heard the myth, "There are three issues important to buyers. The first is price, the second is price, and the third is price." Unfortunately, seller-negotiators often swallow this line of thinking. They focus on the price of the product or service rather than the value of the product or service. They allow buyers to distract the negotiation from areas that empower the seller (problem resolution, pain elimination, etc.) and instead focus on the issues that empower buyers (price, product limitations, etc.).

Sellers determine areas of maximum leverage in the sales process and capitalize on them in the negotiating process. For example, if during the sales process, buyers repeatedly refer to a particular problem, sensitivity, or critical issue, skilled sellers hone in on it. They talk about it. They emphasize it.

I was involved in a sale in which technical support was the dominant issue because the organization did not have an adequate staff of technicians. The *end user* was expected to solve his or her own technical problems. If the software or networking programs crashed, the end users would either have to fix it themselves or wait weeks for a technician to solve the problem, causing major headaches and delays. Because we unearthed this dilemma in the sales process, we were aware of its importance (The power of information). While our competitors focused primarily on product features, we focused on technical support, post sale relationships, and training. We won the sale. When it came time to negotiate price (it was close to a $500,000 sale), we had power. When the buyer attempted to slash prices, we justified our price by explaining the cost of maintaining the industry's best technical support team. We made technical support the primary negotiation issue, not price. We accentuated the value we offered by concentrating the negotiation on areas of maximum leverage.

We were awarded the sale at full price.

Commandment 7: Be Hard on Problems and Soft on People

When dealing with people, remember you are not dealing with creatures of logic, but with creatures of emotion.

—Dale Carnegie

Negotiation can be brutal. Negotiating can be mentally, emotionally, and sometimes even physically exhausting. Patience can wear thin and tempers can sometimes flare. When negotiations get heated or drawn out, it can be difficult to separate the issues from the people, the problems from the players.

Many sellers engage in negotiations over the phone. One disadvantage of telephone negotiations is their less personal tone. It is easier for buyers to say no or to be rude to someone they can't see. As a result, buyers are often more inclined to use adversarial tactics on the phone. When involved in high-dollar negotiations, do everything possible to negotiate face-to-face.

In order for sellers to keep difficult negotiations positive and productive, they should be hard on problems and soft on people. Recognize that you are not negotiating with a company. You are negotiating with a person. It is not American Express or Coca Cola sitting across from you. It is a human being with thoughts, opinions, emotions, and feelings.

Being hard on problems and soft on people sounds fairly simple, but it's often more difficult to implement than it sounds. Being hard on problems means staying focused on issues and topics, not people or personalities. It means focusing on subjects pertinent to the negotiation, not personal insults or ego driven discussions. Being soft on people demands that we be courteous and sensitive to the feelings, positions, and interests of our counterparts.

> **Note:** The most important skill in separating people from problems is listening. Good listeners disarm hostile and/or frustrated negotiators.

Good listeners truly seek to understand the position of their counterparts. They ask questions such as, "Let me make sure I understand what you're telling me. You feel as if..." Good listeners, almost by default, are soft on people.

Contrary to popular belief, the best negotiators are not the best talkers. They are the best listeners. They listen first and talk second. As Stephen R. Covey puts it, they "Seek first to understand and then to be understood." They listen with the intent to understand, not to respond. Good negotiators are good communicators. Good communicators are good listeners.

Not only does listening enable sellers to remain hard on problems (by understanding the prospect's problems) and soft on people (by understanding the prospect's perspectives), it also creates an enormous negotiation advantage. Armed with more information and greater knowledge, sellers are more capable of persuading counterparts and reaching agreement.

Understanding a person's position does not mean agreeing with it, but it does acknowledge that you have taken the time to consider the merits of your counterpart's position. That is what I mean by being hard on the problem and soft on the person.

> **The Point?** Good negotiators dominate listening, not talking. By listening and understanding a buyer's position, sellers keep negotiations focused on solutions, not positions.

Commandment 8: Don't Give Without Getting

⸺⟫◈⟪⸺

British monarch, Queen Elizabeth I, developed a system of *quid pro quo* that was as elaborate as it was informal. Literally translated, quid pro quo means "this for that." She gave select nobles extra time to repay their debts, and she gave certain land owners tax deferred status. To some she granted royal allowances or deeded certain royal properties. Beyond this, she showed a great interest in family affairs and was the godmother to more than a hundred infants. In return, Elizabeth expected undeviating loyalty. In times of political trouble or war, she called upon her nobles to champion her cause and defend her agenda. Her system of quid pro quo fostered a political environment that allowed her to utilize the services and support of the most influential and powerful people in England.

Like Queen Elizabeth, seller-negotiators should use the principle of quid pro quo to negotiate fair and favorable agreements.

One of the cornerstones of successful sales-side negotiation is to never give without getting. Don't make concessions without receiving something in return. When buyers make demands, seller concessions should always be followed with counter demands. This does not mean concessions have to cancel each other out in value. It simply means that something (even if it is of lesser value than what is being conceded) should be given in return.

When buyers get something for nothing, it has no value. The concession was simply a "freebie." The buyer paid nothing. When sellers make counter demands in exchange for concessions, the concession is no longer a freebie. It has value. It has worth. It is exchanged, not donated.

Don't concede without making counter demands or getting something in return, even if it is small. Make concessions conditional. Require buyers to offer something in exchange for the concession. Before making a concession, get a commitment to buy from the prospect. "Suppose we did agree to include the one-year warranty. Are you ready to sign the order?"

The Latin expression *quid pro quo* should be an integral part of every salesperson's vernacular. When buyers make demands, get something in return. Don't give without getting.

Commandment 9: Don't Broadcast Your Willingness to Negotiate

Inexperienced sellers often advertise their willingness to negotiate price (sometimes inadvertently) with statements such as, "Of course, that price is negotiable," or, "I'll work with you on the price."

Sellers do this for one of two reasons: First, because they are in the habit of discounting. To many sellers, discounting and selling are synonymous. They offer discounts because they consider discounting part of their job description as a seller. Second, they broadcast it because they don't have confidence in their ability to establish value. Many sellers are afraid to talk about price related issues without an accompanying statement about discounting because they don't believe buyers will purchase without it.

Experienced buyers exploit sellers who communicate, "I'm negotiable. Come get me. I don't believe my product is worth the price I'm asking; therefore, I'm willing to bargain."

I had a caller on my business radio show ask me about how he could get his sales staff to stop discounting. He was a vice president of marketing for a company that had a sales staff of around ten people. Many of the salespeople offered discounts because they didn't feel their product was worth the published price. This company's problem was not selling clients, it was selling employees. Discounting was the symptom, not the problem. The problem was that they had not convinced their employees of the value of their product. If employees don't believe their product is worth the price, they will feel reluctant (sometimes even guilty) asking for full price.

To ensure sellers don't broadcast a willingness to negotiate, they must first believe that the value of their product or service correlates with the price of the product or service.

Advertising a willingness to negotiate diminishes the power of the seller and builds the power of the buyer. Remember, power is the most crucial element in negotiation. When sellers begin sales or negotiations with statements that show a lack of commitment to a stated price, it's like sharks on blood for experienced buyers. Once buyers know that price is negotiable, their only question is how low can they go?

How much can the buyer get? Their focus is diverted away from value (which empowers the seller) and instead centers on discussions surrounding price (which empowers the buyer).

Don't broadcast your willingness to make concessions. Avoid statements that indicate a lack of commitment to a stated price.

Commandment 10: Negotiate As Little and As Late As Possible

There is no logical reason to start the negotiation process until you have to. When possible, negotiations should take place late in the sales process. Why? Because sellers have a chance to build value by unearthing problems and pains to resolve. It provides sellers with opportunities to deliver presentations which demonstrate the value of their products or services.

Remember, the more value you establish, the easier it is to justify price. In other words, negotiations should not take place until the maximum amount of value is first established.

Negotiations inherently center on price and cost, not value. When negotiations occur early in the sales cycle, buyers are distracted from focusing on what empowers sellers—solutions, benefits, and value.

> **The Point?** Don't negotiate until it becomes necessary. Avoid adjusting your price or modifying your terms until you have no alternative. Negotiate as little and as late as possible.

In Summary

The Ten Commandments of Sales-Side Negotiation are:

1. Negotiate Prepared
2. Focus on Value, Not Price
3. Avoid Making the First Concession
4. Concede Reluctantly
5. Inflate Your Initial Demand
6. Concentrate on Areas of Maximum Leverage
7. Be Hard on Problems and Soft on People
8. Don't Give Without Getting
9. Don't Broadcast Your Willingness to Negotiate
10. Negotiate as Little and as Late as Possible

CHAPTER 16

Implementing Sales-Side Negotiation Skills

---◦◦◦---

In 52 B.C., with the appointment of Gnaeus Pompeius Magnus (Pompey) as sole consul, Rome was thrown into a civil war. Julius Caesar, having conquered most of Gaul over an eight-year campaign, was not about to see Pompey rule Rome. On January 10, 49 B.C., Caesar *crossed his Rubicon* and marched on Rome.

Fearful of directly confronting Caesar's battle hardened veterans, Pompey fled to Greece. Caesar soon followed.

While encamped in Solana, one of Caesar's armies was besieged by Pompey's leading general, Marcus Octavius. Outnumbered, surrounded, and cut off from any reinforcements or supply lines, Caesar's men were trapped. Octavius offered to lift the siege if the troops would foreswear their allegiance to Caesar and join the army of Pompey. Inside the walls, the loyal veterans of Caesar's Gallic Wars replied that they would never surrender under those conditions. The siege dragged on for months. With provisions exhausted and the water supply depleted, every day became a desperate struggle for survival. Outside the walls, the surrounding army had nothing to do but wait.

Finally, on a chosen day, Caesar's soldiers stripped off their armor, buckled it on their women and children, and placed them in the normal guard positions. Then, as the enemy settled down for its traditional noon meal, the gates of the fortress burst open and Caesar's men rushed toward the astonished troops of Octavius. Caesar's men attacked with such fury that they routed not only the first outer post, but the entrenched troops as well. Octavius barely escaped with his life and was forced to flee to his ships.

---◦◦◦---

The historic lesson contained in this experience is this: Those who wait tend to relax and become careless. Those who act, and fight to improve their situation, become more skilled, and more successful.

From Principle to Application

Far better it is to dare mighty things, to win glorious triumphs, even though checkered by failure, than to take rank with those poor spirits who neither enjoy much nor suffer much, because they live in the grey twilight that knows not victory nor defeat.

—Teddy Roosevelt

At the conclusion of our sales and negotiation trainings, I am consistently asked, "How do we implement your training? How do we convert theory into practice? Is there a way for us to turn board room trainings into practical application?"

There is, of course, no easy answer to these questions. Understanding does not necessarily translate into doing. However, there are some fundamental guidelines that will speed up the implementation of sales-side negotiation principles.

Once individuals have mastered the ideas and concepts of *Sales-Side Negotiation*, it is critical to channel the newly acquired information into habits.[1] I have identified five implementation rules that follow skill-learning principles:

- Focus on one skill at a time
- Focus on quantity, not quality
- Set goals and standards
- Plan
- Don't become discouraged

---

1. *Patrick Henry International* has systematized an implementation program that can be customized to the needs of individuals and organizations. To learn how to best integrate sales-side negotiation skills and strategies for your business or situation, contact *Patrick Henry International* at 1 (877) 204-4341.

Focus On One Skill at a Time

In 890, Alfred the Great identified "seven maxims" he strove to follow. He then worked on each behavior individually. Benjamin Franklin did much the same in 1771, outlining thirteen virtues that "occurred to me as necessary or desirable." Franklin then set aside time to focus on each virtue separately. "I determined to give a week's strict attention to each of the virtues successively. Thus, in the first week, my great guard was to avoid every day the least offense against temperance [his first virtue]... Proceeding thus to the last, I could get through a course complete in thirteen weeks and four courses a year. And like him who, having a garden to weed, does not attempt to eradicate all the bad herbs at once... but works on one of the beds at a time, and having accomplished the first proceeds to the second."[2]

Basketball coach Pat Riley outlines in his book *The Winner Within* a program that he used with the Los Angeles Lakers to break down complex skills into component behaviors. "From a list of fifteen possible measures, we selected five that had really cost us the last championship. These defined five 'trigger points,' five areas which comprised the basis of basketball performance for each role and position. We challenged each player to put forth enough effort to gain just one percentage point in each of those five areas."[3] Riley then focused on each skill, one at a time, with each player. The next year, the Lakers won the NBA championship.

---

2. *The Autobiography of Benjamin Franklin* (New York: Barnes and Noble Books, 1994) 106-108.

3. Pat Riley, *The Winner Within* (New York: Berkley Books, 1993) 163.

When softball players work on hitting, they don't attempt to work on their throwing skills at the same time. They focus on one skill at a time. Like successful athletes, successful negotiators do not work on multiple skills simultaneously. They isolate a particular skill and work on it. After mastering the targeted skill, they move on to the next skill.

> **The Point?** Focus on one skill at a time and hammer it. Work on it. Think about it. Write it down. Practice it. Concentrate on developing one skill at a time.

Focus on Quantity, Not Quality

As a young man, I had a basketball coach teach me how to shoot free throws. He showed me the correct mechanics of shooting—bringing my elbow up to a square position, bending my shooting wrist back, following through, etc. After teaching me the correct way to shoot, he then said, "Now go shoot 100 free throws and come back and talk to me again." He understood quantity would lead to quality.

Patrick Henry International refers to this skill-learning concept as *The Quantity Principle. The Quantity Principle* instructs students to focus on skill quantity versus skill quality. New behaviors are learned through a quantity of repetition and practice. Quality comes with time. As new behaviors are learned, adjustments will be made, and skills will be refined. The important part of learning a skill is doing, practicing, engaging.

> **Caution!** In the initial stages of skill learning, don't worry about perfection. Don't worry about making mistakes. Don't worry about quality. Focus on quantity and quality will follow.

Set Goals and Standards

A goal is a desired objective used to motivate and enhance a person's ability to succeed. Goals give people direction and focus and are essential to improving performance.

Setting and achieving goals is not a trivial process. It takes good data, good thinking, and good instincts to set good goals. Inappropriate goals can actually have an adverse effect on a person's performance. Unrealistically high goals that are not achievable not only fail to motivate, they actually discourage people by making them feel unsuccessful. Goals that are too easy to achieve, on the other hand, do not inspire people to stretch and grow.

A seller who wants to improve his or her negotiating skills can set a goal to memorize buyer-negotiator tactics or develop a pre-negotiation worksheet prior to each negotiation. By setting goals, sellers motivate themselves to improve their negotiating skills and behaviors.

The most important aspect of a goal is its means of fulfillment. After establishing a goal, it is necessary to create a game plan to accomplish the goal. Why? Without clearly identifying steps of achievement, people don't have goals—they have hopes.

A *goal* is an objective; whereas, a *standard* is a means of achieving the objective. Goals without standards are like weight loss programs without exercise. An example of a *goal* is to lose twenty pounds. An example of a *standard* is to workout every morning from 6:30 to 7:00. Standards are like "mini goals" fulfilled on a daily or weekly basis that map a clear path to achieving a goal.

When setting goals, a salesperson should set personal standards to achieve the goals.

> **The Point?** Develop goals and standards that are challenging, motivating, and achievable.

Plan

You've undoubtedly heard Benjamin Franklin's oft-repeated maxim, "By failing to prepare, you are preparing to fail." This dictum is scripture in the business world. Plan ahead. Specify what dates, times, and accounts you will implement your new skills.

In order to negotiate well, you must first plan well. Strategic planning is the cornerstone of successful negotiation. If you don't have an effective plan for selling, any success you experience is purely accidental. Plan your negotiations in advance, and anticipate possible problems or potential resistance. Script out questions prior to the negotiation. Use *The Strategic Pre-Negotiation Planner* to plan your negotiations. Plan and analyze the implementation of your newly acquired knowledge and information. Analyze sales calls and negotiations.

- What went well?
- What could I have done differently?
- Which questions had the greatest influence?
- What mistakes did I make?
- What skills could I have implemented?

The key to implementation is to plan and schedule. Map out where work is needed. Week one: Buyer-negotiator tactics. Week two: Seller-negotiator countertactics, etc.

Don't Become Discouraged

A smooth sea never made a skilled mariner.

—English Proverb

In 1832, Abraham Lincoln lost his job in a failing business partnership. Also in 1832, he was defeated for the state legislature. In 1833, a private business failed. Although elected to the state legislature in 1834, he implemented an internal improvement project that nearly bankrupted the State of Illinois. He was defeated twice for the house speaker position in 1836 and 1838. In 1843, Lincoln was defeated for the nomination to the U.S. Congress. Although elected to congress in 1846, he lost the renomination in 1848. In 1849 Lincoln ran for a land-office position and lost. In 1854 he was defeated for the U.S. Senate. In 1856, Lincoln was defeated for the nomination for Vice-President, and, in 1858, he repeated his losing bid for the U.S. Senate. In 1860, he was elected President of The United States of America.

————

Achieving excellence is a journey, not a destination. It's a voyage wrought with bumps and bruises. As Abraham Lincoln's experience illustrates, bouts of failure are part of the path of success. Setbacks and mistakes come with the terrain. It's part of the process. The key is to learn from mistakes and failures and take the lessons to heart.

Many professionals learn new and better ways of selling and negotiating but don't convert the newly acquired knowledge into habits because they become discouraged.

Give new skills a chance. No new skill feels natural the first time you use it. It may initially feel a bit awkward and artificial. That's perfectly normal. Don't quit after only a few attempts. Be persistent. Role-play, think, and practice. Don't become discouraged.

Have High Expectations

Bargain in life for a penny, and life will give you no more.

—Anonymous

Studies indicate that a negotiator's expectations and attitudes prior to negotiation are accurate predictors of the outcome of negotiation. Research has shown that negotiators with high expectations are more successful negotiators. They typically achieve what they expect. Negotiators who expect to be successful usually are. If they mentally and emotionally expect a certain amount out of a negotiation, chances are they will get it. If they walk into a negotiation mentally downtrodden, they are more likely to experience the self-fulfilling prophecy of failure.

This is an important principle to understand. When sellers are accustomed to discounting (a primitive form of negotiation), they expect to discount in order to close a sale. Prior to the sale closing, they expect to offer a price or product related concession. Sellers who do not expect to discount when closing sales don't discount. Because they don't have a preconceived expectation to discount, it's simply not a part of their selling modus operandi.

The essence of this phenomenon is captured in the saying, "Success breeds success." People tend to expect what they experience. People who are highly successful expect to be successful. People who are moderately successful expect to be moderately successful. People who are failures more often than not, expect to fail. The important idea to remember is that achieving success is building success one step at a time. The more success a person experiences, the more success a person expects. Negotiators with high aspiration levels typically accomplish what they set out to achieve. After a seller tastes success, levels of aspiration are raised. If he or she enjoys success, much higher goals and expectations are set and ultimately achieved.[4]

> *Whether you think you can or you think you can't, you're probably right.*
>
> —Henry Ford

Of course, this phenomenon has its limitations. There are people whose expectations exceed their capabilities. The fact that someone expects to beat Michael Jordan in a one-on-one basketball game does not increase his or her likelihood for success. A seller must have achiev-

---

4. For an in depth and excellent discussion on success, see *Success Is A Choice*, by Rick Pitino, 1997, Broadway Books.

able expectations and be equipped with the tools to be successful. As we grow proficient in exercising these tools, winning isn't wishful thinking, it is a forgone conclusion.

Negotiation Success–Deserve It.

No one can guarantee success in war—one can only deserve it.

—Winston Churchill

Negotiation success must be earned. There is no magic potion. In order to be successful, sellers must pay the price. They must sow before they reap. They must deserve success.

Successful negotiators follow a simple success equation:

Sales-Side Negotiation Skills + Power x Work = Success

Goals cannot be wish lists. They have to be work lists. Thinking about your dreams is rarely enough to create the habits to fulfill them. While it is good to start with dreams and goals, before any of your dreams and goals can be realized, you must first deserve your success by acquiring selling skills and working hard. By combining old-fashioned work habits with sales-side negotiation skills, sales professionals are equipped with the tools they need to consistently win.

If you want to succeed—deserve success.

> **The Point?** You can do it. Be patiently persistent, and your skills will improve. Persevere and your selling success will increase. Follow sales-side negotiation principles, work hard and you will be successful. You will have earned it.

Visit www.patrickhenryinc.com to download podcasts, articles, and other sales and negotiation tools.

SELECTED BIBLIOGRAPHY

Adams, Jeremy, Wick Allison, and Gavin Hambly. *Condemned To Repeat It.* New York: 1998.

Ambrose, Stephen E. *Undaunted Courage.* New York: Simon & Schuster, 1996.

Axelrod, Alan. *Elizabeth I, CEO.* New York: Prentice Hall Press, 2000.

Axelrod, Alan. *Profiles in Leadership.* New York: Prentice Hall Press, 2000.

Bailey, Thomas, and David Kennedy. *The American Pageant.* Lexington: Heath and Company, 1991.

Barrett, Erin, and Jack Mingo. *Just Curious About History, Jeeves.* New York: Pocket Books, 2002.

Bernard, Andre, and Clifton Fadiman. *Bartlett's Book of Anecdotes.* New York: Little, Brown and Company, 2000.

Beyer, Rick. *The Greatest Stories Never Told.* New York: HarperCollins, 2003.

Boyd, Katherine, and Bruce Lenman. *Larouse Dictionary of World History.* New York: Chambers Harrap Publishers, 1993.

Caesar, Gaius Julius. *The Conquest of Gaul.* Translated by S.A. Hanford. New York: Penguin Books, 1982.

Churchill, Winston S. *History Of The English-Speaking Peoples.* New York: Wings Books, 1994.

Clausewitz, Carl von. *War, Politics and Power.* Translated by Edward M. Collins. Washington, DC: Regnery Publishing, 1997.

Corvisier, Andre. *A Dictionary of Military History.* Translated by Chris Turner. Cambridge: Blackwell Publishers, 1994.

D'Este, Carlo. *Patton: A Genius for War.* New York: Harper Collins Publishers, 1995.

Dodge, Theodore. *The Great Captains.* New York: Barnes & Noble Books, 1995.

Franklin, Benjamin. *The Autobiography of Benjamin Franklin.* New York: Barnes & Noble Books, 1994.

Greene, Robert, and Joost Elffers. *The 48 Laws of Power.* New York: Penguin Books, 2000.

Helm, P. H. *Alfred the Great.* New York: Barnes & Noble Books, 1995.

Isaacson, Walter. *Kissinger: A Biography.* New York: Simon & Shuster, 1992.

Jimenez, Ramon. *Caesar Against The Celts.* New York: Sarpedon, 1996.

Mintz, Penny. *Thomas Edison: Inventing the Future.* New York: Fawcett Columbine, 1989.

Ritchie, W.F. *Celtic Warriors.* Buckinghamshire: Shire Publications, 1997.

Roosevelt, Theodore. *The Strenuous Life.* Bedford: Applewood Books, 1991.

Rutter, Michael. *Outlaw Tales of Utah.* Guilford: The Globe Pequot Press, 2003.

Shirer, William. *The Rise and Fall Of the Third Reich.* New York: Simon Schuster, 1960.

Strathern, Paul. *Hegel In 90 Minutes.* Chicago: Ivan R. Dee, 1997.

Sun-tzu. *The Art of War.* Translated by Ralph D. Sawyer. New York: Barnes & Noble Books, 1994.

Index

Stating budgetary restrictions, 168
Station manager, 86
Status Quo Not, 91
Steel
    empire, 192
    enterprise, ii, 193
Straining relationships, 210
Strategic
    countertactic(s), 143, 152
    edge, 87
    framework, 241
    negotiation(s), 186
    negotiator(s), 9, 40, 99, 142-143,
152, 154, 189, 197, 247
    planning, 261, 272
    word(s), 4, 20, 135
Strathern, 266
Strenuous Life, 266
Stresses, 189
Strict
    constructionist, 232
    discounting policy, 6
Strong
    businesses, 52
    relationship, 106
    seller(s), 25, 52, 138
    stand, 119
Substantial discount, 50
Success, 1, 5, 9, 11, 13, 24, 33, 49, 76, 194, 239,
261-264
Successful
    athletes, 259
    negotiation strategies, 187
    negotiator(s), viii, 23, 34, 153, 194,
228, 241, 243, 259, 262, 264
    negotiators focus, 194, 228
    presentation(s), 12-13
    sales-side negotiation, 66, 218, 252
    sales negotiation, 218
    seller-negotiators, 156
    selling, ix, 193
    site, 42
Suez Canal, 82, 272
Sun Tzu, 17, 186, 239, 272
Sundance Kid, i, 17, 272
Sunshine
    all, 131, 178
    Buyer Type, 178
    Sunshine, 131
Support proposals, 199
Sustainable relationships, 4
Swaziland, 217
Switzerland, 1, 272

Symbiotic relationship, 28, 223
Sympathy
    Buyer Type, 174
    Sympathy, 127
Syria
    army, v-vii
    king, vi-vii
    monarch, i, v-vi
Systematic approach, 2

T

Tactic buyers, 125, 127, 131
Tel Aviv, 226
Ten Commandments, 15, iii, 239, 255, 272
Texas, 12, 197
Theodore Roosevelt, ii, 194
Thomas
    Edison, iii, 242, 266
    Jefferson, 152, 154, 232
    Mann, 226
    Paine Price, 229
Throw-ins
    intensive relationships, 104
    pressure, 114
Timeframe Buyer, 159, 201
Times, 21, 48-49, 168, 205, 252, 261
Tire kickers, 105
Tom Pollack, 214
Toussaint Charbonneau, i, 45
Trade, ii, 14, 16, 189, 204-205, 213, 215, 231
Trading concessions, 3
Triangulation, 16, 137, 149-150, 180, 201, 272
Trojans, 118
Trophy Sale, 120, 122, 167, 179, 201, 268, 272
Troy, 119
Trump, 98, 272
Trust, ix-x, 58, 75-76, 100-101, 103-104, 204

U

UDM, 272
Unethical tactics, 119
Union leaders, 7
Unique
    approach, 222
    benefit(s), 141, 224
    capabilities, 42, 64, 69, 149
    features, 89
    selling
        Points, 55, 150, 199
        Proposition(s), 54
    solution(s), 70, 113, 145

PATRICK HENRY INTERNATIONAL

CORPORATE SALES & NEGOTIATION TRAINING

TRAINING SUITE

- ◆ **Prospecting**
- ◆ **Selling**
- ◆ **Presenting**
- ◆ **Negotiating**
- ◆ **Keynote Speaker**

POWER PROSPECTING

Generate more leads, set more appointments and fill opportunity pipelines with qualified prospects using PHI's unique lead generation strategies.

THE DNA SELLING METHOD

Implement a proven selling methodology that builds competitive differentiation, prevents traditional "show up, throw up" behaviors and increases sales.

WINNING PRESENTATIONS

Develop compelling content, create unique selling propositions, master effective communication skills and deliver winning presentations.

SALES NEGOTIATION

Build power, recognize buyer tactics, implement seller countertactics and minimize concessions with proven sales-side negotiation strategies.

KEYNOTE SPEAKER

Patrick Henry Hansen is one of America's top business speakers and uses great moments in history to motivate, entertain and educate audiences.

Visit www.patrickhenryinc.com to download podcasts, articles, and other sales tools.

1.877.204.4341 • www.patrickhenryinc.com

PATRICK HENRY INTERNATIONAL

CORPORATE SALES & NEGOTIATION TRAINING

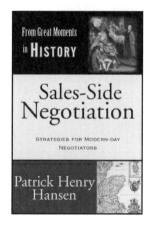

TO ORDER THE COMPLETE

FROM GREAT MOMENTS IN HISTORY

SERIES VISIT

WWW.AMAZON.COM

About The Author

Patrick Henry Hansen is the founder of *Patrick Henry International.* His organization provides sales, prospecting, negotiation and presentation training for corporate sales teams. Mr. Hansen is the author of numerous books and is considered an international authority on sales methodology, sales-side negotiation, lead generation and sales presentations. He is also a recognized expert sales and marketing witness in United States Federal Courts.

Mr. Hansen is a popular speaker, consultant and trainer, and has influenced thousands of professionals in South Africa, Australia, New Zealand, England, Wales, Germany, Canada, Mexico, Spain and forty-nine States.

Prior to starting *Patrick Henry International,* Mr. Hansen was a sales representative, manager and executive. As an executive for multiple technology companies, he introduced advanced selling systems that increased sales more than 100% in each company.

Mr. Hansen is a former radio talk show host, received his BA from Brigham Young University and currently resides in Salt Lake City, Utah with his wife Laura and their six children.

Refer questions to:

Patrick Henry International
1831 Fort Union Blvd., Suite 210
Salt Lake City, Utah 84121
Phone: 1 (877) 204-4341
www.patrickhenryinc.comt

Visit www.patrickhenryinc.com to download sample podcasts, articles, free book chapters and other sales, prospecting, presenting, and negotiation tools.